Irish Fairs and Markets

Irish Fairs and Markets

Studies in Local History

Denis A. Cronin, Jim Gilligan
& Karina Holton

EDITORS

FOUR COURTS PRESS

Set in 10.5 pt on 12.5 pt Bembo by
Carrigboy Typesetting Services, for
FOUR COURTS PRESS LTD
Fumbally Lane, Dublin 8, Ireland
e-mail: info@four-courts-press.ie
http://www.four-courts-press.ie
and in North America for
FOUR COURTS PRESS
c/o ISBS, 5824 N.E. Hassalo Street, Portland, OR 97213.

A catalogue record for this title
is available from the British Library.

ISBN 1–85182–525–8

Printed in England
by MPG Books, Bodmin, Cornwall.

Contents

Abbreviations

Cal. Jus. Rolls	*Calendar of the justiciary rolls or proceedings in the court of the justiciar of Ireland*, (1259–1303) (etc.), ed. J. Mills, (2 vols Dublin, 1905, 1914)
Cal. Doc. Ire.	*Calendar of documents relating to Ireland, 1171–1251* etc., (5 vols London, 1875–86)
Cal. Pat. Rolls Ire., Jas I	*Irish patent rolls of James I: facsimile of the Irish record commissioners' calendar prepared prior to 1830*, with foreword by M.C. Griffith (Dublin, 1966)
Cal. Pat. Rolls Ire., Chas I	*Calendar of patent and close rolls of chancery in Ireland, Charles I*, ed. James Morrin (Dublin, 1864)
CSORP	Chief Secretary's Office Registered Papers
DED	District Electoral Division
H.C.	House of Commons
IFC	Irish Folklore Commission
JRSAI	*Journal of the Royal Society of Antiquaries of Ireland*
Lewis	Samuel Lewis, *A topographical dictionary of Ireland* (2 vols with atlas, London, 1837)
MS(S)	Manuscript(s)
NAI	National Archives of Ireland
NLI	National Library of Ireland
OS	Ordnance Survey of Ireland
PRONI	Public Record Office of Northern Ireland
RD	Registry of Deeds, Dublin
TCD	Trinity College, Dublin
UCD	University College, Dublin
VO	Valuation Office, Dublin

PARLIAMENTARY PAPERS

Return of customs and tolls, 1824: Return of all places where customs, tolls or duties are levied at markets, fairs or ports in Ireland, H.C. 1824 (279), xxi, 703.

Sel. comm. tolls and customs, 1826: Report of the select committee on tolls and customs in Ireland, H.C. 1826 (170), v, 451.

Sel. comm. tolls and customs, 1834: Report of the select committee on tolls and customs with the minutes of evidence, H.C. 1834 (603), xvii, 229.

Royal comm. municipal corps, 1835: Report of the select committee on the municipal corporations of Ireland with supplement and appendices, H.C. 1835 (23), xxvii, 1.

Royal comm. fairs and markets, 1852–3: Report of the commissioners appointed to inquire into the state of fairs and markets in Ireland, H.C. 1852–3 (1674), xli, 79.

Royal comm. fairs and markets, mins, 1854–5: Report of the commissioners appointed to inquire into the state of fairs and markets in Ireland, minutes of evidence, H.C. 1854–5 (1910), xix, 1.

Royal comm. market rights, 1890–1: Final report on market rights and tolls, H.C. 1890–1 (6268), xxxvii to xli.

Illustrations

TABLES

Preface

This collection of essays, like its predecessor *Irish Townlands* (Dublin, 1998), arises out of the M.A. course in Local History offered by the Department of Modern History at NUI Maynooth. Graduates of the course have been meeting regularly since 1994 to share ideas about local history and to undertake studies on topics which might be of interest to students and practitioners of local history.

The authors wish to thank Professor Vincent Comerford and his colleagues in the Department of Modern History at NUI Maynooth for their encouragement and assistance, and in particular wish to acknowledge with gratitude the continuing and unfailing support of Dr Raymond Gillespie. They wish also to thank the directors and staffs of NUI Maynooth Library, National Library of Ireland, and National Archives of Ireland for their assistance. A special word of thanks goes to Dr Noel Murphy, DCU, for his assistance.

The authors also wish to express their gratitude to Michael Adams for his support in agreeing to publish this collection and to his staff at Four Courts Press for their dedication, professionalism and courtesy during the publication process.

Introduction

DENIS A. CRONIN, JIM GILLIGAN AND KARINA HOLTON

This book is the first major collection of studies on trading at local level in Ireland. It reflects not only the continuing growth of interest in local history in general but also the increasing recognition by local historians of the importance of examining economic and social factors when reconstructing the worlds of local communities. The importance of trading in the economic and social lives of local communities cannot be overstated. Fairs and markets brought together people from very different social backgrounds and played an important part in shaping local society. Town met country; farmer met trader; and the influences of the wider world were introduced into the local culture.

The important role which trading plays in society has already been recognised in a number of existing studies. Patrick Logan's *Fair Day* is a useful overview of the history of markets and fairs in Ireland, while Patrick O'Flanagan's examination of the growth of markets and fairs in Ireland between 1600 and 1800 is an essential guide to their importance as indicators of economic development.[1] Anne O'Dowd's *Spalpeens and tattie hokers* explores the world of the hiring fair, mainly through the records of the Folklore Commission.[2] Less work has been done on trading at local level. W.H. Crawford's studies of markets and fairs in Cavan, Donegal and Mayo stand out in particular.[3] A recent work of note is Tom Harris's survey of the markets and fairs of Meath in the nineteenth century.[4] An anthropological approach by Gulliver and Silverman in their study of Thomastown, county Kilkenny, offers valuable insights into various aspects of trading.[5]

The authors of the studies in this collection describe and analyse a range of experiences of buying and selling at local level in Ireland. They include a survey of fairs and markets at provincial level, studies of a number of individual fairs, markets and shops, and an analysis of the household accounts of one particular

---

1 Patrick Logan, *Fair Day – The story of Irish fairs and markets* (Belfast, 1986); Patrick O'Flanagan, 'Markets and fairs in Ireland, 1600–1800: index of economic development and regional growth' in *Journal of Historical Geography* 11, no. 4 (1985), pp. 364–78. **2** Anne O'Dowd, *Spalpeens and tattie hokers* (Dublin, 1991). **3** W.H. Crawford, 'Markets and fairs in county Cavan' in *Heart of Breifne* (1984); idem, 'The evolution of the urban network' in W. Nolan, L. Roynane and M. Dunlevy (eds.), *Donegal: History and Society* (Dublin, 1985); idem, 'Development of the county Mayo economy, 1700–1850' in Raymond Gillespie and Gerard Moran (eds.) *A various country: essays on Mayo history* (Westport, 1987). **4** Tom Harris, 'Fairs and markets in the environment of county Meath' in *Ríocht na Mídhe*, ix, no. 4 (1998), pp. 149–69. **5** P.H. Gulliver and Marilyn Silverman, *Merchants and shopkeepers – a historical anthropology of an Irish market town, 1200–1991* (Toronto, 1995).

family. They range over a wide time-span from early medieval times to the late twentieth century. The topics chosen reflect both the particular interests of the individual authors and a desire to illustrate the diversity of the experience of trade at local level.

Mankind has always traded and markets and fairs developed in response to a local need to exchange surplus produce. This collection of essays takes as its starting point the growth of markets and fairs from Anglo-Norman times. The Anglo-Normans formalised already existing fairs and markets and created new ones to respond to the needs of their economy and society. The majority of fairs and markets were founded on the basis of a grant of charter by the king or by the local lord. A charter gave the founder the right to levy tolls and obliged him to provide institutional support, including the supply and maintenance of weights and measures, the provision of ground and stalls and the preservation of law and order. In her study of medieval Leinster, Karina Holton shows that these services were provided by secular lords such as the Earl Marshall at the medieval fair of New Ross or by the burgesses of towns like Kilkenny. This function continued to be fulfilled in later times by powerful individuals such as the local landlord, for example Thomas Coote at Cootehill, or by town corporations. Brian Ó Dálaigh's study examines the development of the Ennis markets under the patronage of both the O'Briens of Thomond and the town's corporation. As English law became widespread, Gaelic landowners like the O'Briens saw the value of taking out royal patents to develop markets and fairs in their territories.

Part of the function of the patron of the fair was the maintenance of law and order. Disputes were often caused by disagreements over weights and measures, arguments over prices, forestalling and by the rekindling of individual feuds. Temporary courts known as courts of piepowder addressed disputes which arose during many medieval fairs. In other instances, cases were dealt with at the local manor or corporation court. Gatherings of large numbers of people sometimes led to general disorder. Séamas Ó Maitiú in his exploration of the visual representations of Donnybrook fair refers to the violent outbursts that made Donnybrook a byword for riotous behaviour. Paul Connell in his study of an incident at Castlepollard fair demonstrates the sometimes volatile nature of these gatherings. He gives a graphic account of the aftermath of a particularly violent incident which resulted in the deaths of eleven people.

As markets and fairs continued to develop a number began to specialize in response to the economies of the local region. In his study of Cootehill, Patrick Cassidy demonstrates how the linen trade came to be the most important element of the markets there, reflecting the fact that flax and the linen industry were central to the Ulster economy. Denis Cronin traces the evolution of Cahirmee fair in county Cork from a general fair to one specializing in horses, reflecting the importance of horse breeding in the regional economy. A further example of specialization can be seen in Liam Clare's study of the Dublin Cattle Market which developed as a meeting point between the grasslands of Leinster and the large English market.

Figure 1 Map of Ireland showing the locations referred to in the essays.

The development of roads and particularly of railways in the nineteenth century facilitated the distribution of mass-produced consumer goods. This contributed to a significant expansion in the number and geographical distribution of shops both in towns and at strategic locations in the countryside. Jim Gilligan's study of a shop in Dunshaughlin, county Meath and Miriam Lambe's study of a shop at a rural crossroads in county Tipperary both illustrate the range and variety of goods available in the late nineteenth century. Shopkeepers performed an important function in extending credit to customers whose income depended on seasonal factors. Neither proprietor conforms to the stereotype of the rapacious gombeen man. In fact, both of these studies illustrate the often precarious nature of the shopkeeper's existence.

An important element in the success or failure of any marketplace is its catchment area and this is discussed in several studies. These fairs, markets or shops primarily served their immediate areas first but the extent of these localities varied considerably. In the case of the shops examined in this collection, the catchment area was relatively small, with a radius extending little more than five miles into the countryside. The catchment area of weekly markets like the those of Ennis was more extensive. Ennis was regularly visited, for example, by Farmer Lucas, who travelled over eight miles from Drumcavan. In William Gacquin's study of an eighteenth-century household account from Roscommon we are given a rare opportunity to examine the ambit of a consumer of goods and services. The goods and services availed of by the family responsible for this account came from all over south Roscommon, from the immediate environs of Knockcroghery to as far away as Athlone. The catchment area of annual or seasonal fairs such as Cootehill could extend into neighbouring counties. In the case of fairs which specialized, like the horsefair of Cahirmee and the Dublin Cattle Market, the catchment area could extend much further, not only into neighbouring counties but all over Ireland and Britain. British circuses were regular features of Donnybrook fair in the nineteenth century. Certain fairs even attracted customers from continental Europe. Buyers of horses came to Cahirmee from as far away as Germany and Italy. Indeed this was nothing new. Karina Holton demonstrates that the major fairs of medieval Leinster were attended by a wide range of merchants from Britain and the Continent.

A number of factors led to the decline of many fairs in the nineteenth and twentieth centuries. The coming of the railways and of motorized transport along with the improvement of shopping and banking facilities in towns helped to concentrate fairs in the larger centres. An important factor which hastened the demise of the smaller centres was the power granted to local authorities in 1872 to regulate fairs. This led to an increase in the frequency of urban fairs. Many of these new urban fairs tended also to specialize in particular livestock, and so monthly pig fairs and cattle fairs became common. From the 1950s, these fairs and most of the remaining rural fairs were replaced by livestock marts. These regular marts were more convenient for both sellers and buyers, and their auction format removed much of the unpredictability of the traditional fairs.

Virtually all of the fairs examined in these studies are no longer held. The vibrant medieval fairs of Leinster, and the Castlepollard, Knockcroghery, Ennis and Cootehill fairs are no more. Donnybrook fair, with its excesses, fell foul of the authorities and closed in the 1850s. Even the Dublin Cattle Market gave way to local marts, a rare case of a large specialist market being replaced by a number of smaller ones. Of the individual fairs discussed in this volume, only Cahirmee fair in Buttevant, with its long tradition as a horse fair, survives today.

The weekly markets have fared somewhat better. Many of these survive, even if in a somewhat diminished form. In Cootehill and Ennis, as in so many market towns, stalls selling miscellaneous items are still erected on market days. The decline of the small rural and village shop can be largely attributed to specialization and to the concentration of trade in bigger towns now easily reached by car. The rise of the supermarket and the large hardware and DIY store has undermined the traditional general store. The shop at the Cross of Pallas and Murray's of Dunshaughlin no longer function as general stores but specialize as public houses.

A surprisingly wide variety of sources have been drawn upon by the authors in examining these marketplaces and their communities. Some were fortunate enough to find manuscripts which were generated by the act of trading, like account books, as in the case of Miriam Lambe's and Jim Gilligan's shop studies and William Gacquin's household account. Records of central government were among the most widely used, in particular printed parliamentary papers such as the reports of royal commissions and select committees, and statistical returns and accounts. Calendars of medieval government records and later manuscript records such as correspondence to the Chief Secretary's office and even census returns from 1749, 1901 and 1911 were also consulted. Local government records were not as widely available but were particularly valuable in Brian Ó Dálaigh's study of Ennis and in Liam Clare's study of the Dublin Cattle Market. Local newspapers were an essential source also and were widely used, as they carried reports on both routine and unusual happenings at fairs and markets, and even carried advertisements for shops. Other sources used included private documents of record like land deeds and wills and more informal private documents such as letters and diaries. Oral sources contributed in several cases and pictorial sources also were useful, particularly in Seamas Ó Maitiú's examination of changing perceptions of the fair at Donnybrook.

These studies demonstrate the importance of local exploration of the themes of everyday life as it changes over time. They demonstrate also the large range of sources available to the local historian in reconstructing the past world of buying and selling. It is hoped that they are valuable not just as collections of facts about individual fairs, markets and shops but as explorations of the social and economic relationships within communities and between communities. These relationships are at the very core of the work of the local historian.

From charters to carters: aspects of fairs and markets in medieval Leinster

KARINA HOLTON

INTRODUCTION

Throughout much of Western Europe the thirteenth century was a period of tremendous growth and economic expansion. Improvements in farming practices, coupled with an increase in population, led to the development of commerce and trade and ultimately to a more market driven economy. Surplus produce was being created by the predominantly peasant economy. There was also an increasing number of people such as merchants and craftsmen who did not produce the food that they themselves required. Lords and landed tenants had an ever-growing need for cash to spend on military equipment and on luxury items carried by foreign merchants. Peasants too had an increasing need for money to pay rents, fines and taxes.[1] All of these factors contributed to the development of a network of locations for the sale of goods throughout the medieval countryside, culminating in the establishment of organized fairs and markets. The growth of fairs and markets that became the hallmark of the thirteenth century in many parts of England and in those areas of Anglo-Norman settlement in Ireland was an indication of the increasing prosperity of the period. As the river valleys and the fertile plains became more heavily colonized, the number of points of commercial interaction grew even further. Stretches of road located on boundaries of pre-Norman settlements became the sites of market towns, as at Cloncurry in north Kildare. Monastic towns such as Kildare, Glendalough and Kells, which had been centres of economic activity in the pre-Norman era, evolved to become thriving market towns in the Anglo-Norman period. Contemporary documentary evidence contains many references to merchants, particularly in the larger port towns. However, the evidence for medieval fairs and markets is spread so thinly that it is necessary to use information from many decades to gather a useful sample. This study endeavours to examine aspects of the fairs and markets of medieval Leinster, particularly throughout the thirteenth and early fourteenth centuries.

FAIRS AND MARKETS

In modern times the distinction between a fair and a market has been somewhat blurred, but in the medieval period there was a marked difference. The fair was

---

1 R.H. Hilton, 'Lords, burgesses and hucksters' in *Past and Present*, no. 97 (Nov. 1982), p. 3.

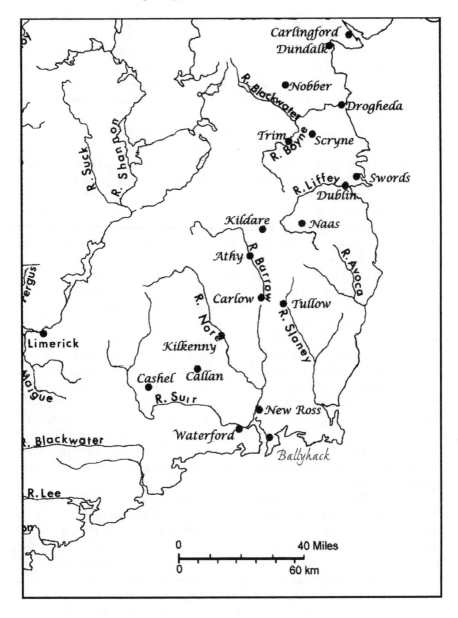

Figure 1 Map of Leinster showing places referred to in this essay.

an extravagant market usually held once a year. It attempted to draw people from afar to purchase the surplus produced in the district and to supply the locals with items that were not readily available in the locality.[2] In some places the fair also provided the opportunity for people to gaze on exotic sights like sword swallowers, jugglers and dancing bears. Fairs of the time 'brought a taste of the outside world to small rural communities and made an exciting break in the normal routine'.[3]

Grants of rights to hold fairs were made at regular intervals throughout the thirteenth century by the king to local lords. In some cases the grant was merely the formalization of a pre-existing informal fair or market, and it is likely that much petty trading took place throughout the countryside without leaving any record. The purpose of the formal grant was to guarantee income from sales for the local lord in the form of tolls. Most of the fairs that were established by grants were associated with religious festivals. Many of these began on the vigil of the religious festival and continued for several days including the festival itself and the following day.

During the thirteenth century an average of three fairs was granted each year. In 1226, ten fairs were granted, while a peak was reached in 1252 with thirteen grants of fairs. The majority of these fairs were held during the months of May, June, July, August and September. July was the most popular month, with fairs being held in various locations throughout Leinster about every two days. There were no grants of fairs for the month of January throughout the thirteenth century. The only documented fair held at this time of the year was the fair of Tuam in Galway which ran from 29 December to 5 January. The vast majority of the fairs ran for eight days. Some continued for fifteen days, such as those in Dublin, Drogheda and Dundalk. Three fairs which were granted to Hugh de Lacy in 1227 at Rotour, Nobber and Carlingford also ran for fifteen days. Most towns which hosted the fifteen-day fairs are located near the eastern and southern coasts and the fairs were more than likely supplied with goods from nearby ports. In smaller settlement areas fairs generally operated for three to five days.

In addition to the more extravagant but infrequent fair where exotic and luxury items were made available, there was a more practical need for regular local markets to cater for the necessities of daily life. Markets provided opportunities for people to buy and sell staple items of diet such as grain and dairy products. Many market grants were issued throughout the thirteenth century. A market charter licensed a market at a named place on a specified day of the week and entitled the holder to collect tolls. An average of two grants per year was made during this period. In 1226, six grants were made while in 1252, a record eight grants were issued. Markets were typically one-day affairs and could be held on any day of the week, although Thursday seems to have been

---

2 W.H. Crawford, 'Markets and fairs in county Cavan' in *Heart of Breifne* (1984), p. 55.
3 Mavis Mate, 'The rise and fall of markets in Southeast England' in *Canadian Journal of History*, xxxi (April 1996), pp. 59–86.

the commonest market day in thirteenth-century Ireland. Over one quarter of all documented markets were held on Thursday.

It is worthy of note that two grants during this period allowed for markets to be held on Sundays. Licences for these Sunday markets were issued to Henry, bishop of Emly and John, bishop of Ferns. Sunday markets allowed labourers the opportunity to buy and sell, as this was the only day when many of them were free. In 1200, the Pope wrote to the king discouraging Sunday trading. From then on, stricter attention was paid to canon law and most grants of markets were issued for weekdays. However, market day in Carlow continued to be held on Sundays until 1311, when it was changed to Wednesday.[4]

Originally, several markets and fairs were held in churches and church grounds. This was a common practice not only in medieval Ireland but also in Britain and in France. The French writer, Philippe Aries, wrote that the medieval French cemetery served as a

> marketplace [a] place for announcements, auctions, proclamations, sentences, scene of community gatherings; promenade; athletic field; haven for illicit encounters and dubious professions … before it was isolated from the church, the cemetery was the public square.[5]

Susan Leigh Fry noted in her study of burial in medieval Ireland that 'the sanctified enclosure surrounding the church – which included the graveyard – was often the focus of a wide range of secular activities … a number of which date from "pre-Christian times".'[6] There are many examples of sacred sites and burial places being used as locations for fairs and markets throughout the literature of early Irish sagas and legends. D.A. Binchy's study of the fair at *Tailten* in county Meath noted that the site of the fair was normally an ancient burial ground.[7] A poem from the year 1006 states that *oenach Tailten* took place around ancestral burial mounds.[8] Fairs and burials are linked again in Joyce's *Social history of ancient Ireland*. He quotes an account from the *Book of Ballymote* in which the origins of the ancient fair of Carman are explained. When Carman the chief was dying, he begged his followers to institute a fair of mourning at his gravesite which should bear his name forever. Joyce states that a fair was held at this site for a long period afterwards.[9] While the function and activity of the early *oenach* differed substantially from the medieval and modern fair, it is suggested that the practice of associating gravesites or cemeteries with fairs and markets continued until the Middle Ages.

4 Robin Flower, 'Manuscripts of Irish interest in the British Museum' in *Anal. Hib.*, ii (1931), p. 335.   **5** Philippe Aries, *The hour of our death* (trans.) H. Weaver (London, 1981), p. 62; originally published as *L'homme devant la mort* (Paris, 1977).   **6** Susan Leigh Fry, *Burial in medieval Ireland, 900–1500* (Dublin, 1999), p. 48.   **7** D.A. Binchy, 'The fair of Tailtiu and the feast of Tara' in *Eriu*, xxviii (1958), pp. 123–4.   **8** *The metrical Dindshenchas part iv*, ed. E. Gwynn (reprint Dublin, 1991 of original edition published Dublin, 1924), pp. 146–63.   **9** P.W. Joyce, *A social history of ancient Ireland* (London, 4 5.

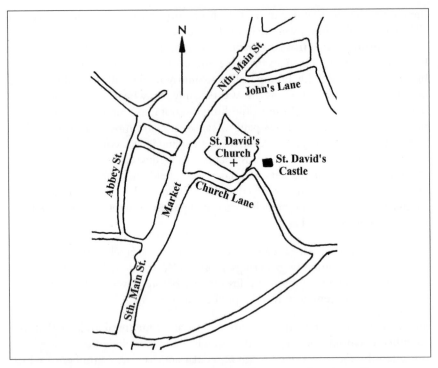

Figure 2 Street plan of Naas, county Kildare, showing market place adjacent to
St David's Church

In 1308, Edward II found it necessary to forbid the holding of fairs and markets in church-yards 'for the honour of Holy Church'.[10] It is recorded that the crypt of Christchurch Cathedral in Dublin was leased to stall-holders during the medieval period and that markets were held there.[11] The French writer, Aries, went so far as to say that 'Undoubtedly it was the appearance of the market in the twelfth and thirteenth centuries that brought about the enlargement of some cemeteries.'[12] Perhaps the rationale behind the association of market places with churchyards was the fact that cemeteries were beyond the arm of the law where taxes were concerned. It was also true that the king's writ held no authority there. It has been argued that in some cases it is possible that the fair or market may predate the church ground on which it was held. William Addison suggests that some churches were constructed on the sites of pre-existing fairs and that the church was then given the patronage of the saint whose festival fell nearest to the time of the fair.[13] One example which may bear this out relates to St

10 *Statutes and ordinances and acts of Parliament of Ireland: King John to Henry V* (ed.) Henry F. Berry (Dublin, 1907), p. 257. Hereafter cited as *Statutes and Ordinances.*   11 James Mills, 'Sixteenth century notices of the chapels and crypts of the church of the Holy Trinity, Dublin' in *JRSAI* xxi (C) (1900), pp. 195–203.   12 Aries, *The hour*, p. 70.   13 William

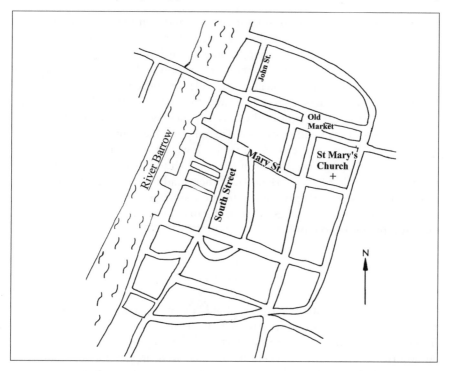

Figure 3 Street plan of New Ross, county Wexford based on P.H. Hore's map of New Ross, *c.*1700 showing the Old Market in close proximity to St Mary's Church.

Colmcille and Swords in county Dublin. The town of Swords is often referred to as Sord Colmcille and the annual eight-day fair, which was granted in 1193, was centred on the feast of St Colmcille.[14] It is possible that the fair had been in existence prior to the grant and there are references to the settlement at Swords in the annals of the tenth century.

In the early Irish context, the ancient *oenach* included a ritual element as well as its legal, commercial and athletic activities.[15] This continued into the middle ages, when medieval fairs opened with solemn church devotions and with the dictum that all trade should be transacted in good faith. All grants for fairs and markets were based on feast days and religious festivals in the Christian calendar. An examination of the layout of medieval towns shows that the market place is often located adjacent to the church site. This is true in the case of the medieval town of Naas, county Kildare (Figure 2), where the market place lies beside St David's Church. Similarly in Nobber, county Meath, the market cross may have

Addison, *English fairs and markets* (London, 1953), p. 6.   **14** John Bradley, 'The medieval boroughs of county Dublin' in Conleth Manning, (ed.), *Dublin and beyond the Pale* (Dublin, 1998), p. 138.   **15** Alfred P. Smyth, *Celtic Leinster* (Dublin, 1982), p. 4.

been located on the junction of Church Lane and Main Street.[16] In medieval New Ross (Figure 3), market stalls were located opposite St Saviour's Church. All of this may indicate that when trading was no longer allowed within the church grounds, following the 1308 statute of Edward II, the traders simply moved their stalls outside the church precincts and trade continued as before. According to Herbert P. Hore, a market cross indicated the site to which the market was relocated.[17] The market cross of the period generally had a base of three steps and an octagonal shaft and crossbeam. The religious element of the fair was not abandoned following the change of venue, however. The saint's festival or the religious feast was still celebrated in the local church from which the people went in procession to the market place where trading commenced. According to L.F. Salzman, the market was protected from outrage and disturbance by these religious conventions that were part of the market ritual of which the market cross was the visible symbol.[18]

PATRONS

Those who were granted charters to hold fairs were generally the local lords who had petitioned the king. An analysis of the founders or applicants for licences for fairs and markets in the thirteenth century yields interesting results. Almost two-thirds of the total fairs and markets were applied for and granted to secular lords. Interestingly however, bishops were granted almost twice the number of markets as fairs.

Table 1 Grantees of fairs and markets during the 13th century.

	Lords	*Bishops*	*Abbots*	*Others*
Fairs	61%	17%	1%	21%
Markets	65%	29%	2%	4%

Based on licences granted 1200–1300 in *Calendar of Documents, Ireland.*

In many cases the grant included permission for the establishment of several fairs or markets by one lord. The market grants were for different days throughout the lordship so that toll collectors and traders could travel from place to place. A grant in 1258 stated that the applicant might establish markets and fairs wherever he wished throughout his estate. The only condition attached was that they would not harm neighbouring fairs and markets.[19] Possession of a licence meant

16 Map of Naas, *JKAS*, vol. xviii (part III), p. 370; map of Nobber, *Riocht na Midhe*, vol. ix, no. 4 (1998), p. 29.   **17** Herbert P. Hore, *History of New Ross – Old and New Ross* (London 1900), p. 114.   **18** L.F Salzman, *English trade in the Middle Ages* (Oxford, 1931), p. 121.   **19** *Calendar of Ormond Deeds, 1172–1350* [etc.], ed. Edmund Curtis (6 vols, Dublin,

that the lord had the power to extract tolls from the buyers and sometimes from the sellers at the fair or market. In return, the licensee provided institutional support for the fair or market in the form of weights, measures, stalls and other suitable premises.

Charters for fairs located in the vicinity of monasteries were applied for by the priors of the monastic establishments. During the thirteenth century, a fair was established at Athassel, county Tipperary, and the grantee was listed as the prior. Many of the fairs were established by the bishops of the period. Henry, bishop of Emly had a fair established there in 1215; Henry, archbishop of Dublin, renewed a grant for a fair in Dublin in 1225; John, bishop of Ferns, established three fairs in his diocese in 1226 while Geoffrey, bishop of Ossory established five fairs there in 1245.

In New Ross in Wexford, the great annual fair was established following the town's first charter from the earl of Norfolk at the end of the thirteenth century. This fair began on 8 December each year. This date was still used for the annual fair as late as 1899. It is believed that the fair of New Ross was located at the site where the Tholsel now stands. According to Hore, this is the site of the old market cross of the town.[20]

The granting of a fair or market does not necessarily signify the origins of regular trading in a village or town, however. Instead, it indicates that trade had become large enough to be formalized.[21] A prohibition on unlicensed markets was issued in 1200. This prohibition implies that markets were appearing in places without the blessing of a royal charter. In 1207 the king forbade the establishment of markets following his visit to Ireland. It is claimed that the medieval fair of Carlingford, county Louth, which received its licence in 1227, was already in existence for some time and that the market of Carlingford, which received its licence in 1358, had probably been in existence for at least one hundred years by then.[22] A weekly Monday market was granted to the archbishop of Dublin at Swords in 1395, but it is believed that this had probably been in existence for many years by that time.[23]

In spite of the fact that many licences were issued for the establishment of fairs and markets, it is not certain if all of these actually came into being. In Skryne in county Meath, it was recorded that 'Richard de Feypo prays a fair at Scren on the day of Saint Luke the Evangelist.'[24] The lands at Skryne had been granted to Adam de Feypo, Richard's father, in the 1170s and the family established a town there. The licence took two years to process and was eventually granted in 1279.[25] In a case before the justiciar five years later in 1284, de Feypo declared

1932–43), i, p. 56. **20** Hore, *New Ross*, p. 115. **21** R.H. Britnell, 'The proliferation of markets in England, 1200–1349' in *Economic History Review*, 2nd series, xxxiv (1981), p. 216. **22** Paul Gosling, *Carlingford town: An antiquarian's guide* (Carlingford, 1992), p. 29. **23** John Bradley, 'Medieval boroughs of county Dublin,' p. 139. **24** Elizabeth Hickey, *Skryne and the early Normans* (Meath, 1994), p. 184. **25** *Cal. Doc. Ire., 1252–1284*, p. 307.

that although he had been granted permission to hold a fair at Skryne, the fair had not yet been established there.[26]

Implicit in the creation of a market or fair by the local lord or monastic abbot was the necessity to create stalls and to maintain standards within the selling place. Unless the founder was willing to provide the necessary infrastructure the market might not expand and develop. In New Ross during the great annual fair, the Earl Marshall held stalls opposite St Saviour's Church. Other stalls were leased to a certain Gallard Maubin to be built up and maintained. Houses were hired for the duration of the fair. Further houses were hired in which court cases would be heard during the fair. In the event of the market being unsuccessful in its original location, the burgesses retained the right to move it elsewhere within the town boundary. In 1289, the community of Market Street paid forty shillings for permission to hold a market at the corner of their street. The earl in turn, hired two houses on that street at a cost of 5s. 2½d. From then on properties in Market Street commanded high rents. Rentals of premises in the main commercial area were twice the rentals of properties further along the street with a house 'in front' costing 2d. a week while another on the same street, but nearer the cemetery, cost 1d. a week.[27] In Kilkenny, houses were let for the duration of the fair. One third of the profits from these was taken by the lord. Plots of land in the street outside these houses were also let during the fair.[28] As trade increased many plots were often subdivided to maximise access to the street. This is true of medieval Trim where properties adjacent to the market place are narrower than those throughout the rest of the town.[29]

HARDSHIPS AND IMPEDIMENTS TO TRADE

It is likely that the stalls in these markets and fairs were temporary erections with wooden frames and canvas or cloth roofs and sides. In some parts of England it was ordained that each booth should be eight feet in length and eight feet in depth.[30] A contemporary account of the Westminster fair gives an idea of the conditions endured by the sellers in their stalls. Matthew Paris, a thirteenth century chronicler wrote in 1248

> … all those who exhibited their goods for sale there suffered great inconvenience because of the lack of roofs apart from canvas awnings; for the variable gusts of wind, usual at that time of year, battered the merchants so that they were cold, wet, hungry and thirsty. Their feet were dirtied by the mud and their merchandise spoilt by the rain. When they sat down

---

26 *Cal. Doc. Ire.*, p. 551. (1284) This fair was subsequently established, as shall be seen later in this article. **27** Hore, *New Ross*, p. 160. **28** *Calendar of inquisitions post mortem* (London, 1904–74), p. 328. **29** Tadhg O'Keeffe, *Medieval Ireland: an archaeology* (Gloucestershire, 2000), p. 95. **30** Salzman, *English trade in the Middle Ages*, p. 149.

there at table, those who normally took their meals at home by the family fireside could not stand the discomfort.[31]

A further insight into the hardships and discomforts endured by retailers is found in the Dublin records. There as in many other market and fair locations, many women retailers sat in the streets and sold goods from baskets.[32]

Several sources declare that trading began at the fair at the ninth hour of the day. This is true of the fairs in Callan and Kilkenny which began 'from the hour of nones on the vigil of Pentecost'.[33] The townspeople were frequently given the first choice of goods. In 1422, it was ordained that nobody should buy corn, oats, barley, peas, beans or any grain in the market of Kilkenny before the tenth hour of the day. The punishment for disobeying this order would be a fine of 40*d*.[34]

Taking goods to and from market often proved to be a dangerous business. Watchmen were necessary both day and night to protect the merchandise. In 1303, Michael de Fernden, who was on his way home from Cashel in county Tipperary with his cart loaded with merchandise, was forced to hire a certain Henry of Norwich to watch over the cart during the night while Michael slept in a nearby lodging house.[35] In another more colourful incident which occurred in 1306 in Kildare, William Douce, a Dublin merchant, was on his way to the fair in Kilkenny when he was robbed at Naas of a pair of linen web, a pair of shoes and a pair of hose. The thief was Cristiana la Sadelhackere who had seduced William's servingman.[36] Penalties for theft from merchants were often very severe. In 1306, Thomas, son of William Fwelewryght, was sentenced to be hanged for having robbed a horse, cloth and other goods from Henry de Kilbeworth, a merchant in Dublin.[37]

In times of war and general disturbance, piracy and robbery were rife along the main roads and rivers. There are many records of complaints from merchants relating to the seizure or robbery of their goods. In 1340, an official complaint was made by a group of merchants who had become reluctant to bring goods to Ireland. These merchants were constantly under attack on the highways and regularly had their merchandise stolen. They themselves were sometimes held captive until large ransoms were paid for their freedom and for the return of their goods.[38] Merchants who came from abroad were also victims of the political intrigues of the time. In 1234–5, the king ordered that all French merchants found in Ireland were to be arrested immediately. This action was in response to the arrest of the king's tailor and other English merchants in France.[39] A mandate issued in 1254 instructed the justiciar to arrest certain merchants at each Irish

---

31 *The illustrated chronicles of Matthew Paris*, trans. Richard Vaughan (Cambridge, 1993), p. 70.   **32** *Calendar of ancient records of Dublin*, ed. John T. Gilbert, (19 vols, Dublin, 1889–1944), i, p. 234.   **33** *Liber Primus Kilkenniensis*, trans. A.J. Otway-Ruthven (Kilkenny, 1961), p. 10. Patrick Logan, *Fair day* (Belfast, 1986), p. 16.   **34** *Liber Primus Kilkenniensis*, p. 61.   **35** *Cal. Jus. Rolls*, iii, p. 461.   **36** *Cal. Jus. Rolls*, ii, p. 502.   **37** Ibid., p. 498.   **38** *Liber Primus Kilkenniensis*, p. 17.   **39** *Cal. Doc. Ire., 1171–1251*, p. 333.

port along with their wines and other merchandise and to hold them until further notice.[40] The following year, in response to the imprisonment of his uncle, the king ordered that all merchants of Lombardy who were currently travelling in Ireland be arrested.[41] A proclamation for the arrest of merchants from Scotland was issued in 1299.[42]

The transport of certain goods from place to place almost certainly posed problems for the travelling merchant. Goods made from metal would have been extremely heavy and cumbersome to transport. The weight and the bulk of animal hides would also have caused problems. Equally, carrying wine must have been difficult. River transport was used where possible but there were regular complaints about the obstruction of boats by weirs on the Barrow, Nore, Liffey and Boyne rivers.[43] Carters were employed throughout the countryside to carry produce to market. In Dublin in the thirteenth century, the wages for carrying salt to the city market were approximately 3d. while a load of iron cost 3½d.[44] A man hired to carry flour from the mill to the town of New Ross was paid 4s. 4d. for carriage for the fifty-two weeks of the year.[45]

The safety and security of the goods on open display at the point of sale in the market and in the fair was also a problem. The townspeople of New Ross hired watchmen at a cost of between 8s. and 10s. per annum for fear of robberies during the fair. In one incident there a customer who spotted a piece of cloth on a market stall began to haggle with the seller. Unfortunately for the seller however, the customer eventually made off with the cloth without paying.[46] Another account refers to eighty horses being stolen from the market of Cloncurry in county Kildare. The market must have been a substantial one if there were at least eighty horses there for sale. Yet, its security was very poor if such numbers of animals could be stolen from it successfully.[47] In Kilkenny, two or three men were hired from the feast of All Saints until Ash Wednesday of the following year to watch from curfew to cockcrow to ensure that market stalls were untouched on the dark winter evenings.[48] In 1285, Edward I commanded that in order to maintain security in the country, the gates of towns should be closed from sunset to sunrise, and that no lodgers should stay in town overnight. Every fifteen days the bailiffs of the town were instructed to inquire about all lodgers in the town. Watchmen were to be employed from Ascension to the feast of St Michael, six at each city gate, twelve at each borough and four to six men in each town. The watch should last from sunset to sunrise. Strangers who passed by were to be arrested until morning. It was acknowledged that the roads and highways were heavily overgrown and in places were almost impassable. It was declared that the highways from one market town to another were to be cleared and widened, particularly where there were woods, ditches and undergrowth.

---

40 *Cal. Doc. Ire., 1252–1284*, p. 56.   **41** Ibid., p. 79.   **42** *Cal. Jus. Rolls*, i, p. 229. **43** Timothy O'Neill, *Merchants and mariners in medieval Ireland* (Dublin, 1986), p. 55. **44** *Calendar of ancient records of Dublin*, i, p. 222.   **45** Hore, *New Ross*, p. 157.   **46** Hore, *New Ross*, p. 52.   **47** *Cal. Jus. Rolls*, ii, p. 198.   **48** *Liber Primus Kilkenniensis*, p. 36.

Clearances of two hundred feet on either side of the road were to be made so that malefactors would be unable to lie in wait for unsuspecting travellers. In the event of the lord's refusal to take such action, he would be held liable for attacks, robberies or murders on his lands.[49] Bridges were to be repaired or rebuilt and then maintained.[50]

As the size and extent of fairs and markets increased, pollution became a significant issue. The sale of fish posed health and sanitary problems in the towns. In Dublin, an ordinance passed by the city declared that fish must be eviscerated at the riverbank and not at the market place. Likewise, waste matter from cattle slaughtered for market was not to be discarded in the market place.[51] In October 1335, the burgesses of Kilkenny ordained that each person should cleanse the pavement outside his house twice weekly on Wednesdays and Saturdays. Two years later it was proclaimed that anyone found washing animal intestines in the town fountains would be punished severely. In addition, it was now also incumbent on merchants selling grain, firewood or turf to clean the street after the market.[52] Women who sold goods from baskets in Dublin were ordered to pay ¼d.-a week towards the cleansing of the streets and stalls.[53] Archaeological excavations have shown that carrion-eating birds and ravens were very common throughout this period. The large quantities of meat and fish debris no doubt contributed to the presence of these birds, which included buzzards, eagles and red kites.[54]

PRODUCTS SOLD

It might be expected that Ireland's location on the western periphery of Europe would have caused her to be isolated in terms of trade and commerce. Yet, this is not the case at all. Throughout the medieval period, many foreign merchants travelled throughout Ireland selling their wares, and goods from as far away as Byzantium and the Orient were available. Traders from Florence were found in New Ross as early as 1217.[55] References to merchants from places as diverse as Germany, France, Spain, Portugal, Navarre, Lombardy, Tuscany, Provence, Catalonia, Aquitaine, Toulouse, Flanders and Brabant are found in the documents of the period. These merchants were obliged to pay customs to the king and in return they were allowed to trade freely. They chartered ships to bring in such goods as wine, wax, jewels, copper pots, spices, furs and cloth. The fact that they used the Latin language for trade enabled them to travel so far afield. Many of these merchants were small-time pedlars. Their stock in trade would have been

---

49 *Statutes and ordinances* p. 256.   **50** Philomena Connolly, 'The enactments of the 1297 Parliament,' in James Lydon (ed.), *Law and order in thirteenth century Ireland: The Dublin Parliament of 1297* (Dublin, 1997), p. 159.   **51** *Calendar of ancient records of Dublin*, i, p. 219. **52** *Liber Primus Kilkenniensis*, p. 28.   **53** *Cal. Ancient Records*, i, p. 234.   **54** Frank Mitchell and Michael Ryan, *Reading the Irish landscape* (Dublin, 1997), p. 73.   **55** M.D. O'Sullivan, *Italian merchant bankers in Ireland in the thirteenth century* (Dublin, 1962), p. 102.

the little luxuries required on medieval estates and villages such as spices, precious metals and gems, furs, silks and fine cloth.[56]

The chief commodities available in the town markets and fairs in Ireland in the early Norman period comprised firstly of agricultural produce such as corn, cattle, sheep and horses. They included such items as salted and fresh hides, skins of horse, ox, sheep, lamb, deer, wolf, marten, otter, squirrel, wild cat, hare and rabbit, sides of bacon, honey, onions, butter, beans and fat pork. Fish featured prominently, with herrings, eels, salmon, oysters, lampreys and mulwell available. Salted, dried and fresh fish were all sold.[57] Heavier metal objects like iron, brass, copper, lead, tin, steel, horse trappings, horse irons and saddles are listed. Household items such as brewers' cauldrons, griddles and grid-irons, platters, dishes and kitchen utensils are mentioned. French and English grinding stones, coal boards, tiles, hemp, white and coloured glass, wood, sumac, alum, copperas, madder, pitch, tar, oils and resin were also imported.[58] In 1306, a merchant on his way to market was robbed of his horse together with its saddle and reins, cloth of Laghton, a *fallaing*, a piece of silver, a robe, shirt, girdle, hat and primer, skins, shearing cloth, copper and a sword.[59] Silks from China, cloth of silk and gold, samite (a heavy silk fabric), diaper (cloth with patterns or repeated figures), carpets, embroidered cloths and covers and woollen cloths of Galloway and Worsted, English and Irish and foreign cloth, canvas, linen, cordwain and the *fallaing* or Irish mantle were also in great demand.[60]

The thirteenth-century poem about the walling of New Ross gives an idea of the trades and skills of the inhabitants of the town at that period. Trades such as vintners, mercers, drapers, tailors, dyers, fullers, saddlers, leatherworkers, tanners, butchers, bakers, porters, carpenters, blacksmiths and masons are all mentioned.[61] John the Goldsmith, John the Wimpler – maker of wimples or ladies veils, the Napper – maker of linen cloth and the Gaunter – maker of gloves – also appear in the Provost of New Ross's accounts in the 1280s. Accounts of shipwrecks off the Irish coast also give some idea of goods being imported for sale in this period. A ship wrecked off the coast of Portmarnock, county Dublin in 1306 included wax, jewels, wine, copper pots, barrels of spices and cloth among its cargo.[62] A wide variety of spices was available throughout the countryside, pepper and cumin being among the most common. However, ginger, galingale, saffron, cloves, mace and many others were also available. Rice, almonds, figs and raisins, dried fruits, garlic and olive oil were also for sale.[63] Perfumes and drugs were

56 M. Postan, 'Trade and industry in the Middle Ages' in *Cambridge Economic History of Europe*, vols. ii, Cambridge, 1952, p. 168. 57 Avril Thomas, 'Financing town walls' in C. Thomas (ed.), *Rural landscapes and communities: essays presented to D. McCourt* (Dublin, 1987), pp. 72–4. 58 *Historical and Municipal Documents of Ireland*, ed. J.T. Gilbert (London, 1870), pp. 124–5. 59 *Cal. Jus. Rolls*, ii, p. 498. 60 *Historical and Municipal Documents*, pp. 124–5. 61 Hugh Shields (ed.) 'The walling of New Ross: A thirteenth century poem in French', in *Long Room*, 12–13 (Dublin, 1975–6). 62 *Cal. Jus. Rolls*, ii, p. 507. 63 Thomas, 'Financing town walls', p. 72. Hore describes 'galingale' as sweet cyperus (*New*

introduced to Anglo-Norman households at this time. Smaller luxury items were also available to those who could afford them. Jewels, *objets d'art*, ivories, gold and silver plate, some of which may have originated in Byzantium, China and Persia were to be found in the houses of the wealthy.[64]

Materials for building and repairs were usually bought locally, possibly directly from the craftsmen. At the end of the thirteenth century, wooden tiles, boards and lathes were purchased at Tullow, Athy and Dunleckny for the repair of the castle at Carlow.[65] Lead for repairs to the gutters was bought in Dublin. Millstones were constantly in need of repair and replacement. Millstones for Carlow were bought at Island in Waterford and were transported upriver to Carlow.

The market at Naas was a centre for the purchase of wool. In 1305, it is recorded that a certain Ricard had purchased nine sacks of wool at the market there. In that same year, Thomas de Cauntelon came to the market at Naas to sell lambs. Sheep and wool were important sources of income on manors of the period. During the last decades of the thirteenth century, attempts were made to encourage the spread of wool production to the southern part of Kildare. The manor of Ballysax, which was then part of the lordship of Carlow, was regularly used to restock other centres throughout the lordship during these years. As a result, sales of wool from the manor of Fothered (now Castlemore) in Carlow increased considerably throughout the years from 1280 to 1288.[66]

OTHER BUSINESS CONDUCTED AT FAIRS

Medieval fairs fulfilled other functions in addition to buying and selling. They also served as places for settling accounts and as centres of social interaction. Indeed, medieval fairs have been described as 'embryonic clearing houses,' as debts were often settled there.[67] At Trim fair in 1280, a sum of £57 10s. 2d. was collected by a messenger of Stephen, bishop of Waterford.[68] A complaint lodged by Geoffrey de Morton in 1302 stated that a debt that was due to be paid to him at the fair of Dublin remained unpaid.[69] A marriage covenant of January 1305/6 included the arrangement that the bride's father would pay off the debts that the prospective groom had incurred at the market of Kilkenny.[70]

A special court called the Court of Piepowder was a feature of many medieval fairs. This term evolved from the French word for pedlar, *pied pouldre*,

---

Ross, p. 202). **64** O'Sullivan, *Italian merchant bankers* p. 110. **65** J. Mills, 'Accounts of the earl of Norfolk's estates in Ireland, 1279–94, in *JRSAI*, 22 (1892), pp. 50–62. Also NLI, pos. 2922, 77*d*. Hereafter cited as Bigod Accounts. **66** Mary C. Lyons, *Manorial administration and the manorial economy in Ireland, c.1200–1377*, unpublished Ph.D. thesis (TCD, 1984) p. 62. **67** J.N.L. Baker, 'Medieval trade routes', in Geoffrey Barraclough (ed.), *Social life in early England* (London, 1960), p. 237. **68** *Irish Exchequer Payments, 1270–1446*, ed. Philomena Connolly (2 vols, Dublin, 1998), i, p. 65. **69** *Cal. Jus. Rolls*, ii, p. 375. **70** *Red Book of Ormond*, ed. Newport B. White (Dublin, 1932), p. 109.

and was also translated as 'dusty foot'.[71] This provided an explicit description of the state of people travelling about on the unsurfaced roads of the period. This court addressed disputes which arose during the fair about prices, contracts, quality of goods or thefts from stalls or merchants. It allowed that

> every person coming to the said fair should have the lawful remedy of all manners of contracts, trespasses, covenants, debts and other deeds made or done within the said fair and within the jurisdiction of the same and to be tried of merchants being of the same fair.[72]

In Kilkenny, four townsmen were chosen as barons to hear the pleas of the fair. Each plaintiff was required to have 'two lawful men' with him to plead his case in regard to transgression, debt, agreements or contracts. Upon proof of his guilt, the defendant was arrested until he satisfied the plaintiff and the court for the amount in question.[73] In New Ross a certain house was rented to accommodate this court. A clerk was also employed to record the pleas heard and the judgements handed down. Parchment, on which the cases were recorded, was purchased at a cost of 6d. A carpet costing 2s. was utilised to record transactions. This was the *tapetum* on which were drawn lines resembling those on a chessboard which was a common medieval system of accounting.

The market place was the centre where news and current affairs were discussed and disseminated. Rumours, scandals and other exciting titbits of information spread like wildfire throughout the market. Announcements and other proclamations of public interest were made at fairs and markets. The apprehension and murder of a felon and the confiscation of his stolen goods quickly became common knowledge at the fair at Tamelog (Templeogue) in 1295.[74] At Naas in 1305, it was claimed that Adam le Tanner had been verbally abused by Thomas de Cauntelon 'before all the people in the market'.[75]

The fair also offered the opportunity to the very rich to purchase on a grand scale. It offered the king's purveyors the opportunity to purchase supplies which could be sent to the armies while they were involved in military campaigns. In December 1298, Henry de Waletone and John Bowet purchased large quantities of corn and malt at the fair in Dublin to be sent to the King in Wales.[76]

PROFITS FROM FAIRS AND MARKETS

It has been suggested that in establishing fairs and markets, patrons were motivated by paternalism and not by profit seeking. It is further claimed that they founded 'small, unambitious new markets more to accommodate the poor

---

71 Addison, *English fairs and markets*, p. 11.   72 Statutes 17 Edward IV, c.2, quoted in Salzman, *English trade in the Middle Ages*, p. 161.   73 *Liber Primus Kilkenniensis*, p. 10.   74 *Cal. Jus. Rolls*, i, p. 63.   75 *Cal. Jus. Rolls*, ii, p. 149.   76 *Cal. Doc. Ire., 1285–92*, p. 272.

than for profit.'[77] An examination of profits from fairs and markets shows however, that they were operated on a very definite profit-making basis and that possession of a fair was a great advantage to a town, and therefore ultimately, to the patron, whether secular or ecclesiastical. Patrons came to appreciate that much could be gained by encouraging and supporting communities in their efforts to regulate trade.

Profits could be made both from tolls and rentals of stalls and houses. The list of goods on which tolls could be charged was extensive. It was intended however, that goods bought for ordinary domestic consumption would be excluded from tolls. By 1220, merchants were complaining to the king that they were so burdened by tolls in Ireland that there was little left for them to live on. These merchants declared that the city of Dublin and other Irish cities had become so hateful to them that they would no longer frequent them to sell their goods.[78] In 1285, in an attempt to alleviate the situation, the king proclaimed that those who imposed excessive tolls in market towns would lose their licences.[79]

The bishop of Waterford exerted such control on the sale of wines and corn in his area that he managed to stock his own cellars with the best wine imported into the country. His own vendors sold this wine and no others were permitted to sell wine in the area.[80] For both secular and ecclesiastical lords, the aim was to raise a certain amount of income from their tenants in cash through tolls, fines, rents and other taxes. This cash would be spent on luxury items necessary to maintain a noble way of life, as well as on military hardware for protection. It was yet another commercial scheme by which they sought to exploit their estates to the full. In order to obtain cash, the tenants had to sell their own produce at the newly established commercial centres in the towns. Consequently, fairs and markets became a vital part of medieval life. Spufford contends that September was the time when most coin was in circulation due to sales of corn.[81] At this time of year, sales of manufactured goods were highest, as farm implements were replaced and repaired in readiness for the following year's harvest.

An examination of the accounts for the Liberty of Carlow for the period 1280–81 gives an idea of the potential income from fairs and markets. Two stalls in New Ross on a street adjoining the Market Street provided an income of 12*d.* Further stalls opposite St Saviour's were worth 4*s.* 4*d.* In the same year, an income of £6 15*s.* 3*d.* was recorded for the Rolls House which became the earl's property during the markets, while the pleas and perquisites of the market came to 26*s.* 10*d.* The accounts for the following year show a deficit for the above-mentioned stalls. It would appear that the stall sites were leased to a Gallard Maubin, who failed to build them up. He was ordered to complete them without delay. The accounts for 1281 record an income of 110*s.* 4*d.* for houses beside the Earl's Gate which were hired at the time of the fair. Pleas and

77 Britnell, 'The proliferation of markets in England', p. 221. **78** *Cal. Doc. Ire., 1171–1251*, p. 148. **79** *Statutes and Ordinances*, p. 71. **80** Ibid., p. 1. **81** Peter Spufford, *Money and its uses in medieval Europe* (Cambridge, 1988), p. 382.

perquisites of the fair were worth 38s. 10d.[82] In 1283–4, houses hired during the fair close to the Earl's gate were worth 54s. 9d. The following year the income had increased again to 60s. 1½d.[83] By 1287, the revenue from these houses had risen to £4 19s. 2d. Stalls hired to Robert Serman produced an income of 10s. These stalls are described as being outside the fair. The toll of the New Ross market was 6d. by 1293–4.[84] In 1307, the perquisites of the market together with the rent of stalls were worth 60s. yearly.[85] This compares very favourably with other fairs which sometimes had perquisites of as little as three shillings annually.[86]

Variations in profits received from fairs imply that the fairs themselves differed in their importance. Miller and Hatcher refer to three differing classes of fair in medieval England. Firstly, there were the great fairs, of which New Ross is probably the best Irish example. Secondly, there were regional fairs such as those held at Drogheda, Kilkenny or Naas, which attracted buyers and sellers from considerable distances. Finally, there were village fairs which had a more local appeal.[87]

The burgesses of the towns maintained exclusive privileges in the fairs and markets. These privileges were embodied in the town charters. Burgesses enjoyed the freedom to buy and sell at the market or anywhere within the town without paying tolls, whereas non-burgesses were restricted to dealing only at the market and were forced to pay tolls on goods brought to market for sale. Burgesses also maintained the right to move the site of the market within the walls of the town at any time if the originally designated site proved unsuitable for commerce. They managed to hold a monopoly on the market as an 'élite core of the richer burgesses constituted the ruling body' of the town.[88] In 1230 for example, the townspeople of Kilkenny came together to 'elect their sovereign and the twelve who are best, and can govern and counsel their sovereign to the profit of the said community.'[89] This measure would ensure protection for themselves and their own goods, as well as control over others permitted to trade or set up business in their town.

Tenants of the king's demesnes in Ireland were also exempted from paying tolls. Despite this, however, in 1306, the mayor and the community of Drogheda were forced by Theobald de Verdun and his men to pay a toll to him in his market at Duleek, county Meath 'to their heavy damage and against custom hitherto enjoyed by men of the king's demesne lands …' A similar incident had occurred the previous year when representatives of Simon de Feypo had demanded tolls from the men of Drogheda at the market of Skryne. Both lords

---

82 Hore, *New Ross*, p. 148.   83 Ibid., p. 152.   84 Ibid., p. 39.   85 *Cal. Jus. Rolls*, ii, p. 348.
86 In 1288 the perquisites of the fair in Youghal in county Cork were 3s. annually, while in other parts of the country perquisites varied depending on the political situation. *Cal. Jus. Rolls*, i, pp. 202, 204.   87 E. Miller and J. Hatcher, *Medieval England: Towns, commerce and crafts, 1086–1348* (London, 1995), p. 169.   88 R.H. Hilton, 'Medieval market towns and simple commodity production' in *Past and Present*, no. 109 (Nov. 1985), p. 15.
89 *Liber Primus Kilkenniensis*, p. 25.

insisted that the tolls were profits belonging to their manors. Following these two incidents an agreement was eventually reached which exempted the burgesses of Drogheda from paying tolls in these markets.[90]

Members of religious communities were also exempted from paying tolls. In 1200, the king had ordered that certain monks be excused from paying tolls when buying goods for their own use.[91] Later, in 1290, the king promised that all members of the Templars in Ireland would be exempt from tolls in any fair or market throughout the realm.[92] In comparison, foreign merchants had very strict conditions placed upon them. Members of the Dublin merchant guild stated that a foreign merchant could only purchase corn, hides or wool from a citizen. No foreigner was permitted to sell cloth within the city.[93] Many town charters also included the proviso that no foreign merchant was allowed to stay within the town for more than forty days at any one time. In Kilkenny and in Moen, (Moone), county Kildare, a foreigner might stay longer if the burgesses agreed and if his stay contributed to the profits of the town.[94] The burgesses of Drogheda were granted the power in 1229 to forbid foreign merchants to sell cloth in cut portions or to sell wine by retail within the town.[95] In Waterford, no stranger was permitted to have a wine tavern unless it was on board a ship within the harbour. Foreign merchants were also forbidden to sell cut portions of cloth, or to stay in the town for more than forty days without the consent of the citizens.[96] Similar conditions applied in the town of Carlow under a charter from William Marshall dated 1209. These conditions were possibly introduced to protect smaller, local retailers by restricting the foreign merchants to wholesale selling only.

DID THE EARLY ESTABLISHMENT OF A MARKET
OR FAIR ENSURE ITS SURVIVAL?

It has been found that the most significant contribution to urban success was an early establishment, and that the towns that proved to be most successful subsequently, tended to be those which were established first by the most powerful lords in their lordships.[97] The same was true in England where the survival rate of markets established before 1250 was much greater than those of later foundation.[98] Where a borough was already established and had a tradition of holding a fair or market, new markets established nearby found it very

90 *Cal. Jus. Rolls*, ii, pp. 66, 188. **91** *Cal. Doc. Ire., 1171–1251*, p. 18. **92** *Cal. Doc. Ire., 1285–92*, p. 328. **93** Roy C. Cave and Herbert H. Coulson, *A Source book for medieval economic history* (New York, 1965), pp. 207–8. **94** *Liber Primus Kilkenniensis*, p. 6. See also *Cal. Jus. Rolls*, i, p. 369. **95** *Cal. Doc. Ire, 1171–1251*, p. 259. **96** Ibid., p. 291. **97** B.J. Graham, 'The High Middle Ages: *c.*1100 to *c.*1350' in B.J. Graham, L.J. Proudfoot (eds.), *An Historical Geography of Ireland* (London, 1993), p. 80. **98** Miller and Hatcher, *Towns, commerce and crafts*, p. 180.

difficult to compete. The borough of Rosbercon, county Wexford, was established in 1290 on the west bank of the Barrow, directly opposite New Ross. A grant for a four-day fair to be held there from 2 May to 5 May was issued to Gilbert de Clare in 1286. A grant was also issued at the same time for a weekly market each Wednesday.[99] However, competition from the already established and very successful New Ross meant that the settlement of Rosbercon did not succeed in becoming a town. The settlement of Newtown near Trim suffered a similar fate due to the proximity of the existing town of Trim. In 1279, the bishop of Meath was granted a fair at Newtown. However, Trim, being the older foundation, continued to attract merchants and traders at the expense of Newtown.[100]

TRADE OUTSIDE THE MARKET

In order to achieve maximum profitability, it was imperative that all trading be carried on in a standardised way within the market or fair. Forestalling was not allowed. This involved the interception of goods en route to market (normally, before the hour when the market could legally begin business), in order to buy them and then bring them to market to sell at a price higher than that for which they would originally have sold. A statute issued at the beginning of the fourteenth century stated that

> ... Forestallers that buy any thing afore the due and accustomed hour against the good state and regulation of the town and market, or that pass out of the town to meet such things as come to the market, and buy outside of the town, to the intent that they may sell the same in the town more dearly ... their names shall be presented distinctly and openly, and they shall be amerced for every default, or to be judged to the Tumbrel.[101]

The burgesses of Kilkenny made it clear that anyone found guilty of forestalling victuals and other saleable items in their town would be committed to gaol and be liable for a substantial fine.[102] Likewise, any merchant selling wine, iron, salt or any other merchandise must only dispose of his goods under licence of the burgesses of the town – that is at the fair or market. Failure to comply would mean confiscation of the merchant's goods. Application of the law against forestalling was intended to protect the privileges of the burgesses as well as to maintain low prices for consumers. In 1333, the burgesses of Kilkenny declared

99 *Cal. Doc. Ire.* 1285–92, p. 109. **100** John Bradley, 'Planned Anglo-Norman towns in Ireland' in H. Clarke and A. Simms (eds.), *The comparative history of urban origins in non-Roman Europe* (Oxford, 1985), pp. 441–67. **101** *The Statutes of the Realm: Printed by command of His Majesty King George the Third, in Pursuance of an Address of the House of Commons of Great Britain, from original records and authentic manuscripts*, ed. A. Luders (London, 1810–1828), i, p. 202. **102** *Liber Primus Kilkenniensis*, p. 9.

that all fish must be brought to the common place ordained for this purpose and that sellers must stand at their stall for the entire day until all fish were sold. No unsold fish was to be kept in any house – it must be taken to the stall and sold the following day.[103] This regulation was possibly put in place to prevent the laying aside of certain fish until all other fish were sold in the market, in order to increase the price when the commodity would become scarce. It was issued on the Monday following Ash Wednesday at the beginning of the Lenten season, when people were not permitted to eat meat. In some towns, fishermen were permitted to sell fish directly from their boats at the quayside without having to pay tolls. However, if the fish were sold from a market stall, the seller had to pay ½*d*. a day for the stall.[104] In spite of these regulations, the problems clearly persisted. By 1352, the Kilkenny fishermen were complaining that they were unable to display or sell their fish as they were being stolen from their stalls by thieves. Three years later, fish had become scarce in Ireland and by 1356, people were finding it impossible to buy fish on the days when fish were eaten. This was as a result of merchants being forestalled on the highways and the fish being subsequently salted, processed and exported at a greater profit. Whatever fish were available were then sold at double or treble the regular price because of the scarcity. It was declared that only *bona-fide* purchasers could buy fish in bulk at the harbours and that they must then display and sell them at market stalls.[105] It was also proclaimed that fish must not be exported from the country. Subsequently, men were employed to supervise all ports between Dublin and Carlingford to ensure that no fish were exported without proper licence.[106] Dublin's fish market also suffered from forestallers. In 1336, it was recorded that, in an effort to regulate trade there, the sale of fish outside the shambles on Fishamble Street was prohibited.[107]

By 1372, there were still problems in the market at Kilkenny. Butchers were selling their meat outside the market. Again the burgesses ordained that all meat and fish must be sold within the market at the appointed place.[108] The problems of forestalling and trading outside the market had still not been resolved by the early fifteenth century. In October 1422, the burgesses declared that nobody should buy corn, oats, barley, peas, beans or any grain in any place in the town outside of the official market. Failure to comply would incur a fine of 40*d*.[109]

The town of New Ross experienced similar problems in the fourteenth century. It had become customary to sell salmon, hides and other merchandise outside of the official markets, thus forestalling the market and frustrating those who sought to regulate prices. In 1391, it was declared that anyone selling salmon, hides or any merchandise must sell them in the market in the town or at the fairs held in nearby towns. Anyone who contravened this order would be

---

103 *Liber Primus Kilkenniensis*, p. 26.   **104** *Cal. Ancient Records*, i, p. 222.   **105** *Statutes and Ordinances*, p. 401.   **106** *Irish Exchequer Payments*, ii, p. 473.   **107** Ian Broad and Bride Rosney, *Medieval Dublin; Two historic walks* (Dublin, 1982), p. 32.   **108** *Liber Primus Kilkenniensis*, p. 39.   **109** *Liber Primus Kilkenniensis*, p. 61.

arrested and would have his or her goods confiscated.[110] In May 1395, William Ilger of Ballyhack, Wexford was arrested for having sold salt, iron, hides, skins, leather and cloth at New Ross in contempt of the king's laws. The variety of goods that Ilger offered for sale indicates that he was possibly a merchant.[111]

THE HINTERLAND OF THE MARKET

It is generally accepted in England that the median distance travelled by customers to market was some 6.66 miles. Thirteenth-century lawyers regarded this distance as a normal day's journey.[112] However, it would appear that in Ireland merchants and goods travelled greater distances to market. A navigable river greatly extended the trading hinterland of a town. The river Barrow was navigable to Athy in the thirteenth and fourteenth centuries thus greatly enhancing the volume of trade in the towns along its course. Oats were brought by boat from Ballysax in Kildare to a 'certain stall in the town of Ross'.[113] William Ilger, mentioned above, travelled about ten miles from Ballyhack to New Ross to sell his merchandise. Kilkenny's success was greatly increased by its location on the Nore at the centre of a rich, agricultural area. It was possible to transport goods down-river from the city to New Ross and Waterford. The Kilkenny fair attracted merchants from far and wide. The records show that a citizen of Dublin regularly sent a packhorse load of merchandise to be sold at the fair there.[114]

EFFORTS TO STANDARDIZE WEIGHTS AND MEASURES

In 1217, Henry III attempted to standardize weights and measures by declaring that there be one measure of wine, one of corn and one of ale throughout the kingdom. He also attempted to create uniformity in lengths for cloth.[115] In 1244, the king instructed the justiciar to standardise all weights and measures throughout the country. These were to be modelled on those used in Dublin. All burgesses were to be informed of this proclamation.[116] Despite the many efforts to standardize weights and measures it was reported in 1253 that standards still varied throughout the country and particularly in Dublin. A further attempt was made to introduce uniformity in 1269. The burgesses of New Ross paid a fee of twenty shillings to have a standard of measurement for their town. The castle at Carlow purchased a gallon measure in Dublin to use as a recognised standard measurement.[117] A fine of 100s. was imposed on Simon Hoser in New

---

110 Hore, *New Ross*, p. 212.   111 Ibid., p. 214.   112 Christopher Dyer, 'Market towns and the countryside in late medieval England' in *Canadian Journal of History*, vols. xxxi (April 1996), pp. 17–35.   113 Hore, *New Ross*, p. 18.   114 *Cal. Jus. Rolls*, ii, p. 502. 115 *Statutes and Ordinances*, p. 15.   116 *Cal. Doc. Ire., 1171–1251*, p. 404.   117 Bigod

Ross for having a false yard measure, while Symon de la Lysere of the same town was fined £5 for a similar offence.[118] In 1277, the king sent his clerk, Elias of Wynton, to inspect weights and measures throughout the countryside.[119] Such inspections were carried out on a regular basis. In 1307, John le Cutayller, custodian of the pleas of the market, fined a town for faults he found there. He claimed that when he came to the town the bailiffs and the community would not produce the measures for examination. Consequently, he declared that he was imposing upon them a fine of 100 shillings. Subsequent to this threat, the weights and measures were immediately produced for his inspection. He then sealed them, as was the custom.[120]

The Statute of Merchants issued in 1285 declared that every fair should have its own seal. This seal should be opened in the presence of two lawful merchants. One piece of the seal should remain with the merchants while the other was to be retained by the clerk of the fair. In 1297, the king presented a seal and counter seal to the merchants of the city of Dublin for this very purpose.[121] The statute further declared that before collection of debts the penalties should be read aloud to the debtor. In order to pay the costs of the clerk and other administrative charges, the king would take three halfpennies of every pound received in a town with a fair. It became apparent in the early fifteenth century, however, that the office of the clerk was open to fraud and the possibility of making personal gains. It was found that some clerks did not examine weights and measures, did not break false measures or seal true ones, and that fines were being cancelled or not accounted for in their accounts.[122]

PHYSICAL LAYOUT OF TOWNS

According to John Bradley's findings, three types of market place occur in medieval towns. Many of the medieval towns whose street plan can be reconstructed are linear, consisting of a single street expanded at one end or in the centre to form either a triangular or oval-shaped market place. The thirteenth-century town of Kilkenny was laid out in this fashion. The single street, High Street, ran northwards towards St Canice's Cathedral. The street was broader in the middle than at either end so that a row of stalls could be erected on market day.[123] Rectilinear market places are found in chequer-plan towns. New Ross and Drogheda are examples.[124] In general, market places in monastic towns were situated to the east or southeast of the monastic enclosures. The

Accounts, 102*d*.   **118** Hore, *New Ross*, pp. 159, 161.   **119** *Cal. Doc. Ire., 1253–1277*, p. 140.
120 *Cal. Jus. Rolls*, ii, p.438.   **121** *Cal. Jus. Rolls*, i, p. 123.   **122** *Statutes and Ordinances*, p. 418.   **123** John Bradley, 'Kilkenny-the Faire City' in Howard B. Clarke (ed.), *Irish cities* (Cork, 1995), p. 159.   **124** John Bradley, 'The Medieval towns of Tipperary' in W. Nolan and T. McGrath (eds.), *Tipperary, History and Society* (Dublin, 1985), p. 38. See also Bradley, 'Planned Anglo-Norman towns,' p. 439.

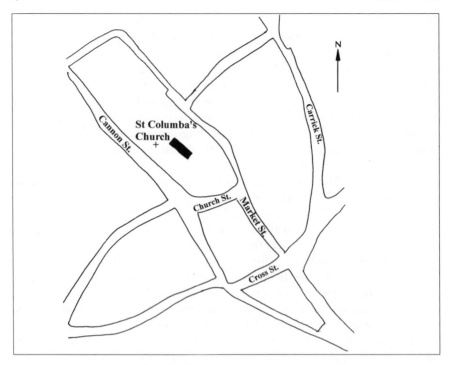

Figure 4 Street plan of Kells, county Meath showing Market Street
to the southeast of St Columba's Church.

market place at Kells in Meath is an example, lying to the southeast of the
Columban monastery.[125] Medieval Wexford's market place was situated outside
the town wall to the southeast of the monastic enclosure. The market place and
the monastic site were connected by a road.[126] Similarly, Kildare's market square
lies to the southeast of its monastic site. The site of the marketplace at
Glendalough was located to the northeast of the enclosure.[127]

   In some towns, the main street was expanded at one end to form a triangular
shape. This is true of Naas in county Kildare.[128] Suburbs of medieval Dublin also
had triangular market places. Oxmanstown's market lay outside the north gate
of St Mary's Abbey. The suburb that developed around St Patrick's Cathedral had
a triangular market place at the northern end of New Street.[129] The markets of

125 Anngret Simms, 'Kells' in William Nolan and Anngret Simms, (eds.), *Irish Towns:
A Guide to Sources* (Dublin, 1998), p. 180.   **126** Billy Colfer, 'Medieval Wexford' in *Journal
of the Wexford Historical Society*, no. 13 (1990–71), p. 9.   **127** Leo Swan, 'Monastic Proto-
towns in early medieval Ireland: The evidence of aerial photography, plan analysis and
survey' in H. Clarke and A. Simms (eds.), *The comparative history of urban origins in non-
Roman Europe* (Oxford, 1985), p. 99.   **128** Bradley, *Planned Anglo-Norman towns in Ireland*,
p. 439.   **129** Howard B. Clarke, 'Myths, magic and the Middle Ages: Dublin from its

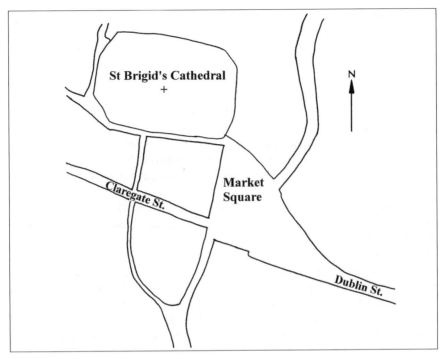

Figure 5 Street plan of Kildare showing Market Square to the
southeast of St Brigid's Cathedral.

the city of Dublin appear to have been well spread out. A map of the later
medieval city shows the meat market to have been quite separate from the fish
market, which was located near the riverside.[130]

REASONS FOR SUBSEQUENT FAILURE

The decline of marketing activity due to the population fall of the later Middle
Ages, was responsible for the failure or demise of many medieval fairs and
markets. The excessive optimism of lords who believed growth would persist
indefinitely and who speculatively sought market charters for villages which had
little chance of generating sufficient trade to support a market also contributed
to their downfall. By the early fifteenth century the unstable political position
of the Anglo-Norman towns greatly affected the commerce of these towns. In
1403, the king, in reply to a petition from the townspeople of New Ross,
granted them permission to trade with their 'Irish enemies' in such goods as

beginnings to 1577,' in Clarke (ed.), *Irish cities*, pp. 91–2. **130** *Viking and Medieval Dublin*,
Curriculum Development Unit (Dublin, 1978), p. 24.

victuals and other necessary articles. In 1402, the burgesses of the town of Kilkenny were forced to follow suit. They obtained the king's permission to sell victuals or merchandise to their enemies on market days in times of peace or truce. However, they were not permitted to sell them horses or arms.[131]

CONCLUSION

The dearth of documentary evidence makes it impossible to carry out an in-depth study of the fairs and markets of medieval Leinster. Yet it is possible to gain some idea of the trading and commerce of the period by combining the available sources. The survival of many calendared records of fair and market grants allows some examination of the frequency and distribution of these events throughout the east and southeast of the country. However, some of these fair and market charters may never have been put into effect. Others were already in existence for many years before the advent of the Anglo-Normans and it is possible that no licence or charter was ever issued for them. Therefore it is impossible to ascertain with any degree of accuracy the exact number and distribution of fairs and markets during this period. Yet, it is certain that there was indeed much trade in Leinster in the Middle Ages and that the fairs and markets attracted merchants from many parts of Europe and goods from all over the known world.

The quest for profit was the main motivation behind the foundation of most fairs and markets. However, unless many elements were in place, the venture was doomed. Those fairs and markets that were established earliest by the Anglo-Normans were destined to survive longer than those established later (Newtown, Trim and Rosbercon in Wexford). Support in the form of stalls, standardised weights and measures, and protection for both sellers and buyers were vital to the success of the fair or market. The variety of goods available at the fairs and markets of the medieval period was indeed wide and extensive. As transport and accessibility improved, the tastes of the wealthy for luxury and exotic items increased. Markets and fairs began to attract customers and sellers from further afield both within the country itself and from many parts of the European continent. One disadvantage of this increase in sales and profits was the environmental impact of the trade on the towns in terms of pollution and sanitation. Those who governed the towns were constantly under pressure to ensure the smooth operation of the markets and fairs as well as the maintenance of law and order. Transactions conducted outside the official market place caused many problems for those who stood to gain from the profits of the fairs and markets. Yet, despite the difficulties and the obstacles, many of the fairs and markets survived and proved to be very profitable commercial ventures for their founders.

131 Hore, *New Ross*, p. 217, note 3.

APPENDIX I

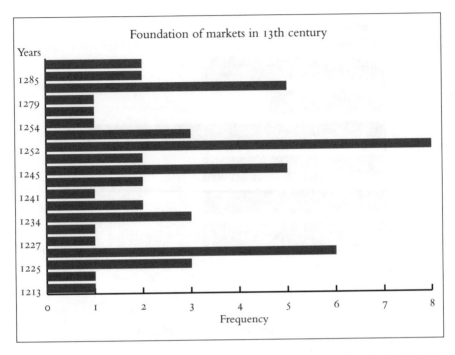

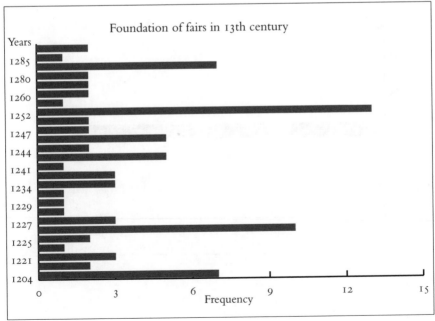

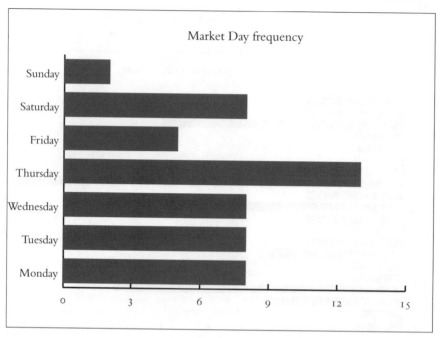

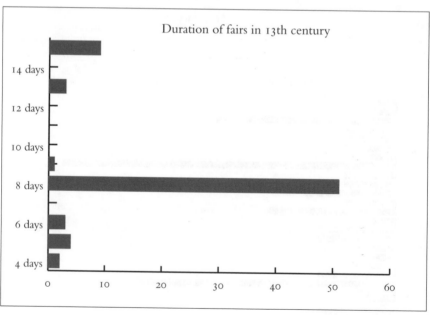

The origins, rise and decline of the Ennis fairs and markets

BRIAN Ó DÁLAIGH

At the summer assizes of 1844 Colonel George Wyndham, the owner of the Ennis fairs and markets, prosecuted a case against Alexander Bannatyne, the biggest corn merchant in county Clare, over his refusal to pay the market tolls of Ennis. By 1831 Ennis Corporation had ceased to function and there was a widespread determination among townspeople not to pay tolls or customs. Bannatyne questioned Wyndham's right to levy tolls and challenged him to produce the licences on which his claims rested. Wyndham's counsel laid three documents before the court: the first was a patent granted in 1609 to Donough O'Brien, fourth earl of Thomond, confirming his right to hold a Tuesday market and a fair twice yearly at Ennis. The second was a patent of 1620 granting the earl ownership of the soil on which the town was built and on which the markets were held. The third was a patent issued in 1835 giving permission for the collection of tolls on every day of the week except Sunday. Wyndham pointed out, however, that the royal patents were not the origin of his right to levy toll, but rather an additional entitlement to a prescriptive right that had been in existence long before the first licence was issued. A prescriptive right was defined as 'an uninterrupted enjoyment of a right, which is presumed to have been [in existence] from the earliest period whereof the memory of man runs'. The court found in favour of Wyndham but only awarded him the nominal sum of one farthing.[1] The tolls were quickly re-introduced and levied on all transactions at the Ennis fairs and markets for the remainder of the nineteenth century.

ORIGINS OF THE MARKETS

It is difficult to say when the Ennis markets began. In the early thirteenth century, the O'Briens, kings of Thomond (North Munster), located their principal stronghold at Clonroad on the eastern approaches to the town. Under their patronage a fine Franciscan friary was established on the island of Ennis. Franciscan foundations were normally located near urban centres; friars were dedicated to the pastoral care of the community so that their presence in Ennis

---

1 Petworth House Archives (hereafter PHA) 1223, Transcript of evidence in court case concerning Ennis market tolls at summer assizes 1844; see also *Clare Journal*, 10 July 1844.

presupposes a population of some size. In the fifteenth century Thomond experienced a period of unprecedented prosperity: many new churches were built, a tower and transept were added to Ennis friary and canopied altar tombs of great beauty housed the noble dead.[2] In the countryside the landed elite utilized their wealth in the construction of well-appointed tower houses. It was in the fifteenth century also that some Gaelic lords, following the example of the Anglo-Normans, attempted to develop the economic potential of their lordships by establishing towns. The towns of Longford and Granard, for instance, were developed by the O'Farrells of Annaly and attracted merchants from the Pale. Further north the O'Reillys founded the town of Cavan, even going so far as to issue their own coinage. In 1480, a complaint was made in parliament that these towns were attracting business from the Pale 'which if they are long continued will bring great riches to the king's enemies and great poverty to the king's subjects'.[3] The O'Briens of Thomond, with the examples of Limerick and Galway on the edges of their territory, cannot have been blind to such developments, so it is perhaps to the fifteenth century that we should assign the origins of the Ennis markets.

Ennis began its life on a low ridge overlooking the river Fergus where the road from Limerick (now O'Connell Street) intersected the road from Galway (Abbey Street) and the road from north Clare (Parnell Street). The river played a key role as a channel of communication. Manufactured goods were traded up river in return for unprocessed materials. Iron, salt, cloth, wine and luxury items were exchanged for corn, wool, hides and furs. In the early days there was little formality, as traders from Limerick and Galway gathered at the junction of the roads above the Fergus to display their wares. The Franciscan friary provided the peaceful environment necessary for the market to take place. On particular days, the traders erected stalls along the well-beaten track ways. At first the stalls were removable but gradually as the traders competed for the best sites, the stalls became fixtures. Finally the stalls gave way to small shops with living accommodation overhead. The rough trodden track way in front of the stalls would eventually be dignified with a street name.

In the second half of the fifteenth century a gatehouse was built over the southern entry to the town.[4] The gatehouse marked the boundary between town and country and facilitated the collection of tolls from country people entering the urban precinct. No town wall was ever built, presumably because the island setting of the town afforded sufficient protection and perhaps also because the volume of trade was never enough to finance the building of a town wall. The O'Brien castle of Clonroad protected the eastern approach to the

2 Brian Ó Dálaigh 'Canopied wall tomb of Ennis Friary, 1460–70' in *The Other Clare*, 20 (1996), pp. 20–4. 3 Raymond Gillespie, 'The O'Farrells and Longford in the seventeenth century' in R. Gillespie and G. Moran (eds), *Longford: essays in county history* (Dublin, 1991), p. 18. 4 Ristéard Ua Croinín and Martin Breen, 'The hidden towers' in *The Other Clare*, 16 (1992), pp. 5–6.

town. There is no evidence of a tower or castle protecting the western approaches. It is likely that a fortification of some kind stood at the point where the secondary channel of the Fergus, which formed the island of Ennis, intersected the road from north Clare.[5]

The surviving documentary evidence dates from the sixteenth century and shows the kind of trading that occurred. In a letter to the town of Galway in 1538, Henry VIII commanded that no merchant was to go with merchandise into the country

> save only to our market towns; but suffer the inhabitants of the country to resort to the market of our said town to sell their wares and cattle ... Moreover, if O'Brien, or any other Irishman, be at war with our Deputy or our subjects of the city of Limerick, that in no wise ye suffer victuals, iron, salt or other commodity to pass from you to them.[6]

Clearly, the O'Briens traded with both Galway and Limerick merchants. The insistence of the king that countrymen bring their produce to the market towns was a way of ensuring that the English interest benefited from whatever commercial activity ensued. In a petition from the mayor and citizens of Limerick to Queen Elizabeth in 1575, it was requested that no ship coming into the estuary of the Shannon be allowed to discharge its cargo of 'munition, shot, powder, wines or other wares' at any port save that of the corporation of Limerick.[7] Notwithstanding the petition of the Limerick merchants, cargoes continued to be traded up the Fergus. Connor O'Brien, third earl of Thomond, requested Queen Elizabeth in 1577 that he be allowed to charge custom on wines and ale being discharged at his castles of Clare and Clonroad as his ancestors had done.[8] Perhaps the best evidence for local markets in the sixteenth century comes from an inquisition *post mortem* taken at Ennis to determine the possessions of Murrough O'Brien, fourth baron of Inchiquin. The young O'Brien had been killed at Ballyshannon, county Donegal, during an expedition against O'Donnell in July 1597. O'Brien and all his ancestors, 'as long as men's memory could reach', were the owners of a weekly market held every Saturday near the church of Coad in the Manor of Inchiquin.[9] As at Ennis, the church precinct provided the peaceful conditions that allowed the market to function and presumably disputes arising in the marketplace were adjudicated on by the clergy. Following

---

5 An entry in the corporation book for 1752 refers to an old structure that stood in Mill Street that could have had such a function. The entry requests that the walls of 'the old ruined building' be pulled down, as it was a danger to people walking in the street. Clearly the structure was much more substantial than the houses townspeople usually occupied. See Brian Ó Dálaigh (ed.), *Corporation book of Ennis* (Dublin, 1990), pp. 161–2. Hereafter cited as *Corp book Ennis*. 6 Constantia Maxwell (ed.), *Irish history from contemporary sources, 1509–1610* (London, 1923), pp. 365–7. 7 Ibid., p. 370. 8 John O'Donoghue, *Historical memoir of the O'Briens* (Dublin, 1860), pp. 527–8. 9 Quoted in George McNamara, 'Inchiquin county Clare' in *JRSAI* xxxi (1901), p. 352.

the completion of the English conquest in the early seventeenth century, Gaelic lords took out royal patents on such markets to protect their interests and to allow them to continue drawing income under English law.

COMMERCE IN THE EARLY SEVENTEENTH CENTURY

The ending of the Nine Years War in 1603 ushered in a period of peace and stability. The earl of Thomond, determined to develop the economic potential of his estates, invited large numbers of English settlers to reside on his lands in county Clare. English settlers had capital and were skilled in commerce and agriculture – skills that were in short supply among the native population. The influx of skilled farmers and traders would modernize agriculture, exploit economic opportunity and hasten the urbanization process. In 1609, to regularize his position under English law, O'Brien sought a patent for the Ennis markets. The patent granted him the right to hold a Tuesday market and a fair twice yearly at Ennis. Disputes arising in the marketplace would be settled at the manor court of Ennis and Clonroad.[10]

However, Ennis still lacked a town law with an urban constitution. This was to come in 1613 with the granting of a royal charter, which laid down the rules under which the town should be governed and granted the precious right of self-rule to a body of burgesses. The charter established a corporation with authority to elect two members to the Irish parliament. Under a provost and twelve free burgesses the corporation was empowered to keep a borough court, admit freemen and appoint minor officials.[11] It was also entitled to hold a weekly market which it held on Saturdays. The burgesses named in the charter were all drawn from the new English elite that had settled in the vicinity of the town. Surprisingly, no native families were included among the burgesses. This may have been because of the need to elect Protestant members to the parliament of 1613 or perhaps because no local families of sufficient mercantile status had emerged in Ennis. The burgesses preferred to live on their estates in the countryside rather than reside in the town with the result that from the outset the day to day running of the corporation was left to others; the burgesses met only when they needed to appoint a provost or to elect the parliamentary members.

From the early seventeenth century, Ennis had two market days. The corporation controlled the Saturday market, whereas the manor court had charge of the Tuesday market. Inevitably, there were clashes between the two bodies. The corporation was held to be subordinate to the manor court because it was established in 1613, four years after the issue of the first market patent.

10 *Calendar of Irish Patent Rolls of James I* (Irish Manuscripts Commission, Dublin, 1966), p. 155. 'Grant from the king to Donogh, earl of Thomond. Licence to hold a Tuesday market and two fairs on Easter Monday and St Bartholomew's day and the day after each at Inishe. Rent £1. 27 February [1609]'.   11 *Corp book Ennis*, pp. 386–93.

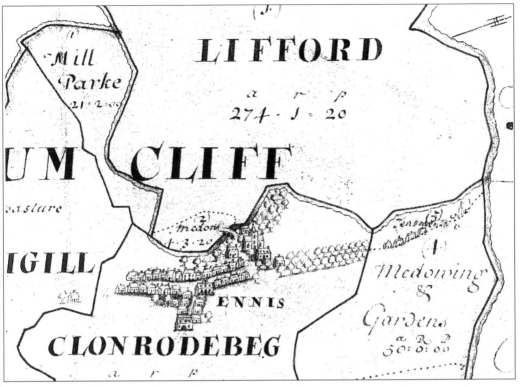

Figure 1 Thomas Moland's drawing of Ennis, 1703. Note the arcaded market house with cupola at the junction of the main streets and the gateway at the southern entry to the town (photo: courtesy Petworth House Archives, West Sussex).

This was to lead to many problems, which, as shall be seen, were never really successfully resolved. Whether or not there was sufficient trade to sustain two market days is an open question. Market days needed to be held at least once a week in the smaller towns and more often in the larger ones to provide sufficient supplies of fresh food for the inhabitants. The well-being of urban dwellers depended on the productivity of the rural population. There is little evidence, unfortunately, as to how the Ennis markets functioned in their first fifty years of operation.

A county courthouse was erected overlooking the marketplace sometime prior to 1641.[12] The courthouse was built by the county grand jury, the body charged with the administration of the county and with the upkeep of roads and bridges. It was the venue for the spring and summer assizes where the most serious criminal cases were tried. The courthouse also made an important

12 Mentioned in the depositions of the dispossessed Protestant settlers in 1641. See James Frost, *The history and topography of the county of Clare* (Dublin, 1893), pp. 342, 364–70.

contribution to the conduct of the markets. The ground floor was arcaded and functioned as an exchange where produce could be weighed and traded on market days. The courts were held above the exchange on the first floor of the building, where on alternate market days, the seneschal of the manor or the provost of the corporation adjudicated on disputes arising in the market place.

The steady stream of English settlers into county Clare and the favourable treatment they received caused much resentment among the native population, which eventually manifested itself in the rising of 1641. The work of the earl of Thomond was largely undone by the rising of 1641 and most settlers left the town never to return. In the absence of the settler community the corporation did not function during the war-torn years of the 1640s.

The depositions of the displaced settlers provide considerable detail on the number of English merchants and traders resident in Ennis and the variety of trades they plied at the time of the uprising. The most prominent merchant family was the Cuffes, originally from Minehead in Somerset. They were sufficiently wealthy to be able to afford the luxury of a lakeside castle residence at Ballyalia, a few miles outside the town. Another merchant, George Waters, claimed he lost the huge sum of £2,047 during the hostilities. Henry Woodfin who ran the town's principal inn, became a Catholic for the duration of the rebellion in order to stay in business. Many merchants of Old English origin were also present in Ennis. Surnames like Stritch, Oliver, Bourke and Galway attest to the Limerick origins of these families. Besides the merchants there were many other Englishmen present. These were mostly tradesmen such as carpenters, weavers, shoemakers, millers, clothiers, dyers and saddlers. An indication that the town was expanding is the number of stonemasons that are recorded. Nearly all the native Irish about whom we have information, engaged in agriculture-related trades such as tanners, butchers, shoemakers, husbandmen and labourers. About 150 Englishmen took refuge in Ballyalia Castle when the uprising began. If we add to this the number of Old English and native Irish inhabitants of the town, the population of Ennis in 1641 bore favourable comparison with many of the planted towns of Ulster.[13]

ENNIS MARKETS, 1651–82

Following the fall of Limerick to the Cromwellians in 1651 many merchant families were expelled from the city and came to reside in Ennis. The years following the Cromwellian conquest were extremely disturbed and we may only guess the extent to which markets operated. A certificate of marriage banns issued to a couple in Ennis is the first indication that the markets were functioning in the 1650s. The certificate required that the marriage banns be proclaimed on three consecutive market days, ending 19 October 1658. This date fell on a Tuesday, so clearly the manor court market continued to operate.[14] In 1659, Patrick White, a

13 Above section based on Ciarán Ó Murchadha, 'Ennis in the seventeenth century' in *The Other Clare*, 8 (1984), pp. 65–8.   14 Brian Ó Dálaigh, 'Notice of marriage banns of

recently transplanted merchant, paid a half-yearly rent of £5 for the 'fairs and markets of Innish and Six Mile Bridge'.[15] The earl of Thomond had fled the country in 1647 and now resided permanently in England. He leased out the markets to a series of individuals who collected tolls on his behalf. In 1676, the earl set the duties and customs of the fairs and markets of Ennis, Clare and Sixmilebridge for thirty-one years at an annual rent of £20 to John Gore, a Cromwellian army officer who had settled in Ennis. If war or troubles intervened no rent was to be paid during such disturbances.[16] This lease governed the Ennis fairs and markets until 1707.

It is fortunate that a record survives of the proceedings of the manor court for the years 1672–85. They record the concerns of the court in organising the weekly markets. One of their principal concerns was keeping the river and highways open and free of encroachment. In 1674 Laurence Lillis was ordered to pull down a weir or mill dam, which he had erected in the river Fergus, on pain of a fine of forty shillings. Pigs roaming in the streets were a major nuisance. It was ordered that the pigs 'who daily spoil the gardens, trees and quicksets in rooting them up, shall not be permitted in the streets of the town'. The town's bakers also caused concern. The bread exposed to sale 'was not the full weight and ordered in goodness as it ought to be'. It was decreed that for the future all bread should be made of sound and wholesome corn and that a penny loaf must weigh at least sixteen ounces. Tree bark was an important ingredient in the tanning process but the stripping of trees had so denuded the countryside that a ban was placed on the sale of bark. The clerk of the market was ordered to seize all bark coming into the town and to bring the owners before the seneschal to be dealt with according to law. In 1674, Domnick White, possibly a relative of Patrick who rented the market tolls from Thomond, was fined for having charged excessive tolls on goods brought to market.[17]

It is not, however, until Hugh Brigdale's account of Ennis in 1682, that one gets a more complete picture of the town, its merchants and the trade that was the mainstay of its markets:

> [Ennis] derives a considerable trade in hides, tallow and butter, which are sent thence by boat to Limerick. It consists of about 120 houses whereof a score are good slated buildings, the rest covered in thatch. The number of inhabitants may be five or six hundred, whereof not above a dozen English families, the rest (for the better sort) are of the birth of Limerick, who settled here upon their turning out of that town by Ireton anno 1651 and now thrive and grow wealthy by the trade aforesaid.[18]

Owen McConsidin and Una Clanchie, Ennis 1658' in *The Other Clare*, 18 (1994) p. 32. **15** PHA 1223, Transcript of evidence. **16** *Corp book Ennis*, p. 373. **17** *Corp book Ennis*, pp. 350–66. **18** Quoted in Brian Ó Dálaigh (ed.), *The stranger's gaze: travels in county Clare 1534–1950* (Dublin, 1998), p. 71.

Evidently the river continued as the principal channel of communication with the outside world. Perhaps more surprising is the extent to which Ennis, despite being a county town, had, in terms of its trade, become a satellite of Limerick city.

The 1680s saw the first stirrings among the citizens for a reinstatement of Ennis corporation. The chief disadvantage of the manor court was that it did not provide an urban constitution or a set of rules under which the town could be governed. With growing prosperity in the 1680s there was a demand for self-rule among the merchant class and a call for a revival of the corporation that had ceased to exist in 1641.

REVIVAL OF ENNIS CORPORATION, 1682–91

At a meeting of the burgesses and principal merchants of the town in March 1682, the old corporation was reactivated. A copy of the original charter was procured and translated into English, and a set of maces, seal, uniforms and hats were brought from Limerick.[19] The Saturday market was revived and a basic list of byelaws was compiled. The first law was that no person coming into the town during the time of a fair or market should be served with a summons for debt but should have twenty-four hours liberty. The purpose of this law was to allow country people sell their produce and discharge their debts without fear of arrest. Clearly, country people in debt would be discouraged from attending the market if they could be arrested on setting foot in the town.[20]

The corporation legislated against the forestalling or re-grating of the market. Forestalling occurred when produce intended for sale was purchased before the market began and was then resold in the marketplace at a higher price. It was a strict rule that markets should begin at ten o'clock in the morning and that no transaction should take place before that hour. The purpose of the legislation was to stop profiteering and to ensure that townspeople had full access to the open market. There were few shops and people depended on the market for supplies of fresh food. Milk, corn, butter, meat, vegetables and cheese were traded. Keeping the narrow streets and laneways clear of rubbish was a major problem. Citizens were obliged to clean and carry away the dirt from the front of their premises, on every Saturday after the market on pain of a fine of six pence.[21]

A body of freemen was created. Theoretically, only freemen were entitled to open shops and transact business within the town. Freemen were free of the markets tolls and they had special privileges in the borough court. The system of urban freemen, however, never functioned properly in Ennis. While freemen were recognized by the corporation, they were subject to all the tolls and charges of the manor court. In time, the rank of freeman became an honorary title and while it continued to be conferred, it held little practical value.[22]

19 *Corp book Ennis*, p. 67.   **20** *Corp book Ennis*, p. 55.   **21** *Corp book Ennis*, pp. 56–7. **22** *Corp book Ennis*, pp. 30–32.

Following the accession of James II, a new charter was imposed on the town in 1687. The intention of the new charter was to permit greater participation of Catholics in municipal affairs. The old corporation, a largely Protestant body, gathered in the court house and declared that they would not allow 'countrymen' to become burgesses or freemen but that they would retain all such rights themselves.[23] Notwithstanding their protests, a new corporation was installed which took charge of local government. The franchise continued to be limited to a provost and twelve burgesses but now most new burgesses were merchants resident in the town. It is not known if the markets operated following the hostilities that broke out in 1689 between the followers of James II and William of Orange. They may well have continued but with interruptions. In any event, the profits of the Ennis markets did not accrue to their usual beneficiaries because John Gore, the lessee of the earl of Thomond, had to be allowed two-and-a-half years rent in 1691 for his inability to collect the tolls during the hostilities.[24]

MUNICIPAL GOVERNMENT IN THE EIGHTEENTH CENTURY

Following the defeat of James II and the treaty of Limerick in 1691, the old corporation of Ennis was quickly restored. However, the burgesses, being largely non-resident, took little part in municipal affairs, only meeting for the election of the parliamentary members. A special byelaw had to be enacted levying a fine of £40 on a burgess, who refused to serve as provost when elected.[25] In the absence of a provost, an officer called the vice-provost was appointed. There was no provision in the charter and thus no legal basis for such an appointment. However, in time, it was the vice-provost who became the most effective officer of the corporation, overseeing the markets and acting as magistrate in the borough court. In the absence of the burgesses, a town council called the grand jury was established. The grand jury was comprised of twenty or so of the town's principal merchants. Like the position of vice-provost, the grand jury had no standing in law. However, it was this body, meeting four times a year that enacted byelaws, admitted freemen and collected the town tax. In conjunction with the vice-provost, the grand jury controlled the Saturday markets and oversaw the commercial development of the town.

During the eighteenth century the manor court went into decline and the corporation's borough court came to the fore. The borough court could impose fines to the value of five marks or £3 6s. 8d. Two uniformed sergeants at mace executed the civil process, usually through the confiscation of goods. In January 1710, Martin Nihill, a town butcher, bought eight quarters of mutton from a country butcher in the open market at six pence a quarter. At his own stall

---

23 *Corp book Ennis*, pp. 66–7.   **24** PHA 1707, Rental of the Irish estates of Henry, earl of Thomond, 1711, no. 111.   **25** *Corp book Ennis*, pp. 63–4.

Nihill refused to sell the mutton to Peter Rice at six pence a quarter but sought a higher price. Rice complained to the borough court and Nihill was fined five shillings, which was levied on his goods, under the byelaws of the corporation against forestalling and re-grating.[26]

In 1711, the corporation ordered that the stones of the market cross in the middle of the street be used for the construction of a new public quay. The market cross was the focal point of the marketplace, where people gathered and where public announcements were made. The cross may have been erected in 1609 when the town received its first market patent. Its removal relieved congestion in the overcrowded marketplace.[27]

An important part of the corporation's duties was maintaining the town clock. The clock hung on the facade of the courthouse while the bell was housed in a cupola, which surmounted the building. A timekeeper was employed to regulate the clock. The clock provided the time for the townspeople but it also played a significant role in the operation of the markets. To allow as many people as possible to participate in buying and selling, the market could not begin until ten o'clock in the morning. In May of 1719, a complaint was made to the vice-provost that three meal women, contrary to the laws of the borough, had purchased wheat in the marketplace at eight in the morning. In court both buyers and sellers were fined the sum of five shillings.[28]

The markets and fairs of the county were clearly expanding in the early eighteenth century because, in 1712, the earl of Thomond leased the Ennis markets to Francis Gore for thirty-one years at an annual rent of twenty pounds.[29] This was the same rental for which Gore's father had leased the markets and fairs of Ennis, Clare and Sixmilebridge in 1676. Clare and Sixmilebridge were now set to other individuals. This new lease was to govern the Ennis markets until 1743.

DIARY OF FARMER LUCAS

In a diary kept by a Mr Lucas of Drumcavan for the years 1740–1, we get a rare glimpse of how country people interacted with the town and the use they made of the fairs and markets.[30] The Lucas family lived in the parish of Ruan, about eight miles north of Ennis. They lived too far away to attend the markets weekly. However, family members were regular visitors to the town. They were present on no less than forty occasions between the beginning of January and the end of October 1741. It is instructive to examine the reasons that brought the Lucas family to Ennis. Fourteen visits related to the sale of produce, twelve were to avail of town services, eleven to visit relatives and three to purchase goods. In the

26 *Corp book Ennis*, pp. 89–90.   **27** *Corp book Ennis*, p. 91.   **28** *Corp book Ennis*, p. 101.
29 PHA 1707, Rental of the Irish estates of Henry, earl of Thomond, 1711, no. 111.
30 NLI, MS 14101. The diary survives in copy form only made about 1890. The diary has been edited and indexed with a view to future publication.

ten-month period, Lucas came to town on eight Saturdays and four Tuesdays, showing perhaps that Saturday was the pre-eminent market day. He rarely made use of the markets, using the Saturday market twice only to sell butter. He also purchased goods on these occasions. Having sold a firkin of butter on 18 February 1741, he bought a pair of red breeches from James McNamara and the pattern of a coat and waistcoat from the draper, James Honan.[31]

Lucas was a more regular attender at the fairs. Fairs were held twice a year on the streets of Ennis and twice a year at Clonroad, in the eastern suburbs of the town. He had mixed fortunes at the fairs. He attended the April fair in Ennis but did not sell or purchase animals. At the July fair in Clonroad he sold thirty bullocks for a total of £50 12s. 6d. In August, his servants brought 30 two-year-old bullocks to the Ennis fair but failed to sell a single animal. At the October fair in Clonroad he again made no sale and had to return home with his twenty cattle. When he did sell his animals he immediately paid off his bills, such as the £13 he paid, following the July fair, to James Armstrong and Robert Crowe, two of the principal merchants of the town.[32]

Lucas also engaged in extensive tillage and sold his corn to the brewers and corn merchants of Ennis. There was no special day for the cornmarket and Lucas appears to have sold his corn on days most suitable to himself. He did not sell his corn immediately it was harvested, but at the time of the year when it was most likely to command the highest price. In March, he sold ten barrels of barley, at 23s. a barrel, to Bethy Tomkins, a meal woman of the town. When the new barley crop was harvested at the end of July the price had fallen to 15s. a barrel.[33] Lucas was prepaid for his corn, which was to be delivered within one month. Taking money in advance for one's produce broke the corporation's byelaws against forestalling and re-grating, as the corn never reached the open market. However, paying in advance worked to the mutual advantage of both buyer and seller. For the merchant it ensured supply, while for the farmer it was a form of credit that helped him over those difficult periods of the year when his crops were not ready for the market. The corporation continued to enact laws against forestalling and re-grating but never succeeded in eliminating the practice.

OWNERSHIP OF THE MARKETS

Henry O'Brien, the last earl of Thomond, died without issue at his residence in Jervis Street, Dublin in 1741.[34] His large estates in county Clare (37,292 acres) he left to his relative, Murrough O'Brien, son of the earl of Inchiquin. However, Murrough O'Brien also died in 1741 and, as a result, the estates passed to Percy Wyndham, who had been named as the remainder man in the will. Wyndham was a nephew of Thomond's wife; he had no connection whatsoever with Clare

31 NLI, MS 14101, 18 Feb 1741. **32** NLI, MS 14101, 21 July 1741. **33** NLI, MS 14101, 14 and 15 March and 24 July 1741. **34** *Pue's Occurrences*, 21 April 1741.

and had few prospects until he inherited the Thomond estates.[35] For the next century and a half the Wyndham family controlled the Ennis fairs and markets.

The lease of the tolls of the markets expired in 1743. Rather than lease them again to the Gore family who had held them since 1676, the tolls were let on a yearly basis to Richard Griffith, a corn merchant of the town. Griffith quickly fell foul of the corporation. In 1744, he was accused of weighing corn in the hucksters' houses before it reached the market, contrary to the laws against forestalling and re grating.[36] He was warned that if he persisted in the practice he would be fined the maximum penalty the borough court could impose. Despite disagreements with the corporation the leasing of the tolls became a long-term arrangement in 1749 when Wyndham leased the customs of the fairs and markets to Griffith for thirty-one years at a yearly rent of £30.[37] As the markets expanded, there was intense competition for the lucrative market tolls. Griffith quickly realized that his right to collect toll was superior in law to that of the corporation. He based his right on a declaration made by the manor court in 1683, which claimed authority to levy tolls of the provost, burgesses and freemen of the corporation, as well as on strangers, every day of the year.[38] Matters did not come to a head until 1769, at a special meeting convened before the vice-provost, grand jury, freemen and principal inhabitants of the town. Griffith was accused not only of collecting the tolls that belonged to the Thomond estate, but also the tolls that of right belonged to the corporation.[39] A report of the proceedings was sent to Percy Wyndham in England.

Wyndham visited the town in the following year – his one and only visit to his Irish estates. The corporation greeted him with all the pomp and ceremony a provincial corporation could muster and presented him with the freedom of Ennis in a silver box.[40] The corporation came to an agreement with Wyndham whereby the vice-provost was made weigh master of the markets and shared the tolls between himself and the lessee of the Thomond estate. Thereafter, a double toll was exacted at the public scales, one toll going to the municipal authority and the other to the private proprietor.[41]

GROWTH OF MARKETS, 1750–1820

The trade and commerce of the town expanded rapidly after 1750. In 1752 the corporation levied £10 on the citizens for the erection of a new Milk Quay 'because the trade of the town had so much increased there was not sufficient

35 Ivar O'Brien, O'Brien of Thomond (Chichester, 1986), p. 238.   36 Corp book Ennis, pp. 142, 147.   37 Corp book Ennis, p. 226.   38 NLI, Inchiquin MSS 2776, Papers re a dispute between the Corporation of Ennis and Lord Thomond's toll gatherer.   39 Corp book Ennis, p. 226.   40 Corp book Ennis, p. 227.   41 First report of the commissioners appointed to inquire into the municipal corporations in Ireland, Appendix part 1, HC 1835, [27] xxvii, p. 314.

quayage or landing places for merchants goods turf and other necessaries'.[42] Similarly, in 1755 the market place in front of the courthouse had become so congested that the corporation was compelled to lay out a new market square:

> Whereas it appears to us that the standings of potatoes and milk in the public streets are very detrimental to the inhabitants ... and coaches, chairs and other carriages are daily in danger of being overturned by the vast number of horses, baskets and other lumber that on market days take up the whole of the street ... we therefore present that for the future no person shall expose to sale any potatoes, milk or other gross goods in the public streets but that the same shall be sold at Cloughaneagour.[43]

Cloughaneagour (*Clochán na ngabhal*, stepping stones of the forked stream) was the triangular area of ground at the western end of the town, between Gaol Street and Mill Street, where the secondary stream of the Fergus flowed (now Lower Market Street). It was ordered that the watercourse be flagged over with 'good broad lintels'. A rectangular area of ground was levelled and paved, house plots were laid out, and merchants invited to build houses around the new market square.[44] Milk and potatoes had clearly become an important element in the urban diet by the 1750s. The change from corn to potatoes as the staple food occurred relatively quickly. Potatoes are first mentioned in the municipal minutes in 1726 when the inhabitants were prohibited from collecting the dung of the streets to manure their potato gardens.[45] The laying out of a specific square for the sale of potatoes indicates that in a few short decades they had become one of the principal commodities traded at the Ennis markets.

The rapid expansion of the markets meant that the vice-provost, with the limited manpower at his disposal, was no longer able to oversee the buying and selling of produce. A body called the market jury was established in 1752. The jury consisted of twelve merchants whose job it was to ensure that the market byelaws were enforced.[46] They were to detect and seize all light weights and measures including turf baskets, and to prosecute people leaving dunghills or rubbish in the streets and back lanes. There was no provision in the charter and thus no basis in law for such a body, yet the market jury was to regulate the affairs of the Ennis markets for well over half a century.

As the eighteenth century drew to a close the volume of trade continued to increase. Commodities were removed from sale at the congested marketplace in front of the courthouse and sent instead to the Milk and Potato Market at Cloughaneagour. In 1792, the fish jolters, straw sellers and root and vegetable vendors were directed to move to the new market place. The standings of fruit and vegetable baskets were ordered to be removed from the streets in 1802 and to be likewise set up at Cloughaneagour, on pain of a fine of two shillings; the

---

42 *Corp book Ennis*, p. 167.   **43** *Corp book Ennis*, pp. 181–2.   **44** *Corp book Ennis*, pp. 183–4.   **45** *Corp book Ennis*, p. 108.   **46** *Corp book Ennis*, pp. 170–2.

fine was to be levied on the offender's goods and chattels by the sergeants-at-mace.[47]

In 1805, a second square of ground called the Pig Market was laid out at Cloughaneagour. There is no record of the corporation expending any money on this project. Therefore the new market was almost certainly provided at the expense of the private proprietor, George Wyndham, third earl of Egremont. (Egremont had inherited the Thomond estates on the death of his uncle, Percy Wyndham, in 1775). The provision of the new market place necessitated a rearrangement of venues for the sale of produce. The new square of ground (now Upper Market Street) was to be used for the sale of all live oxen, cows, calves, sheep and pigs. The crane or public weighing scales was set up in the centre of the new square and all supplies of potatoes coming into the market would in future be weighed there.[48] The sale of milk, fruit, vegetables and fish continued in the old square (Lower Market Street). It is of interest to note that, with the exception of the sale of potatoes, the arrangements as laid out in 1805 are the ones that still prevail at the Ennis markets to this day.

William Turner De Lond's beautiful painting *The Market Place and Court House at Ennis* provides the best picture of the markets in the early nineteenth century. Turner was an itinerant artist, apparently from London, who visited the town in 1820.[49] His painting depicts the old county courthouse built in 1732. A clock is fixed to the pediment of the courthouse; the time is twenty minutes to four in the afternoon. As the Limerick mail coach arrives, the market is in full swing. On the left-hand side of the picture a stallholder sells brightly coloured cloth and fabric to two ladies attired in black; sitting on the ground beside an adjacent stall, three market women offer eggs and farmyard fowl for sale. Near the central foreground a woman displays her cabbages, fruits and vegetables. Here and there women are depicted carrying jugs or hooped wooden vessels probably for the sale of milk. Donkeys with baskets of turf stand patiently on the periphery of the market. Near the corner of the courthouse a man examines what appears to be the carcass of an animal carried on the back of a horse. The arches of the courthouse are fenced off by iron railings, indicating that the arcaded ground floor of the building no longer functioned as the exchange or market house. Above all, the painting shows the very crowded conditions that obtained at the Ennis markets and which compelled the corporation to move the sale of produce from the front of the courthouse to other parts of the town.

COINAGE AND EXCHANGE

Shortage of suitable coinage was a continual impediment to the transaction of business. In the absence of coins of smaller denominations, merchants resorted

---

47 *Corp book Ennis*, pp. 282, 311–12.   **48** *Corp book Ennis*, p. 325.   **49** Brian Ó Dálaigh, 'An early nineteenth century painting of Ennis' in *The Other Clare*, 10 (1986) pp. 12–13.

Figure 2 The Market Place and Court House at Ennis, 1820 by
William Turner de Lond (photo: courtesy of NLI).

to issuing their own tokens particularly to facilitate petty transactions. As early
as 1679 David White, a merchant of Ennis, issued his own penny and half penny
trade tokens.[50] The well-worn tokens that survive indicate that they remained
in circulation for many years. In the first half of the eighteenth century French,
Spanish and Portuguese gold coins circulated freely in Ireland. Foreign coins
were legal tender by weight only and official weights and scales were issued to
determine the value of coins. In March of 1741, Farmer Lucas was compelled to
accept an unweighed gold coin at the Ennis market as payment for his produce.[51]
Because of the scarcity of coin, traders were often unable to complete transactions.
In July 1741, the merchant Robert Crowe could not give 4s. 2d. in change to
Farmer Lucas as he did not have enough small coins.[52]

50 Peter Seaby, *Coins and tokens of Ireland* (London, 1970) p. 113.   **51** NLI, MS 14101, 7
March 1741.   **52** NLI, MS 14101, 21 July 1741.

The problem had become particularly acute by the first decade of the nineteenth century. In 1805, the Bank of Ireland, in order to put an end to the shortage of small change, minted thousands of five and ten pence silver tokens. The appearance of the new coins caused immediate problems at the Ennis markets, as people refused to accept the old worn-down disks that had previously circulated and demanded the new silver coins instead. The affairs of the market were so disrupted that the corporation was compelled to enact a law stating that the refusal of good mint sixpences and copper halfpennies was very injurious to the trade and business of the town and ordered that the old coins should be accepted to the value of one shilling in each transaction, on pain of a fine of five shillings.[53]

In the absence of suitable coinage, traders in Ennis had long resorted to issuing paper money for small amounts, ranging in value from sixpence to ten shillings. There was often insufficient capital to cover the value of these notes with the result that people who could least afford it, sustained heavy losses. Despite the widespread circulation of silver coins by the Bank of Ireland, paper money continued to circulate at the Ennis markets. 'It will be scarcely credited in Dublin', observed Hely Dutton in 1807, 'that notes of the value of 1s .1d. to a guinea are publicly negotiated in Ennis'. To put an end to the practice, Dutton suggested that all land holders should refuse to accept any notes other than those drawn on the Bank of Ireland or the Bank of Limerick.[54] It was not until the opening of the commercial banks in the town in the 1840s that the problem of coins and notes as a medium of exchange was finally resolved.

GRAND JURY, ROADS AND BOUNDARIES

Perhaps the best insight into the burgeoning Ennis markets is obtained by examining the value of the annual rents paid to the Thomond estate by the lessees of the tolls and customs. The rents of the markets increased in value by a factor of twenty over a period of two centuries. The annual rent, which began as £10 in 1659, had tripled in value by 1749; the rents more than tripled again by 1812 and were to double further in value by 1844 (See Table 1) What factors were responsible for this phenomenal growth?

---

53 *Corp book Ennis*, p. 322.   **54** Hely Dutton, *Statistical survey of county Clare* (Dublin, 1808), p. 247.

Table 1 Annual rents paid by the lessees of the Ennis markets to the Thomond estate, 1659–1845.[55]

Date	Lessees	Rent	Markets
1659	Patrick White	£10	Ennis, Sixemilebridge
1676	John Gore	£20	Ennis, Sixemilebridge, Clare
1712	Francis Gore	£20	Ennis
1749	Richard Griffith	£30	Ennis
1781	John Stack	£76	Ennis
1812	Patrick Kean	£100	Ennis
1844	John Macbeth	£200	Ennis

The Clare Grand Jury was undoubtedly the most powerful force for growth in the county. By 1800, the grand jury had been responsible for a century and a half of road construction and bridge building. The road network linked the rural settlements and allowed the surplus produce of the countryside to be conveyed to the market towns. Roads also had the reverse effect of allowing the market economy to penetrate the countryside: rural areas were opened up for settlement and agricultural improvement, and a demand created for manufactured goods that could only be supplied by the towns.

The achievement of the Clare Grand Jury is best observed in Henry Pelham's *Grand Jury Map of county Clare* published in 1788. Pelham shows that the road network had penetrated the most remote districts of the county. The map depicts Ennis at the hub of the county's road system. Roads radiate from the town to every part of the county like the spokes of a great wheel.[56] The development of the road network facilitated the expansion of the Ennis markets, and while other factors – the prolonged period of peace, the growth of population, the increasing effectiveness of central government – were important, it was the improvement in transport facilities that was the key factor in the markets' phenomenal growth.

As the population increased there was growing pressure on space within the urban boundary. Apart from a scarcity of building land, few suitable areas remained to accommodate the expanding markets. New land outside the town's limits could not be purchased, as the patents specified that markets and fairs had to be held within the urban boundary. From the mid eighteenth century there was a demand for the expansion of the borough boundaries. The corporation also had a vested interest in boundary extension as a way of increasing the tax base. Many of the town's most opulent houses were built outside the borough

55 Statistical information drawn from MSS in Petworth House Archive, West Sussex; PHA 1223 for leases of 1659, 1749, 1781, 1812; PHA 1707 no. 111 for leases of 1676 and 1712 and PHA 357 for 1844 lease. **56** *Henry Pelham's map of county Clare, 1787* (reprint by Phoenix Maps, Dublin, 1989).

limits with the result that those residents were not liable for any of the town's taxes. The borough boundary was first extended in 1752. This facilitated the laying out of the two new market squares at Cloughaneagour – the first in 1756 and the second in 1805. The limits were again extended in 1807. On this occasion, land on the opposite bank of the Fergus was, for the first time, included within the town boundary. The 1807 extension also facilitated the development of the area leading to the Mills of Ennis which eventually became known as Cornmarket Street. The town boundary was extended for a third time under the Electoral Reform Act of 1832. The new boundary enclosed an area of 469 acres which essentially remained the urban district until 1988.[57] The 1832 extension permitted the buying of thirteen acres for a fairgreen. The purchase of the fairgreen in 1868 meant that cattle fairs no longer needed to be held on the streets of the town.

DEMISE OF ENNIS CORPORATION, 1810–42

The Ennis charter drawn up for the requirements of local government in 1613 was wholly unsuited to the conditions that prevailed in the early nineteenth century. Over the years, custom and practice had grown up that bore little relation to the provisions in the original franchise. To amend the terms of the charter the corporation would have had to sue out and purchase a new charter confirming additional powers. In practice, however, municipal government was so haphazard that very few authorities went to the trouble and expense of taking out new charters. The result was that by the early nineteenth century Ennis corporation, in common with many municipal authorities, was vulnerable to legal challenges in the courts. Although taxes had been levied on the town since the revival of the corporation in the 1680s, it was uncertain whether they were specifically allowed for in the charter. The charter was written in Latin and problems arose with translation and interpretation. In any event, the Ennis charter survived in copy form only and so it was impossible to know what precisely was specified in the original. Because of such difficulties, no town tax was collected in 1802 or in 1807. In 1809, with the continuing refusal of inhabitants to pay tax, the grand jury employed counsel to ascertain the right of the corporation to impose taxes under its charter.[58] The legal opinion was that the grand jury had no such right. Consequently, after 1810 no further taxes were levied and the municipal minutes ceased to be recorded. The vice-provost, however, continued to regulate the markets and to act as magistrate in the borough court. In a legal challenge brought against the vice-provost in 1823, it was pointed out that under the charter, only the provost had the power to hold the borough court. As the provost had always been a non-resident and had never presided as magistrate in

57 Brian Ó Dálaigh, 'The old urban boundaries of Ennis' in *The Other Clare*, 12 (1988), pp. 25–30.   **58** *Corp book Ennis*, pp. 339–40.

the town, the borough court quickly ceased to function.[59] Worse was to follow. The grand jury, although not able to levy tax, had apparently continued to meet. It met in 1825 to sanction a new schedule of tolls for the vice-provost at the public scales. However, in 1827, the thirteen burgesses of the corporation, who had never resided in Ennis and whose only contribution had ever been to elect the town's parliamentary members, refused to recognize the proceedings of the grand jury and consequently this body finally disbanded.[60]

The vice-provost alone continued to act as weigh-master of the markets. The market tolls provided the vice-provost with an income of some £200 to £300 a year.[61] However, the affairs of the market were in a state of disarray. The lessee under the earl of Egremont claimed complete ownership of the tolls, although he was not the weigh-master of the market. By 1831, the market traders refused to pay any tolls because they believed that neither the corporation nor the lessee of Egremont had any legal right to levy them. In the case of the corporation, the opposition arose from the fact that the original charter could not be produced. A story circulated which claimed that the charter had, a long time ago, been pledged by the corporation to a person in Galway for a sum of money and had never been redeemed.[62] While the story was manifestly false (the original charter was lost prior to 1641), it was indicative of the low esteem in which the corporation was held. The loss of the market tolls, the only remaining property of the corporation, precipitated the final collapse of the municipal authority.

Following the collapse of the corporation, a number of attempts were made to establish a town council under an 1828 act of parliament which empowered any borough in which the services of lighting, watching, cleansing and paving were not provided, to elect commissioners for that purpose. All inhabitants of houses rated at £5 or more within the town, or within one mile of its boundaries, were entitled to vote at a public meeting.[63] However, the enmity towards the old corporation combined with the resolve of the £5 freeholders not to pay tax and the fear of a new Protestant power base being established in the town ensured that the act was not adopted. Opposition was led by Dean Terence O'Shaughnessy, parish priest of Ennis, who dominated proceedings at the public meetings in the courthouse.[64] The old corporation had been a predominantly Protestant body in an overwhelmingly Catholic town. While some Catholics had penetrated the lower echelons of the administration by being admitted to the grand jury, the burgesses had remained an exclusively Protestant body. It was not until 1842, after the town had been without any form of municipal government for a number of years, that the citizens finally agreed to the setting up of a body of town commissioners under the Lighting and Cleansing Act of

59 *Municipal corporations in Ireland report*, 1835, Appendix 1, p. 310. **60** Ibid., p. 311. **61** Ibid., p. 310. **62** *Report on parliamentary representation in Ireland*, HC 1831–32, xliii, pp. 68–72. **63** Virginia Crossman, *Local government in nineteenth-century Ireland* (Belfast, 1994), pp. 65–8. **64** *Ennis Chronicle*, 22 Nov. 1828; *Morning Register*, 24 Nov. 1828.

1828.[65] In the subsequent election, twenty-one town commissioners were elected, including Dean Terence O'Shaughnessy, the only time a Catholic priest was elected to public office in the town.[66] While municipal government was now in Catholic hands for the first time since the reign of James II (1687–91), the new body, in terms of its powers, was a mere shadow of the former corporation. It had no power to elect members of parliament, to hold a borough court, to enact byelaws or to regulate the markets. Its sole remit was to oversee the cleaning of the streets and the lighting of the town.

CORN MARKET TOLL DISPUTE, 1844

Following the refusal of the people to pay the market tolls in 1831, George Wyndham, third earl of Egremont, went to the trouble of suing out a new patent for the Ennis markets. The new patent, issued in 1835, confirmed on him the sole right to collect tolls at the Ennis markets on every day of the week except Sunday.[67] Egremont died in 1837 and the Thomond estates devolved on his eldest illegitimate son, Colonel George Wyndham. Because of his illegitimacy, Wyndham could not assume his father's title. However, unlike his father, Wyndham became very active in the administration of his Irish estates and set about developing his interests in county Clare with considerable vigour. As market owner he had a duty to provide a service for the tolls he received. Prior to this the markets were held in the open streets and, with the exception of the weighing scales, no facilities were provided. In 1841, Wyndham purchased half an acre of ground off Cornmarket Street at a cost of £400. He spent a further £200 constructing a high wall, intersected by three gates, around the property. He built sheds, set up four weighing scales and erected a large toll-board setting out the charges for weighing corn.[68]

   Corn had become the largest single commodity traded on the markets. Vast amounts of grain passed through the markets each year. In 1831, 60,000 barrels of wheat, 30,000 barrels of barley and 100,000 barrels of oats were sold in Ennis.[69] The cornmarket had moved to the northwestern periphery of the town with the extension of the borough boundary in 1807. A space off Cornmarket Street was set aside and a weighing scales put in place. Four pence was levied on each barrel of wheat and two pence on every barrel of barley and oats. The vice-provost and the lessee under Egremont attended on the first Monday of every month to collect their share of the tolls.[70] With the growing quantity of corn there was little room around the scales and the market soon spilled out onto the street. Cars lined up along the road towards the Mills of Ennis to wait their turn

65 Kieran Sheedy, *The Clare elections* (Dublin, 1993), pp. 727–8.   66 Ibid., p. 728.
67 *Royal comm. fairs and markets, mins 1852–3*, pp. 146–52.   68 PHA 1223, Transcript of evidence.   69 *Municipal corporations in Ireland report*, 1835, Appendix 1, p. 313.   70 PHA 1223, Transcript of evidence.

Figure 3 Map of the Upper and Lower Markets, Ennis, 1840. Note the
crane or public weighing scales in the Upper Market.

at the scales. After 1831, when tolls ceased, farmers sold their corn directly to the cornstore owners. Each cornstore weighed the corn it purchased but the farmer had no independent means of verifying the weight of his produce.

After Wyndham built the new cornmarket, which was directly across the road from the old scales, farmers continued to line up along Cornmarket Street in the usual manner and refused to enter the new premises. Wyndham, determined to make an issue of the matter, called on Alexander Bannatyne, owner of the Mills of Ennis and largest corn merchant in the town, to pay the market tolls. Bannatyne refused, stating that he had only come to Ennis in 1836 and that the tolls had been discontinued since 1831. In the court case that followed at the summer assizes of 1844 no less a person than James Morrin, editor of the *Calendar of Patents and Close Rolls of Chancery in Ireland, Henry VIII to Elizabeth I* (Dublin, 1861) was called on to translate the old Latin patents for the court.[71]

Counsel for Wyndham declared that his client was anxious only for the prosperity of the town and concerned that the farmers should have an independent means of verifying the weight of their corn before it was sold. Among the many witnesses called was the small farmer, Thady Glynn. Glynn could speak Irish only and was examined through a court interpreter. He brought two bags of wheat for sale to the market. He went first to the new market where he received a ticket from John Macbeth stating the weight of his corn. He then brought his corn to Bannatyne's store where it was weighed again. There was a discrepancy of one and a half stone between Bannatyne's ticket and Macbeth's ticket. Glynn refused to accept payment for his corn on the Saturday but returned on the Tuesday following and received 2s. 6d. more for his grain. When asked by Bannatyne's counsel if he expected the court to believe that Macbeth spoke with him in Irish, Glynn replied, 'Macbeth did not speak to me in Irish, many understand English that cannot speak it'.[72] Bannatyne was also accused of forestalling the market, of sending his agents out to intercept cars coming into the market and directing them to his own cornstores instead – a charge he hotly denied. The jury, drawn exclusively from the Protestant landowning gentry of the county, was largely sympathetic towards Wyndham and in the end he won his case. The tolls of the Ennis markets were re-introduced after a break of thirteen years.

REPORT ON MARKETS AND FAIRS, 1852

In 1852, the government established a commission to enquire into the state and condition of the fairs and markets of Ireland. The commissioners were to enquire by what authority fairs and markets were held, the tolls and fees that were levied, the diversity of weights and measures used and the frauds committed. They were also required to examine the possibility of obtaining

71 Ibid., f. 30.   72 Ibid., f. 37.

accurate returns of the quantity and price of all agricultural produce.[73] The commission sat at Ennis in November of 1852 and interviewed several people associated with the markets and fairs of the town. The efficiency and good management of the markets immediately struck them. Dennis Curtin, Clerk of the Cornmarket, gave evidence that the cornmarket was enclosed. There were six scales for weighing corn, six clerks, six assistant weigh-masters and twelve porters employed in the market. Tolls were charged only if the article was sold and weighed. The tolls were 6*d*. for cows, 3*d*. for pigs and 1*d*. for sheep. Wheat was levied at 2*d*. per barrel, barley and oats at 1*d*. per barrel, wool at 5*d*. per pack and butter at 2*d*. per firkin.[74] The amount and nature of all produce sold in the market was recorded in the market books. The books, laid before the commissioners, contained the date, name of market, name of buyer and seller, description of the article sold and weighed for every day of the previous seven years. When examining the statistics published in the report, the diversity of weights and measures becomes apparent. There were three different measures employed for barrels of corn. A barrel of wheat weighed 280 pounds, a barrel of barley 224 pounds and a barrel of oats 196 pounds. For purposes of comparison all the quantities in the table below have been converted into metric tons, at the rate of 2204.6 pounds per metric ton.

Table 2 Quantity of corn sold at the Ennis Market, 1845–51 expressed in metric tons.[75]

Date	Oats	Wheat	Barley	Totals
1845	6,959	5,219	0,556	12,734
1846	7,406	5,741	0,776	13,923
1847	5,079	1,949	0,320	7,348
1848	3,777	2,793	0,593	7,163
1849	3,054	1,394	1,018	5,466
1850	3,058	1,955	1,232	6,245
1851	3,504	1,362	1,182	6,048
Totals	32,837	20,413	15,677	58,927

These figures are of particular interest, as they allow us to see the volume of grain traded in the market during the Great Famine. In terms of quantity, oats was the largest commodity sold over the seven-year period, followed by wheat and then barley. The failure of the potato crop in 1846 did not affect the supply of corn as the volume of grain actually increased. However, the failure of the potatoes again in 1847 had a dramatic impact. There was a switch by those who

73 *Royal comm. fairs and markets, 1852–3*, pp. 1–3.   **74** *Royal comm. fairs and markets, mins 1852–3*, pp. 146–52.   **75** Ibid.

could afford it from the consumption of potatoes to corn, with the result that
the surplus of grain available for the market almost halved.

It is interesting to see how average prices fluctuated during the crisis. The
large increase in prices in 1846 encouraged the sale of corn and in famine
conditions the volume of corn traded actually increased. Prices rose steeply again
in 1847 but as the third year of famine took effect the quantity of corn decreased
dramatically. It was a blow from which the market never fully recovered.

The price rises in corn are revealing. Between 1845 and 1847, oats, the grain
of the poor, rose by 66 per cent, wheat by 61 per cent and barley by 46 per cent.
Prices cannot be said to have reached an equilibrium again until 1850.

Table 3 The average price per metric ton of oats, wheat and barley at the Ennis
Cornmarket and the total of receipts and tonnage for the years 1845–51.[76]

Date	Oats	Wheat	Barley	Total Receipts	Tonnage
1845	£5.76	£8.77	£6.52	£89,450	12,734
1846	£6.83	£10.51	£6.77	£116,192	13,923
1847	£9.58	£14.09	£9.55	£79,168	7,348
1848	£5.51	£9.49	£6.31	£51,038	7,163
1849	£5.41	£10.00	£6.20	£36,766	5,466
1850	£4.69	£7.67	£4.70	£35,139	6,245
1851	£4.90	£8.50	£5.42	£35,166	6,048
Total				£442,919	58,927

However, the figures for the sale of potatoes, the staple food of the vast
majority of people illustrate the awful impact of the famine. A ton of potatoes
cost less than a fifth of the price of a ton of wheat. Almost 4,000 tons of potatoes
were sold in 1845. This decreased by 1,000 tons with the onset of famine in
1846. In 1847, the supply fell to less than one tenth of the quantity that had been
traded in 1845. One may only guess at the appalling human suffering concealed
behind these cold statistics. Prices went way beyond what ordinary people could
afford. There was a five-fold increase in the price of potatoes between 1845 and
1847 and even after this prices remained stubbornly high. The famine had a
long-term impact upon the market and the pre-famine levels of trading were
never again achieved.

76 Ibid.

Table 4 The quantity and price of potatoes at the Ennis Market for
the years 1845–51.[77]

Date	Metric Tons	Price per Ton	Total Receipts
1845	3,910	£1.48	£5,722
1846	2,955	£2.62	£7,755
1847	384	£7.55	£2,898
1848	1,248	£6.89	£8,596
1849	1,285	£5.74	£7,379
1850	1,863	£3.62	£6,752
1851	1,546	£4.26	£6,595

One of the last witnesses interviewed by the commissioners in 1852 was a stonemason, Thomas O'Connor, who complained about the frauds being committed in the sale of milk. He alleged that milk coming into the market was bought up by the forestallers so that poor people could not buy milk except at inflated prices. Women going about the town selling milk had a large quart measure for buying and a small quart measure for selling, in addition to diluting the milk with water.

FAIRS IN THE STREETS OR IN THE FAIR GREEN?

In the post famine period, fairs continued to be held in the narrow streets of the town. A rare glimpse of an Ennis fair is provided by a Quaker, Spencer T. Hall, who came to Clare in 1849 to report on the social conditions in the wake of the Great Famine:

> At the Ennis fair there was a considerable supply of stock, consisting of horses, mules, asses, cows, goats, pigs and poultry – which might have been had almost at any price, but there were scarcely any buyers. I never saw a fair so melancholy as this. The few bargains I saw were made with much clamour, in the Irish language, and in the presence of two witnesses, who confirmed them by uniting their hands over or with those of the buyer and seller – thus forming a cross ...
>
> On our nearing Ennis again, it was a moving sight – that of the crowds of people returning to the country from the fair, many of them taking back their unsold stock, others sad from having been compelled to part with it at most ruinous prices.[78]

All prices fell in the wake of the famine and it only gradually became apparent that the price of livestock would fall less drastically than that of grain. The rising

77 Ibid.   **78** Quoted in Ó Dálaigh (ed.) *The strangers gaze*, pp. 219–20.

standards of living in Britain created a demand for Irish meat, while the growing accessibility of European and American grain to the same market greatly reduced the demand for Irish corn. The Ennis cornmarket went into long-term decline and the new emphasis in agriculture was on the production of livestock.

One of the principal recommendations of the 1852 commission was that market owners provide fair greens with proper facilities for the sale of livestock. Thomas Crowe, the agent of Colonel Wyndham, agreed with the commissioners that fairs in the streets were objectionable and that the owner of the fairs and markets should in all cases provide accommodation for the public in return for the tolls he received. Wyndham was anxious to purchase land within the limits of the borough to hold fairs but there was a difficulty in getting clear title. Fairs in the streets were a nuisance which interfered with traffic and disrupted town life. At the Ennis fairs, two men stood at each of the entrances. One man recorded in a book the description, price and number of cattle sold and the other collected the tolls. Tolls were levied only on livestock sold and were collected when the sellers were leaving the fair. No swearing or touching of a bible was required of people departing. 'Under the present system', Mr Crowe informed the commissioners, 'a great number of sellers pay no toll on livestock'.[79] It was not until 1868 that Wyndham, bearing the newly conferred title of Lord Leconsfield, was able to buy suitable ground for a fair green. Leconsfield's agent, Wainright Crowe, paid £1,000 for thirteen acres of firm ground behind the new county court house. 'It would be one of the best and driest fair greens in Munster', trumpeted the *Clare Journal*. 'Lord Leconsfield by his noble example has conferred a substantial boon on the Clare capital'.[80] The fair green, however, was rarely used for fairs. Farmers continued to exhibit their animals in the convivial atmosphere of the streets rather than in the comparative isolation of the fair green. Taking over the town on a fair day gave the farmer status and emphasized the dependency of the urban dweller on the countryman. Publicans, too, objected to fairs being moved to the edge of the town as it interfered with their business. After the 1870s, with the growing demand for Irish beef in the British markets, the number of cattle fairs in Ennis substantially increased.

NEW BUTTER MARKET

By the 1860s, most of the county towns in Munster had enclosed markets for butter. Large quantities of butter were sold at the Ennis market. Between 1845 and 1851 some 1,208 tons of butter, valued at £84,997, passed through the market.[81] However, no special provision was made for the sale of butter in Ennis. 'The only protection the farmer has is to know that his produce is

---

79 *Royal comm. fairs and markets, mins 1852–3*, pp. 146–52.   **80** *Clare Journal*, 25 June 1868 and *Limerick Chronicle*, 30 June 1868.   **81** *Royal comm. fairs and markets, mins 1852–3*, pp. 146–52.

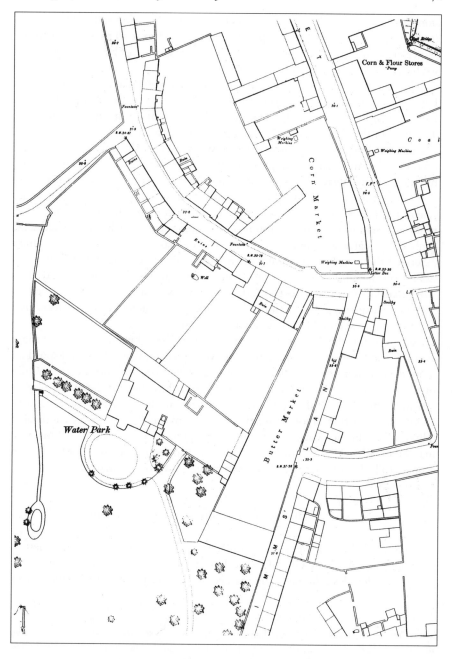

Figure 4 Map of Corn Market Street, Ennis, 1894. The Corn Market
was built in 1841 and the Butter Market in 1862.

honestly weighed'.[82] Butter was generally sold by the lump rather than by the firkin, with the result that most producers preferred to send their butter to the Limerick market. It was requested that a sworn inspector of butter be employed so that farmers would get a fair price.

The recommendations of the 1852 commission were taken seriously by Lord Leconsfield and in 1860 he purchased a plot of ground on the corner of Simm's Lane and Mill Street for £264 from John Macbeth and John Busteed Knox.[83] The new butter market, which opened in 1862, was in close proximity to the cornmarket built in 1841. Little expense was spared in the construction of the premises. Entrance gates were provided with impressive cut-stone piers and the buildings within were of dressed limestone. At the top of the new market stood the butter house, a building about one hundred feet long and forty feet wide, where the firkins of butter were weighed, inspected and branded. The butter house was surmounted by an iron roof of a single span which was sheeted with timber and slates. At the apex, large panes of glass formed a skylight which extended the length of the building and by which means the butter house was lit and ventilated. The cast iron was painted in light blue – which displayed its workmanship to great effect – and the timber was stained and varnished to present a clean and polished finish. The whole was designed by Mr Petty, a civil engineer, and executed by the builder, Mr Sexton.[84]

According to the *Clare Journal* in 1868, a very large business was done there every week.[85] Seven butter merchants were recorded in Ennis in 1866. The number had risen to eleven by 1870 but had fallen back to four by 1881. Only one was recorded in the town directory of 1895, showing that the butter market was in decline.[86] With the rise of the creameries in the early twentieth century and the introduction of lorries for the transport of milk, there was a considerable falling off in home-made butter and consequently in the sale of firkins. The market nevertheless continued to operate and between 1927 and 1933 an average toll of £196 per year was taken at the Ennis butter market.[87]

DECLINE OF MARKETS AND THE RISE OF FAIRS

By the 1850s, Ennis's markets had experienced almost two centuries of continuous growth. The Great Famine, however, marked a decisive turning point and, in the decades following, the markets went into irreversible decline. Across

---

82 Ibid., pp. 146–52. **83** RD, 1860/19/21, 483. **84** See '135 years ago' in *Clare Champion*, 18 July 1997. **85** *Clare Journal*, 25 June 1868. **86** George H. Bassett, *Directory of the city and county of Limerick and of the principal towns in the counties of Tipperary and Clare* (1866), p. 100; *Directory of Ireland* (1870), pp. 104–5; Slater's *royal national commercial directory of Ireland* (1881), p. 128; Francis Guy, *Postal directory of Munster* (1893), p. 44. **87** Conrad M. Arensberg, Solon T. Kimball, *Family and community in Ireland* (2nd edition, Massachusetts, 1968), p. 297.

the country there was a steep fall in land under cultivation. The corn acreage in Ireland fell from about 3.3 million acres in 1850 to 1.3 million by 1910. Wheat declined especially quickly, from a high of three quarters of a million acres in 1850 to less than 48,000 by 1910.[88] The Ennis cornmarket declined accordingly. Related to the decline in tillage was the phenomenon of mass emigration. In the wake of the famine, people abandoned agriculture and fled farmland. In a period of just seventy years there was a staggering fall in population levels. The population of Clare had fallen from a high of almost 287,000 in 1841 to 104,000 by 1911.[89] The introduction of the railway to the county in 1859 merely accelerated the emptying of the countryside. The railways also permitted the penetration of the local markets by foreign foodstuffs. Tea, sugar, bread and butter became the new staple diet and the consumption of potatoes declined. In Ennis, as elsewhere, there was a gradual transfer in the purchase of food from the marketplace to the shops. Increasingly people bought their food as groceries over the counter rather than in the open market.

With Irish agriculture concentrating on the production of cattle for the English market, there was a considerable rise in the number of fairs. Four fairs had traditionally been held in Ennis since the early seventeenth century, two in the eastern suburbs at Clonroad and two on the streets of the town. George Stacpoole, attorney of Ennis, sued out a new patent for the Clonroad fairs in 1775, increasing the number of fairs at Clonroad from two to four per year.[90] The two Ennis fairs were held on the third Tuesday in April and on 2 September respectively. To cope with the increasing demand for the sale of livestock, the period over which the street fairs were held, was extended from one to two days.[91] Under the Local Government Board Act of 1872, however, the power to alter and fix the days on which fairs were held was given to local authorities.[92] By 1881 the Ennis Town Commissioners had initiated monthly fairs, held on the first Saturday of every month.[93] With the introduction of monthly fairs, there was a marked decline in the number of places around the county at which fairs were held. Cattle buyers preferred fairs in the larger urban centres where a wide selection of stock was on offer and especially where railway lines were located. The result was that the largest fairs of the county were concentrated in Ennis and the fairs in all but the largest rural centres declined. The attendance of many buyers attracted large numbers of sellers, as competition among purchasers inevitably resulted in keener prices. Large-scale buyers had neither the time nor the inclination for the old rituals of deal making at fairs. Instead, a ticket was given to the farmer as a record of the transaction and an arrangement made to meet him later in the day when payment was made.[94] Ennis, in addition, could offer a range of services available in no other town in county Clare: banking

88 F.S.L. Lyons, *Ireland since the Famine* (London, 1971), pp. 47–8.   **89** *Census of population report*, Munster 1911.   **90** *Royal comm. fairs and markets, mins 1852–3*, p. 66.   **91** Slater's *Directory* (1881), p. 127.   **92** C. Walford, Fairs, *past and present* (London, 1883), pp. 52–3.   **93** Slater's Directory (1881), p. 128.   **94** Arensberg and Kimball, *Family and community*, p. 292.

facilities, hotels for the accommodation of cattle dealers and a wide range of shops where purchases could be made.

The increased number of fairs greatly disrupted town life. Farmers continued to buy and sell in the streets and refused to go to the fair green. A determined effort was made by the police in 1899 to move the fairs off the streets. Individual farmers were brought before the courts and fined for blocking the thoroughfares.[95] However, in a spirited campaign organized by the newly elected urban district council on behalf of the shopkeepers of the town, the attempt to move the fairs to the fair green was successfully resisted. It was agreed that in future the fairs would be held in the old market area of the town and that Jail Street and the road to the railway station would be kept open.[96] There was a further rationalization in 1905, when the monthly fairs were restricted to the first five months of the year.[97] By the first decade of the twentieth century then, cattle fairs had come to dominate the commerce of the town.

PURCHASE OF THE MARKET TOLLS

With the rising tide of nationalism in the second half of the nineteenth century, townspeople found it objectionable that an absentee aristocrat resident in England should have the permanent income of the Ennis fairs and markets. As early as 1859, a letter from Michael Considine, the respected secretary of the Ennis Trades' Association and the man responsible for the erection of the O'Connell Monument in the town, requested that the town commissioners should take control of the Ennis tolls.[98] The question arose at several council meetings over the years but, without an act of parliament, nothing could be done to compel the owner to relinquish possession of the tolls. The Local Government Act of 1898 transformed the Boards of Town Commissioners into Urban District Councils. Under the act the councils were given enhanced responsibilities including power to purchase market tolls or any franchise or right to hold a market or fair. One of the first acts of the Ennis Urban District Council was to petition Henry Wyndham, the second Lord Leconsfield, for control of the tolls and customs associated with the fairs and markets of Ennis. Leconsfield's reply was unfavourable. The act, while empowering the council to purchase the tolls, did not compel the owner to sell them. A resolution was passed in May 1899 which declared Leconsfield's ownership of the tolls 'an intolerable nuisance' and the government was requested to bring in legislation to transfer the ownership of all such tolls from private ownership to local authorities.[99]

95 *Clare Journal*, 23 Feb. 1899 and 22 June 1899.   **96** Sheedy, *Clare elections*, p. 751.
97 Kelly's *Directory of Ireland* (1905), p. 231.   **98** Sheedy, *Clare elections*, pp. 734–5.
99 Ibid., p. 751.

Figure 5 The Lower Market (the Mall), Ennis, *c.*1900. The square of ground was
originally laid out in 1755 for the sale of milk and potatoes
(photo: courtesy of the NLI).

The question did not arise again until April 1906, when the interest of the
tolls was advertised for sale by Miss Macbeth, a relative of John Macbeth, who
had first leased the tolls in 1844. At a special meeting of the urban council it was
decided not to lease the tolls, but to make an offer instead for their outright
purchase. A sum of £3,000 was offered to Charles Wyndham, the third Lord
Leconsfield.[100] A reply was received in November 1906 stating that Lord
Leconsfield was prepared to sell the tolls for the sum of £3,300.[101] The council,
after much argument, finally agreed to the amount and in March 1907 made an
application to the Local Government Board for a loan of £3,300. The board,
however, refused to sanction a loan for such a purpose. In the end, both
Leconsfield and the council agreed that the purchase price would be paid out of
the income of the tolls over a period of years.[102] This finally ended the Wyndham
connection with the Ennis fairs and markets, a connection which had begun in
1741 when the family, almost by accident, had inherited the Thomond estates.

100 *Clare Journal*, 16 April 1906.   **101** *Clare Journal*, 1 Nov. 1906.   **102** *Clare Journal*, 18
March 1907; Sheedy, *Clare elections*, pp. 753–4.

And so for the first time since 1609, when the first market patent had been granted to the town, ownership of the tolls and customs of Ennis was in the sole possession of the elected local authority.

CONCLUDING REMARKS

In the twentieth century, the story of the Ennis markets was one of continuing decline. The cornmarket remained open until the late 1950s, but little corn was traded. In its latter years it was used mainly for weighing and selling small quantities of potatoes. Today a shopping complex stands on the site. The butter-market closed in the 1940s. Its buildings housed a woodwork joinery until recently and at present the old buildings are being renovated to house the new offices of the Ennis Urban District Council. By contrast, the story of livestock sales has been one of unprecedented growth. The fair green was used for cattle and sheep fairs until the early 1960s. Today it has been transformed into the town's municipal park. Fairs are no longer held on the streets. The agricultural business of the region is now concentrated in the Ennis mart which opened for its first livestock auction on 16 January 1957.[103] The mart was built adjacent to the railway station, near the green where the old Clonroad fairs were held. Initially boycotted by cattle buyers, the business grew slowly in the early years. However, by 1968, the company trading as Clare Co-operative Livestock Mart Ltd, was selling 25,000 head of cattle valued at over £1.5 million per year.[104] With Ireland's entry to the European Economic Community in 1972, the livestock industry flourished. In 1988, one of Clare Marts best years in operation, 91,998 cattle were sold for a total of £48.88 million.[105]

What remains of the Ennis markets are held in Lower and Upper Market Street – the two squares laid out in 1755 and 1805 respectively. Amazingly, the byelaws laid down in 1805 are still generally obeyed. Vegetables are traded in the lower market and pigs and calves in the upper market. In Ennis, on Saturday mornings, vendors of miscellaneous merchandise still gather and lay out their stalls, more or less in a row, along the market street, for which they pay tolls. Traders little realize that they continue a tradition that has persisted in Ennis for more than five hundred years.

---

103 Information provided by Maura Green of Clare Marts Ltd.   104 Ibid.   105 Clare Marts Ltd, Clonroadmore, Ennis, *Annual Report and Accounts 1988*.

The markets and fairs of Cootehill, county Cavan

PATRICK CASSIDY

Cootehill is a picturesque market town nestling among the rolling drumlin landscape of northeast county Cavan. An unsuspecting visitor may view it as a quiet and relaxing place to spend a few days, 'far from the madding crowd'. A quick glance at a modern map reveals that the town is not located along a main National Primary route. However, this was not always the case. During the eighteenth century, Cootehill was the most prosperous town in both counties Cavan and Monaghan and it had road links with all the main urban centres in the region. The town also formed part of the rail network which wove its way through the Irish landscape during the nineteenth century. Today, like many other small provincial towns, Cootehill no longer possesses a rail link with the outside world. The last train pulled out of its train station in 1960, adding a severe blow to the prosperity of the town.

I

Cootehill's story commences in the middle of the seventeenth century. Colonel Thomas Coote was granted an estate consisting of 17,000 plantation acres in the barony of Tullygarvey in northeast county Cavan in the 1650s as part of the Cromwellian land settlement.[1] He married Frances Hill, a daughter of Moses Hill of Hillsborough, county Down and named his new Cavan estate 'Coot-Hill' to immortalize their names.[2] This was a common practice in the late seventeenth and eighteenth centuries as new landowners attempted to create a lasting imprint on the landscape. Mr Coote died without an heir in 1671 and his Cootehill estate was left to his nephew and namesake, Thomas Coote, son of Lord Colooney in county Sligo[3] (see appendix 1).

The new estate proprietor was eager to create a successful and profitable estate on his lands in county Cavan and subsequently, as no town already existed on the estate, he began to construct one on a site close to his residence in the townland of Magheranure. Thomas Coote obtained a patent on 3 July 1725, for a weekly market on Friday and for four annual fairs to be held on 1 March, 28

---

1 Revd A. De Vlieger, *Historical and genealogical record of the Coote family* (Lausanne, 1900), p. 23. **2** Ibid., p. 23. **3** Ibid., p. 23.

May, 1 September and 25 November and the day after each of these dates.[4] This was a crucial step in the development of the town. County Cavan was going through a phase of economic growth during this period, as three other local landlords took out patents for fairs and markets at that time.[5] This followed a national trend of economic expansion as the country settled down after the turbulent final decades of the seventeenth century. Another incentive for promoting the new town of Cootehill was that main roads could be constructed using county funds, provided that they were built between market towns. Cootehill was able to benefit from an improved transport network which connected it with all the towns and villages in the surrounding counties and further afield.

The Irish linen industry had originated in the northeastern counties of Ulster during the later half of the seventeenth century. This was the region of Ireland which had been most heavily planted with Protestant settlers from Scotland and the north of England during the Ulster and subsequent plantations. Many of these settlers became involved in the linen industry and, as the settlements spread, skilled linen workers were encouraged to relocate to new urban centres like Cootehill with the inducement of favourable leases and the other attractions a new town could offer.[6]

Thomas Coote, as well as being a successful lawyer in Dublin, was also keenly interested in commerce. He had a particular interest in the expanding linen trade in Ireland. Consequently, he developed Cootehill into a thriving linen centre during the course of the eighteenth century. The linen industry was then a cottage-based one and it required workers who were skilled in the arts of spinning and weaving. It also depended on tenants who were familiar with the production and processing of flax, the raw material of the industry.

Landlords such as Thomas Coote attracted new tenants to their estates by advertising in newspapers like the *Belfast Newsletter*. The Revd Dean Richardson's description of the new town, dating from 1740, states:

> There are a great number of weavers and bleachers in this town and neighbourhood, and no less than ten bleach yards, the least of which bleaches a thousand pieces of cloth every year. All which was brought about by means of a colony of Protestant linen-manufacturers, who settled here on the encouragement given them by the Honourable Mr Justice Coote, who with a great deal of good management and care to have this new town so tenderly nursed and cherished in its infancy, that many of its inhabitants soon grew rich and brought it to the perfection which it is now at.[7]

---

4 Ibid., p. 43.   **5** W.H. Crawford, 'Markets and fairs in county Cavan' in *The Heart of Breifne* (Cavan, 1984), pp. 55–65.   **6** W.H. Crawford, 'The reshaping of the borderlands *c.*1700–1840' in R. Gillespie and H. O'Sullivan (eds) *The Borderlands* (Belfast, 1989), pp. 93–105.   **7** Armagh Public Library, 'Lodge MSS' (An account of Cootehill in 1740 by Revd Dean Richardson, p. 1).

Cootehill continued to flourish as a linen market and centre of production throughout the eighteenth and early nineteenth centuries. Thomas Coote's grandson, Charles, who inherited the estate in 1750 after the death of his father, also took a keen interest in his town.[8] He controlled the estate from 1750 until his death in 1800 and it was during his lifetime that Cootehill's markets and fairs reached their peak in activity.

II

Charles Coote, who became earl of Bellamont in 1767, was directly involved in the promotion of the linen industry in the Cootehill area. *Faulkner's Dublin Journal* includes an article on a parade which took place in Cootehill in September 1760.[9] Charles Coote took part in the festivities along with five hundred linen weavers, linen drapers and other members of the local gentry. The celebrations culminated with parties for the linen weavers in the local public houses and a 'grand ball' in the new assembly rooms. Mr Coote hosted a party for the local gentry and linen merchants in his Palladian residence, 'Coot-Hill'. This stately home was later renamed 'Bellamont Forest' after Charles Coote obtained the title earl of Bellamont in 1767.[10]

Like many other improving landlords of his generation, Charles Coote was eager to expand his town and he realised that trade was the key to this expansion. Trade depends on an effective network of communication and Cootehill's communication links with the outside world were an essential part of its success as the premier market town in the Cavan – Monaghan area during the eighteenth century. Cootehill was well serviced with roads at that time. It was located along the main road between Dublin and Clones, as indicated on Herman Moll's 1712 map of Ireland.[11] This map also indicates that Cootehill had a direct road link with Cavan town and a connection with Monaghan town, via Killevan, on the Clones road. In the following decades, Revd Richardson's account of Cootehill also refers to the importance which the Cootes placed on road building in the area. He noted

> There are not better roads to be met with anywhere, than those which these two public-spirited gentlemen both the father and the son have taken care to be made about Cootehill.[12]

The evolution of the road network serving Cootehill can be followed by examining Taylor and Skinner's *Maps of the Roads of Ireland*, which was first published in

8 De Vlieger, *Genealogy of Coote family*, p. 167.   **9** *Faulkner's Dublin Journal*, September, 1760.   **10** G.E. Cokayne (ed.), *The complete peerage* (Gloucester, 1987), ii, no. 108. **11** Herman Moll, 'A new map of Ireland, 1714' in *The world described* (London, 1718). **12** Armagh Public Library, 'Lodge MSS', Cootehill account, p. 3.

1778.[13] Towards the end of the eighteenth century an extensive network of roads had emerged around Cootehill. In addition to the roads already listed, the town now also had direct links with Rockcorry and Monaghan town and with Ballybay and Bailieborough. (See map of Cootehill in its regional context) These new roads provided suppliers and linen drapers and merchants from the surrounding areas and further north with a more direct route to and from Cootehill.

The new roads to the north also gave the town easier access to the important ports of Drogheda, Dundalk and Newry. They also made the markets and fairs of Cootehill much more accessible to the people who inhabited the surrounding countryside. The town had become a hub for the linen trade towards the end of the eighteenth century and, because of its well-established road network, it soon emerged as one of the most important brown linen markets in the province of Ulster.

Cootehill's linen industry provided the town and its environs with a great deal of employment. Being a labour-intensive industry it involved many families in the various processes of producing the finished product in the form of linen yarn. Sir Charles Coote noted in his *Statistical Survey of the county of Cavan* in 1802 that there was a considerable population in the Cootehill area at the beginning of the nineteenth century.[14] Most townlands contained between twelve and fifteen families. Certain townlands had as many as twenty to thirty families with an average of six persons per household. This thriving population helped to sustain the weekly markets and the less frequent seasonal fairs.

The town itself expanded greatly during the course of the eighteenth century and this building boom had reached its height in the early decades of the nineteenth century when Cootehill acquired its most prominent public buildings. These buildings included a new market house (which also served as a town hall), a new courthouse, a shambles area and a new Church of Ireland at the end of Market Street.[15] Information contained within a series of leases dating from the 1750s, between the earl of Bellamont and his urban tenants, indicates that construction was constantly in progress along the principal streets of the town.[16] It was during this period that Market Street became the most important commercial street in Cootehill.

Using these leases along with trade directories from the first half of the nineteenth century, it is possible to get an impression of the types of business that existed in the town at that time. The leases list a variety of business establishments, including shopkeepers, merchants, apothecaries, saddlers, publicans, licensed tanners, a tobacconist, a surgeon, a cooper and an inn-keeper.[17]

---

13 George Taylor and Andrew Skinner, *Maps of the roads of Ireland 1778* (Reprint, Shannon, 1969) p. 52. 14 Sir Charles Coote, *Statistical survey of the county of Cavan* (Dublin, 1802), pp. 239–40. 15 Ordnance Survey Memoirs, parish of Drumgoon, county Cavan, 1834–35, pp. 5–6. 16 NLI, D 6791–6875, Leases & renewals of premises in Cootehill granted by Sir Charles Coote and other members of the Coote family 1766–1830. 17 NLI, D 6791–6825.

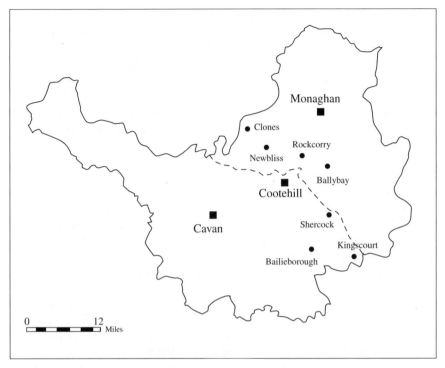

Figure 1 Cootehill regional context.

The town's shopkeepers and professionals relied on the markets and fairs for much of their commercial activity. A more complete picture of the businesses and professions in Cootehill can be found in Pigot's *Commercial Directory of Ireland* in 1824. Cootehill is described as 'a neat town' whose 'regular weekly market on Friday is plentifully supplied with provisions of all kinds from the adjacent country.'[18] Pigot's directory of 1824 shows that the town had a population of about one thousand and it was able to support a variety of professions including four doctors, three apothecaries, two linen officers and two lawyers. There were also twenty-four public houses in the town. The markets and fairs attracted large numbers of people and the large number of public houses would not have survived had they depended solely on the townspeople for their trade. These establishments formed an important role in the social aspect of the fairs and markets.

A wide range of other businesses are listed under the heading, 'Shopkeepers, Traders, & c.' This group included grocers, bakers, spirit dealers, woollen drapers, leather sellers, boot and shoemakers, haberdashers, watchmakers, saddlemakers and cartmakers. All of these merchants depended on the markets and fairs to attract large numbers of people to Cootehill from the surrounding countryside.

18 J. Pigot, *Commercial directory of Ireland* (London, 1824), p. 376.

Part of the wealth generated at such gatherings would then find its way into the coffers of the local businessmen as country folk spent some of their earnings on supplies, provisions and services.

Market Street contained six grocery shops and four bakeries. Church Street had four grocery shops and two bakeries. Cavan Street had one grocery shop and Bridge Street had one bakery. These entries indicate that the majority of trade was carried on in two of the four principal streets of the town, Market Street and Church Street in the early part of the nineteenth century[19] (see appendix 2).

III

Towns do not exist in splendid isolation. Cootehill, as a planned, market town, emerged out of an increasingly densely populated, fertile, rural landscape. It was designed as a service centre for the Coote estate and the surrounding estates in the region. Pigot's *Commercial Directory of Ireland* states in its description of Cootehill in 1824 that the town received a plentiful supply of provisions from its hinterland, 'which is well cultivated'.[20]

As well as the linen trade, agriculture played a crucial role in the very existence of the town from its infancy. The townspeople of Cootehill depended on their country neighbours for essentials such as fresh milk, butter, meat and other foodstuffs. Likewise, the large landholders and the smaller tenant farmers relied on the merchants, professionals and craftsmen of Cootehill for their groceries, general supplies and a range of other essential services, ranging from that of the shoemaker to that of the blacksmith and apothecary. This symbiotic relationship can best be explored by focusing on the markets and the fairs which attracted people to Cootehill.

The weekly Friday market was facilitated by the construction of a market house in the town. The Revd Richardson refers to it in his 1740 account of the town. He noted:

> Here is a Church in decent order, a good Market-House, a large market kept on Fridays, in which there is plenty of provisions and abundance of good yarn and green cloth sold.[21]

The exact construction date and the location of this building is uncertain owing to the lack of cartographic evidence for the town during the eighteenth century. However, it may be assumed that the market house was located on the site of

19 An examination of the earl of Bellamont's will, dating from 1800, indicates that developments along Bridge Street and Cavan Street were to be prohibited in order to keep the town to a fixed plan. A copy of this will is held at PRONI, D/3406/B/2. 20 Pigot, *Commercial directory*, 1824, p. 375.   21 Armagh Public Library, Lodge MSS, Cootehill account, p. 1.

the one replacing it in the early part of the nineteenth century. The impression given by Revd Richardson is that the town was a thriving centre of commercial activity and that the surrounding countryside was keeping the market well supplied with both linen and agricultural produce.

Evidence of the booming linen market at Cootehill can be found in a number of contemporary sources. Apart from Revd Dean Richardson's account of the market in 1740, Revd Daniel Beaufort, who visited county Cavan in 1792, described the county town of Cavan as 'neither large nor commercial', while he noted that 'Cootehill has the advantage of a well-frequented linen market, in which great sums of money are weekly circulated'.[22]

Statistical surveys of Cavan and Monaghan were carried out by Sir Charles Coote in the opening years of the nineteenth century under the auspices of the Royal Dublin Society. The Monaghan survey was published in 1801 and the Cavan survey appeared the following year. The principal aim of these surveys was to collect data on agricultural practice, land use, soil type, the main commercial centres and other general information. Owing to its geographical location, Cootehill features in both these surveys.

The *Statistical Survey of the county of Monaghan* devotes an entire chapter to the linen industry and it lists Cootehill as the principal linen market in counties Cavan and Monaghan.[23] The Monaghan survey also states that the average weekly value of linen webs and sheetings sold at the market in Cootehill was £4,000.[24] The *Statistical Survey of the county of Cavan* describes Cootehill in more detail.[25] Sir Charles comments on the importance of the linen market to the economic success of the town and claims that without this thriving market, the town would not survive. The market at Cootehill so impressed him that he wrote, 'it should and might be the best inland town in Ulster'. He also noted that Cootehill's market attracted buyers from 'all the linen markets of Ulster.'[26] Sir Charles Coote was in fact a half-brother of the Cootehill estate proprietor of the early 1800s. His comments may thus suggest a slight bias in relation to his father's former estate.

To facilitate the steady influx of linen drapers from other parts of Ulster and from further afield, a new inn, complete with post chaises opened at the beginning of the nineteenth century.[27] Buyers from as far away as England were attracted to Cootehill's linen market. There is evidence of such buyers attending the linen market in Cootehill as late as 1816, when many of the other linen markets had already gone into decline.[28] This proves that Cootehill's reputation as a centre of excellence for the purchase of webs of brown linen was still attracting such buyers up to the 1820s.

Trading at Cootehill's linen market reached its peak around the beginning of the nineteenth century. Estimates of annual sales in brown linen at Cootehill

22 Revd Dr Daniel A. Beaufort, *Memoir of a map of Ireland* (Dublin, 1792), pp. 35–7. 23 Sir Charles Coote, *Statistical survey of the county of Monaghan* (Dublin, 1801), pp. 202. 24 Coote, *Monaghan Survey*, p. 202.   25 Coote, *Cavan Survey*, p. 255.   26 Ibid., p. 255. 27 Ibid., p. 256.   28 Conrad Gill, *Rise of the Irish linen industry* (Oxford, 1925), p. 176.

around this time are given in Table 1.[29] The term 'brown linen' refers to unbleached linen cloth.

Table 1 Estimated brown linen sales at Cootehill's market.

YEAR	1783	1803	1816	1820
TOTAL	£52,000	£114,400	£52,000	£55,762

In 1803, the town's linen market ranked sixth in Ulster, the province where the linen trade was most prominent in the country. Cootehill's market was in the same league as top markets such as Lisburn, Lurgan and Belfast. This prosperity coincided with the nationwide economic boom which had occurred as a result of the Napoleonic wars in Europe.

Table 2 Estimated annual brown linen sales in leading Ulster markets in 1803.

Market	Sales (£'s)
Armagh	208,000
Dungannon	182,000
Belfast	156,000
Lisburn	145,600
Lurgan	130,000
Cootehill	114,400
Derry	104,000
Tanderagee	88,000

In 1809, Thomas Bell, a Dublin artist and architect, published an account in the *Dublin Evening Post* of an excursion he had taken to Cootehill. He noted 'Market Street receives its name from a neat market-house for the sale of corn and being the place where the great weekly market and also the fairs are held.'[30] His description of the town includes a section on market day. He observed that there was a large influx of people on market day and that the main articles for sale were linen and yarn. However, the market day also attracted a host of sellers and 'there is scarcely an article of general consumption which is not exposed for sale in the public street and at very little higher than they would bring in the metropolis'.[31]

Mr Bell made an interesting observation on the gender of traders in the town. Commercial activity was by no means the exclusive preserve of men.

29 W.H. Crawford, *Domestic industry in Ireland – the experience of the linen industry* (Dublin, 1972). See appendix.   **30** TCD, Ref. 54 U.2. Extracts from Thomas Bell's 'Rambles Northwards' in *Dublin Evening Post* (1809).   **31** Ibid.

Here the women are equally industrious; even young girls, many of whom in other places, are scarcely considered out of their tutelage are here extensively embarked in speculations of commercial enterprise.[32]

The explanation given for this high level of both male and female participation in trading relates back to the linen trade. The thriving linen trade encouraged an entrepreneurial spirit in many of the inhabitants of both Cootehill and its environs. The poorest tenants could acquire a small quantity of flax, which could then be spun into yarn. This yarn could then be sold at the market and a small profit realised. Mr Bell noted,

They, consequently, are early initiated in the mysteries of buying and selling and acquire a knowledge of business which as their capital increases finds new channels in which to exert itself.[33]

IV

This boom period for the town did not last. In little more than a decade, the linen market saw its sales decrease by over 50 per cent. There were slight improvements in sales between 1816 and 1820 and again in the late 1830s.[34] However, the market never regained the prominent position it had held at the turn of the nineteenth century. The fall in prices after 1815 was not the main factor in the decline of Cootehill's linen market. The most serious threat came from within the province of Ulster itself.

During the 1820s a transformation in the manufacture of linen had taken place. Throughout the eighteenth century the linen industry had been a cottage-based one. Contemporary records, such as Coote's survey of 1802, show that the vast majority of the population in the Cootehill area was involved in manu-facturing linen in the home. However, by the 1820s, this trend of cottage-based industry had begun to disappear in the Lagan Valley district. It was superseded by a mechanization of the industry, which resulted in a transformation from home-based production of linen to one centred on linen mills.

With the advent of the linen mills and the rapid centralisation of the industry in the Lagan Valley region, linen markets such as that at Cootehill began to decline in importance. Cootehill was geographically too far from the new epicentre of the industry and subsequently its linen market suffered a swift decline. The mechanization of the linen industry had additional repercussions for Cootehill and its economic and commercial prosperity.

The barony of Tullygarvey in northeast county Cavan was one of the most densely populated areas in Ireland at the beginning of the nineteenth century. Its population depended on the linen industry for survival. The labour-intensive

32 Ibid. **33** Ibid. **34** Crawford, *Domestic industry in Ireland*, see appendix. Lewis,

nature of the domestic linen industry had encouraged larger families which, in turn, increased pressure on landlords to subdivide their land. Tenant farmers who engaged in the linen industry were able to survive on a small amount of land.

Sir Charles Coote commented on the very small percentage of land being utilized for farming in both the Cavan and Monaghan surveys. Most of the land was used for the growing of flax and provisions for the manufacturers. He also noted in his Monaghan survey that a typical farm in the barony of Dartrey, which lay directly across the county boundary from Cootehill, consisted of five acres. Two acres were given to the growing of oats, half an acre to potatoes, half an acre to flax and two acres were left as pasture and meadow.[35] Large families could thus survive on farms of this scale, provided the price of linen remained high.

Weavers earned twice as much as farm labourers, and the prosperity which this created was a major factor in the growth of the local population and of the weekly market.[36] It was also a reason why more people were involved in the domestic manufacturing of linen than in agriculture at the beginning of the nineteenth century in the Cavan and Monaghan areas. Accordingly, the following remark by Sir Charles Coote is justifiable; 'nowhere in Ireland are there more slovenly modes of farming or more bleak, bare and unadorned fields than are to be seen in the manufacturing counties.'[37] Agriculture was in such a neglected state in this area simply because linen production, which was more profitable, dominated the markets. Most families were almost self-sufficient and 'provisions very seldom appear for sale, as the weavers till just enough of land to afford them potatoes, oats and the flax plot.'[38] However, once the linen industry began to decline in the Cootehill area, the Friday market, which had been dominated by sales in linen webs and sheetings, began to adapt to a changing shift in market supply.

This trend reflects the shift in Cootehill's rural economy from that of a cottage-based linen industry to that of an agricultural economy. This transformation in favour of agriculture was to have a radical effect on Cootehill's markets and fairs from the 1830s to the 1960s. The town gradually lost its famous linen market and was forced to adapt its market focus and increase the frequency of its fairs in order to survive.

V

An examination of sources for the decades preceding the Great Famine of 1845 indicates that, despite the rapid decline in the linen trade in Cootehill, the town was still relatively prosperous. Lieutenant P. Taylor conducted a statistical report on Cootehill in 1835 to accompany the first Ordnance Survey six-inch maps of Ireland.[39] The *Ordnance Survey Memoirs* for the parish of Drumgoon provide the

Dictionary, i, 398.   **35** Coote, Monaghan Survey, p. 96.   **36** Ibid., p. 214.   **37** Ibid., p. 213.   **38** Coote, *Cavan Survey*, p. 240.

reader with a unique picture of the town in the aftermath of the collapse of its linen market. Cootehill is fortunate to have been included in the survey memoirs before this project was discontinued.

Lieutenant Taylor noted that 'during the flourishing condition of the linen trade, [it was] one of the most prosperous towns in this division of the kingdom.' He also stated that 'from its central position and means of communication [it] ought now to be the depot of the agricultural produce of an extensive sur-rounding district.'[40] He observed that the town was well supplied with meat, poultry and butter. Later in his report he noted that 'the corn trade is much more extensive now than at any former period.'[41] An estimated 15,000 barrels of corn were sold annually at Cootehill's market and this was ground into meal and exported to Liverpool and Glasgow via the port of Dundalk.[42] The local tenant farmers had begun to grow more oats, the local corn crop, to replace the flax crop when the linen trade declined in the Cootehill area.

Agricultural produce and livestock had so increased in importance by the 1830s, that the town now hosted twelve annual fairs.[43] This increase in fair days reflects the changing pattern of agriculture in the Cootehill region, as the economic activity of the town attempted to adapt to the decline in linen production and the increase in cattle exports to England. The fairs focused principally on livestock and they took place on the second Friday of each month. Horses, cows, sheep, pigs and asses all featured in the monthly sales which took place at various locations throughout the town. Horses sold for between £8 and £15, cows from £4 to £6, asses from £1 to £2, sheep from 35s. to 55s. and pigs were sold by their weight, at from 2d. to 3d. per pound. It was noted that the cattle 'were of a very inferior description.'[44]

A specific market for pigs developed in an area of Bridge Street, which became known as 'the pig market.' This market developed in the square in front of the Seceding Meeting House and on fair days this area, along with the whole of Bridge Street, was filled with carts containing pigs for sale. This market was not controlled by the Horan family and it tended to be very disorganised. Dr T.H. Moorehead gave the following evidence to the Royal Commission on market rights and tolls inquiry held at Cootehill in 1888: 'that market is a great public nuisance. On the days upon which it is held, the street is occupied from one end to the other by men holding on to their pigs by hay and straw ropes, and traffic up and down the thoroughfare is a matter of impossibility.' Another witness noted, 'I have seen the public roads so crowded on many occasions that the earl of Dartrey could not get up the street on his way to the poor house, where he acted as a guardian.'[45]

39 Angelique Day and Patrick Mc Williams (eds), *Ordnance Survey Memoirs of Ireland: Counties of South Ulster 1834–8*, vol. 40, (Belfast, 1998), p. viii.   **40** *O.S. Memoirs: South Ulster*, vol. 40, p. 4.   **41** Ibid., p. 9.   **42** Ibid., p. 9.   **43** Ibid., p. 10.   **44** Ibid., p. 10. **45** *Report of commissioners, inspectors and others of the royal commission on market rights and tolls*, 1889 [c.5888] xxxviii, p. 401.

Despite these problems, Cootehill was one of the most prominent pork markets in the northeast counties in the decades after the famine.[46] Lieutenant Taylor noted in 1835 that pigs were bought by 'jobbers', who drove them to Belfast, Newry and Dublin for the English markets,[47] thus indicating that Cootehill's pig market was thriving even prior to the famine.

A further reference to Cootehill's pork market appears towards the end of the nineteenth century in *The Belfast and Province of Ulster Directory 1899*. Cootehill then played host to two pig markets. In its description of the town, the directory states that 'a large dead and live Pork Market' takes place in Cootehill. The pork meat market took place each Wednesday from the third week in September until the first week in May and the live pig market was held on the third Thursday of each month at the market house.[48]

Mr James Mc Cudden, a Dundalk man, settled in Cootehill towards the end of the nineteenth century. He was one of the town's butchers and pork dealers and his name appears in *The Belfast and Province of Ulster Directory*.[49] Pigs bought at the market were taken to the rear of his premises where they were slaughtered. The carcasses were then hung on wooden beams in the garden awaiting collection. 'Carters' loaded the meat onto carts, which were then taken to the market house for weighing, prior to being transported to the train station for transport to Dundalk and onwards to Glasgow, where the Mc Cudden family had business connections.[50]

Cattle were the principal farm animals sold at the town's fairs. The four annual fairs in Cootehill had remained unchanged from 1725 until the 1820s. *Pigot's Directory* of 1824 noted that fairs still took place on 12 March, 9 June, 12 September and 6 December annually.[51] However, as stated above, this number had increased to twelve by the 1830s reflecting the change in market focus from linen to agriculture.[52]

Cootehill's fair green, also referred to locally as the 'cow green', now assumed a more prominent role in the commercial life of the town. The herds of cattle were driven into town on foot and they assembled on the 'cow green' awaiting sale. Several townspeople remember observing this scene. The dealers arrived and inspected the cattle. A 'tangler' was employed as an intermediary between the buyer and the seller.[53] A 'luck-penny' was given with cattle, varying from 5 shillings to 1 shilling. Once a deal had been done, the animals were driven away. When the train station opened in 1860, the cattle could be herded out to the station and loaded onto cattle trucks for transport to ports along the east coast.

46 Interview with Mr Andy Adams, Cortober, Cootehill in February, 1999.   **47** *O.S. Memoirs: South Ulster*, vol. 40, p. 10.   **48** *The Belfast and Province of Ulster Directory* (Belfast, 1899), p. 1312.   **49** *Belfast and Ulster Directory*, p. 1313.   **50** Interview with Miss Veronica Blessing, Market Street, Cootehill on 8 July, 1999. Mr McCudden was this lady's grandfather.   **51** Pigot, *Commercial Directory*, 1824, p. 375.   **52** *O.S. Memoirs: South Ulster*, vol. 40, p. 10.   **53** Interview with Mr Colm Smith RIP, Bridge St., Cootehill on 12 July, 1999.

Figure 2 Cootehill's Market House and Town Hall, built in 1806.

Lieutenant Taylor was unimpressed with the cattle being sold at the monthly fairs in Cootehill in the 1830s. He states that 'the breed of cattle is of the very lowest class' and that they were 'low priced'.[54] This may have been the result of the depressed state of the land in general at that time. Subdivision was rife in the parish of Drumgoon and farms varied in size from two to ten acres. All the landlords in the area, together with their agents, were absentees, apart from Mr Charles Coote, the proprietor of Bellamont Forest. The majority of tenants were tenants at will who were unused to cattle rearing, and in the decades prior to the famine, there was little opportunity for investing in livestock improvement.

Under a sub-heading entitled 'Remarks on Improvement', Lieutenant Taylor noted that although the parish of Drumgoon had a wealth of natural resources and a well-developed network of communication in the form of roads,

> Its surface presents a more wretched and desolate appearance generally than appears in any other parish of the surrounding district, arising entirely from the deplorable system of agriculture and the minute sub-division of the farms which so unhappily prevails.[55]

54 *O.S. Memoirs: South Ulster*, vol. 40, p. 10.   **55** *O.S. Memoirs: South Ulster*, vol. 40, p. 11.

The tenant farmers of Drumgoon were clearly suffering from the virtual collapse of the linen trade. The entire community had prospered during the golden days of the linen industry. Subdivision hadn't posed a major problem. There was neither a deep-rooted interest in nor a reliance on agriculture. However, once the linen industry began to decline in Cootehill, the now over-populated parish of Drumgoon was forced to eke out a living from agriculture. The Great Famine of the 1840s greatly exacerbated this depressing scene. The changes wrought by the declining linen industry were also reflected in Cootehill's weekly markets. Market day had taken place each Friday in Cootehill since Thomas Coote had obtained his patent for markets and fairs in 1725. This tradition still applied in 1824, as evidenced in *Pigot's Directory*. While linen remained the principal product sold at Cootehill's market, one weekly market day was sufficient for the local population to sell their yarn and purchase the supplies they required.

However, in *Slater's Directory* of 1846, there were now two weekly markets in the town. 'The markets are Friday and Saturday, the former for general produce, the latter for grain.'[56] The new Saturday corn market took place in the market house. The market house (Figure 2), which was rebuilt in 1806, was described as 'a large, oblong commodious building'. Lieutenant Taylor reported that during the prosperity of the linen trade 'the upper range was used for the measuring and stamping of linen whilst the lower was, and still is, employed as the general mart of potatoes and corn'.[57]

The Coote family exercized control over the markets held at the market house and they collected tolls on all goods sold there. Patrick Horan leased the markets from Richard Coote in January 1841. This lease included the market house, cranes, scales, weights, tolls and a number of stores adjoining the market house.[58] Members of that family controlled business at the market house until it was closed in the 1950s.

Cootehill's Saturday grain market was very successful. A report on the Greville Estate, which included a number of townlands in the parish of Drumgoon to the southeast of Cootehill, confirms that Cootehill had an 'extensive exportation' of oats in the early 1840s.[59] This reflects a trend which was prevalent throughout county Cavan and further afield. Cavan's major export in the decade prior to the Great Famine was oats. While no figures are available for Cootehill, the Railway Commission valued Cavan's market at 7,500 tons per annum, which was worth £55,000.[60] It may be assumed that similar figures applied to Cootehill's grain market.

56 Isaac Slater, *National commercial directory of Ireland* (Manchester, 1846), p. 446. **57** *O.S. Memoirs: South Ulster*, vol. 40, p. 5. **58** Report of commissioners. Inspectors and others of the *Royal commission on market rights and tolls, 1889*, p. 397. **59** NA, Greville Estate Papers, MSS 6178 (64). **60** Kevin O' Neill, *Family and farm in pre-Famine Ireland* (Wisconsin, 1984), pp. 83–4.

County Cavan suffered greatly during the famine years and its population fell from 243,158 in 1841 to 174,064 in 1851, a decline of almost one-third.[61] Cootehill had a population of 2,425 in 1841. This had dropped to 2,105 by 1851. While a decrease of 320 people may not seem like a huge disaster, a broader look at the wider geographical area paints a much bleaker picture. The population of Tullygarvey barony, where Cootehill was the principal market town, was given as 37,532 in 1841. In 1851, this figure had decreased to 25,955, giving a decline of 30.8 per cent.[62] Demographic changes exacerbated by a new and increased wave of emigration must have taken their toll on Cootehill and its markets and fairs in the years after the Famine.

The Great Famine had a major impact on Cootehill and its hinterland. In *Sketches of the highlands of Cavan* which was written shortly after the Great Famine, Revd Randal Mc Collum, a Presbyterian minister in the neighbouring town of Shercock, noted that the famine had wiped out most of the smaller farms in the county.

> The four pauper houses in this one county are standing evidence of the state of the country parts, which had been cut up and subdivided into tiny fields and gardens, with cabins attached, most of which have been forsaken and levelled since the failure of the potato.[63]

He also noted that the Coote estate had not been well managed in recent years and that the majority of the small tenant farmers were struggling to pay their rents and make ends meet. Prior to the famine, the decline in the linen trade had resulted in emigration from Cootehill and its hinterland. This exacerbated the decline in the local population. Revd Mc Collum estimated that hundreds of families had been left unemployed as a result of the failure of the linen trade and that they were 'broken up and scattered for want of lucrative employment in their own neighbourhood.'[64]

Despite this, Cootehill's markets and fairs continued to function relatively prosperously. The ravages of the famine may have decimated the rural population but Cootehill retained an air of affluence. The Revd Mc Collum observed that 'Cootehill is still a fine-looking town, with a good market every week on Friday.' The commercial life of the town, including its markets and fairs, was assisted by the large number of 'gentlemen's seats that thickly stud the face of the country for three miles around.'[65]

The large concentration of strong farmers and landowners in the vicinity of the town was a result of the linen trade. Although this had now declined, it left behind a rich legacy of affluence in the Cootehill area. Revd Mc Collum lists

61 *Report of commissioners appointed to take the census of Ireland of the year 1841*, H.C. 1844 [504] xxiv; and *The census of Ireland for the year 1851*, part vi, H.C. 1856 [2134] xxxi. **62** Ibid. **63** Revd Randal Mc Collum, *Sketches of the highlands of Cavan and of Shirley Castle* (Belfast, 1856), p. 257. **64** Mc Collum, *Sketches*, p. 257. **65** Ibid., p. 255.

many of the strong farmers in the area. Bellamont Forest, Dawson Grove, and Ashfield were the three principal estates in the area. These and other properties were important to the survival of the town as they had a strong impact on the local economy. The gentlemen who occupied these properties still contributed large sums of money to the commercial life of the town, 'even other days beside the market and fair days, and the town is again resuming its healthy business appearance after the famine.'[66]

VI

A major boost to Cootehill's markets and fairs came in 1860 with the opening of a branch line of the Dundalk to Clones railway via Ballybay, county Monaghan. Cootehill was now served by three trains each way, connecting it via Ballybay to all the major towns, cities and ports in the country. This rail link gave Cootehill the edge over other towns and villages in the area, such as Bailieborough, Shercock and Rockcorry, which did not possess a rail link with the outside world.

In the decades after the Great Famine, the principal crops to appear at Cootehill's markets were oats and potatoes. Flax remained an important cash crop and there were still at least two flax dealers in business at the end of the century.[67] The flax market took place in every street of the town and it commenced at 9 a.m. Business was brisk and it usually finished by 10 a.m. As already noted above, a separate grain market had emerged by the second half of the nineteenth century and it continues to appear in trade directories at the close of the nineteenth century.[68]

The other main agricultural commodities for sale were poultry, eggs and butter. Poultry was sold at the junction of Church Street and Market Street, and also at the Market Street end of Cavan Street. 'Fowlers' or 'cleavers', who were businesspeople involved in the poultry trade, visited Cootehill from different parts of Ulster to purchase the local stock. They were also known to intercept farmers and their wives en-route to market and strike a deal prior to their reaching the town.[69]

Eggs and butter were sold at various locations in the town on market day. Eggs were originally sold at the town cross, and the egg market commenced at 10:30 a.m. once the flax market finished.[70] Later on, egg dealers assembled at a store in Chapel Lane behind the market house and also in a number of yards along Market Street, including those of Hugh Fay, John Rice and Blessing's.

66 Ibid., p. 255.   67 *Belfast and Ulster Directory*, 1899, p. 1313.   68 Ibid., 1899 p. 1312.
69 An interview with Mr Packie Dempsey, Latton, county Monaghan, revealed that certain fowlers waited at a junction along the Cootehill to Ballybay Road leading to Latton in the early decades of the twentieth century and dealt there with people on their way to the market in Cootehill.   70 *Royal commission on market rights and tolls, 1889*, p. 398.

Figure 3 A hiring fair in Cootehill, 1890s.

Several Cootehill residents remember these sites.[71] According to the inquiry of the Royal Commission on market rights and tolls in 1888, Cootehill had a prosperous butter market in the market house with sellers coming from Meath and outlying towns in county Cavan like Virginia, Ballyjamesduff and Mullagh. Butter was sold by the firkin, with 75 lbs per firkin. A firkin of butter cost £3 in 1888. Butter was also sold to the local grocers or bartered for groceries. *The Belfast and Province of Ulster Directory* 1899 lists a Mr James Mc Cullagh of Market Street, a provision merchant who was also involved in exporting eggs and butter. This indicates that a certain proportion of the butter sold on market day was for the export market. The Woods family established a poultry and egg store in a disused maternity hospital in Church Street at the beginning of the twentieth century.

VII

The story of Cootehill's markets and fairs would be incomplete without reference to the hiring fairs. Hiring fairs were a common phenomenon in the

71 Miss Veronica Blessing remembers her mother letting their yard to a large egg dealer called McCormack.

north of Ireland between the last few decades of the nineteenth century and the middle of the twentieth century. Changes in agricultural practises together with a reduction in the rural population, due to the Great Famine and the flood of emigration which followed it, led to an acute shortage of manual labourers. This labour shortage was addressed at two of the annual fairs in Cootehill. The hiring fairs took place on the last Friday of May and November each year. On those days, young men and women gathered in the town to find work for the following six months.

On the last Friday of May and November each year, a steady stream of young men and women made their way into Cootehill. They congregated around the 'top corner' at the junction between Market Street and Bridge Street. They were dressed in their best attire and waited for prospective employers to approach them.

The hiring fairs in Cootehill were principally for the hire of farm labourers. However, residents of the town also attended these fairs in search of a servant boy or girl. The encounter generally followed a similar pattern. The farmer or merchant approached his prospective employee and asked if he or she was for hire. The young man or woman answered in the affirmative if they were interested. The farmer or merchant then asked the person how much money they wanted for the six months.

Wages varied depending on the skills and type of work involved. In the 1920s, £6 plus board and lodgings was the average sum earned for general farm labourers and housemaids while skilled workers like ploughmen received as much as double that amount.[72] During the 1930s, wages for labour in the Cootehill area had increased to £8 for girls, £10 for general farm workers and £16 for ploughmen.[73]

Once a price was agreed upon, the deal was done. Both parties to the arrangement shook hands and a token, known as 'earnest money', was given to the new employee. Earnest money varied, depending on who was giving and receiving it. Most workers received a shilling, and the acceptance of earnest money was a sign that a deal had been done. Five shillings or half a crown was considered to be 'big' earnest.[74]

The hiring fairs started around 9 a.m. and once contracts had been arranged, the parties involved made arrangements to meet the following day. Those who failed to find a suitable employer returned to Cootehill the next week in a last effort to secure work. This was known as the 'runaway'.[75] The bargaining power of such unfortunate individuals was, no doubt, considerably reduced and they were forced to take whatever work they could find.

Generally, when the hiring contract terminated, a 'loosening fair' took place. The loosening fair coincided with the monthly fair. This gave both parties to the

72 Harry Bradshaw, 'A hiring fair in Cootehill' in *The Heart of Breifne* (Cavan, 1985), p. 13.   **73** Interview with Mr Andrew Adams, Cortober, Cootehill in February 1999. **74** Ibid.   **75** Ibid.

Figure 4 Market Street, Cootehill, 1830s.

contract a week before the next hiring fair took place. This interim period allowed those seeking employment an opportunity to search for alternative positions and to visit their families before commencing a new term of employment.

Few residents in Cootehill remember hiring fairs in the town. The practice appears to have virtually died out during the 1940s. Numbers attending hiring fairs began to decline during the Economic War as a result of the agricultural depression. Added to this, the introduction of the Ford Ferguson tractor in 1941 enabled many farmers to farm their land without the help of a hired hand. In the late 1940s, new models of tractor such as the Ferguson Standard and the David Brown appeared in Ireland. These advances in agricultural mechanization led to a reduction in the numbers employed on the land, and hastened the demise of the hired hand. Heightened emigration in the 1950s also accounted for the disappearance of the hiring fairs in Cootehill.

VIII

Although the linen trade had been the main source of employment and wealth in the town and dominated the town's markets and fairs for over a century, it was not the sole source of commercial activity in Cootehill. The weekly markets and the fairs also enabled the local farmers to sell their produce to both townspeople and visiting buyers. Cootehill was still a rural market town which relied on the local farming community for its survival and prosperity.

An early nineteenth-century sketch of Market Street helps to recreate the atmosphere which prevailed at Cootehill's markets and fairs (see Figure 4). It reveals a streetscape devoid of tarmacadam, footpaths, streetlights and electricity poles and wires. It creates the impression of a wide, spacious boulevard, which provided an ideal setting for markets and fairs. The elegant, slated, two storey buildings which lined the main streets of the town gave the visitor an impression of affluence and prosperity. It also provided a fine backdrop for the commercial activities being pursued at the market and fair days. Prior to the advent of cars and trucks, there would have been plenty of space on the streets to engage in buying and selling. On a fair day or market day, the main streets were filled with cartloads of provisions, a variety of farm animals and a wide selection of stalls and hawkers claiming to sell everything from a needle to an anchor.

Cootehill's markets and fairs were not solely the preserve of the buyers and sellers. They also provided an important opportunity for the country people of the surrounding region to assemble in the place and interact socially, as well as conducting commercial activities. Lieutenant P. Taylor, while compiling his statistical report on the parish of Drumgoon, noted that 'attendance at markets and fairs are the principal amusements of the people'.[76] The same gentleman made a similar observation in the neighbouring parish of Kildrumsherdan, adding that such gatherings were occasions for 'mirth, jollity and dancing'.[77]

Markets and fairs provided both townspeople and their country neighbours with a variety of amusements and those old enough to remember do so with fondness. School was closed on fair days in Cootehill and once the cattle sales had concluded in the early afternoon, the shopping and carnival atmosphere continued along the main streets. The 'eating houses' did a brisk trade in herrings, eggs, bread and tea and the public houses provided the weary dealers and traders with a respite from their toils before they faced their homeward journeys.[78]

In the middle of the twentieth century, the importance of both fairs and markets to Cootehill's economic survival began to decline. Firstly, the hiring fairs ceased during the 1950s. This was soon followed by the closure of the train station in 1960. This had a profound effect on the town's fairs and markets. In 1965, a new livestock mart opened in the recently deserted railway station and the focus of livestock sales shifted from the town centre to the new premises on the Station Road. The two weekly marts soon eliminated the need for fairs and markets in the centre of the town itself.

---

76 *O.S. Memoirs: South Ulster*, vol. 40, p. 9.   **77** Ibid., p. 36.   **78** Fair day took place on Friday in Cootehill, which was a fast day for many who attended, hence the absence of meat on the local menu.

The frenetic days of Cootehill's bustling markets and fairs have now ceased. Friday is still looked upon as 'market day' by the older generation of the town's citizens, but the fair days only linger in the mind's eye. Today, Cootehill is readjusting to its new role as a service centre for the surrounding catchment area. Its essential morphology may not have altered radically, but sadly, the demise of its traditional markets and fairs have lost the town an important part of its essence and its urban heritage. Today, there are no hawkers or pedlars to be found in the town. The market house has vanished and the fair green has been redeveloped for car parking and recreational uses. Apart from one or two stalls along Market Street there is little evidence that Cootehill's streets were once hives of activity on fair and market days. It is now difficult to imagine how Cootehill could once have been such a thriving commercial centre whose famous linen market and fairs attracted buyers from all parts of the country and from across the Irish Sea.[79]

APPENDIX I: GENEALOGY OF THE COOTE FAMILY

Sir Charles Coote (*d.*1642) was involved in the Nine Years War and later became marshall of Connaught for life under James I.

|

Col Thomas Coote (*b.*1621–*d.*1671) married Frances Hill and named his new estate in Co Cavan, 'Coot-hill'. He died heirless and left the estate to his nephew and namesake Thomas, son of Richard Coote, 1st lord Coolooney.

|

Thomas Coote (*b.*1655–*d.*1741) founded the town and got a patent to hold fairs and markets there in 1725.

|

Charles Coote (*b.*1695–*d.*1750) built 'Bellamont Forest' in the 1720s, the Palladian villa designed by Sir Edward Lovatt-Pearse.

|

Charles Coote (*b.*1738–*d.*1800) was created earl of Bellamont in 1767 and married Lady Emily Fitzgerald, daughter of the duke of Leinster. He influenced the morphology of the town. The estate passed to one of his illegitimate sons in 1800 and was eventually sold in 1874.

79 The market house was demolished in the 1960s to provide for a car park at the White Horse Hotel. A discotheque now occupies this site.

APPENDIX 2

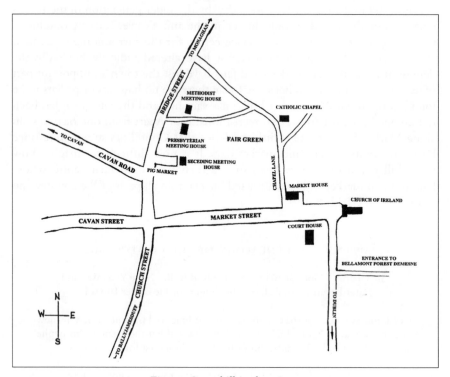

Figure 5 Cootehill in the 1830s.

A household account from county Roscommon, 1733–4

WILLIAM GACQUIN

The document which forms the basis and inspiration for this short article has proven something of a mystery (see appendix).[1] A copy of it arrived on the desk of the Roscommon county librarian in October 1996 from the archivist of the Argyll and Bute Council in Scotland. The covering letter described it as a household account for the years 1733–4, in which the placenames mentioned suggested a Roscommon origin. Further correspondence with the lady who deposited the material in the Argyll and Bute Archive has shed some light on the origin of the document. The aim of this study is, firstly, to determine to what part of Roscommon the document refers, and then to use the material contained in the document to give a picture of the life of an early eighteenth-century household in county Roscommon. Other sources will be used to give a more complete picture of life in the locality referred to in the document.

The document, consisting of four pages, each with two columns of accounts, was found at the beginning of a book later used as the rental book for the Kilberry estate in Argyllshire. The opening entry of the accounts, dated 1 September 1733, is as follows: 'An accont of what money I laid out for the use of my co-partners in [this] house' and seems to imply that the household involved is some kind of joint venture between the writer and others. The introduction to the second year of the accounts refers to 'money laid out this year for the use of the house and family'. The writer does not say that the family concerned is his own, which confirms some kind of partnership arrangement. As will be seen later, the placenames confirm the Roscommon connection, but unfortunately there is no clue as to who the writer of the accounts was, or why they exist for those two years only.

The next question is how and why it made its way from county Roscommon to Argyllshire. From information supplied by the depositor of the material, it seems reasonable to suggest that the person referred to as 'My sister Cathy' no less than eight times in the accounts was Catherine Glass or Glasse. A Catherine Glass, the daughter of an Edward Glass from Ireland, married a Colin Campbell of Kilberry (*c*.1722–98) as his first wife.[2] She apparently brought the material with her to Scotland. However, as she died giving birth to her first child (as did the child), no knowledge of the accounts survived in the Campbell family. It is

1 Campbell of Kilberry papers (Argyll and Bute Council Archive, DR/14/1/5).
2 Letter from Miss Marion Campbell, Kilberry to William Gacquin, 22 October 1998.

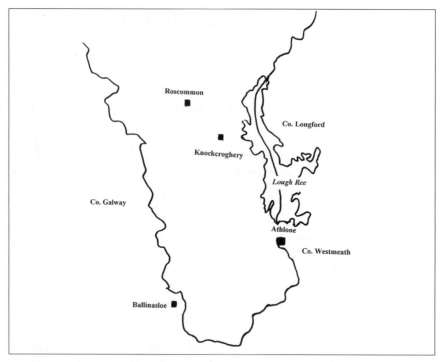

Figure 1 Location Map: Knockcroghery in south Roscommon.

possible that Colin Campbell met with Catherine Glass while he was in Ireland during his military career, which began in 1745. While he married again in 1772, he left no descendants and his estates passed to a cousin. It was one of this family who had possession of the accounts.

If we accept that Catherine Glass was the person referred to as 'My sister Cathy' then the mystery of the bookkeeper's identity still remains. It has not been possible to trace a Glass family to the part of Roscommon mentioned in the accounts, but there was a Glass family on the west side of Athlone town in the eighteenth century, and indeed there was a street named after them in the town in 1744 and throughout the nineteenth century.[3] The religious census of Elphin diocese, dated 1749, lists an Edward and Loftus Glass, 'Protestant Esquires,' apparently living in the same house in St Peter's parish in Athlone.[4] There were two children in the household, one aged over fourteen and the other under fourteen and five servants in all. The fact that this house in Athlone was occupied by two people, possibly brothers, as joint occupiers fits the notion of the joint venture mentioned above. This evidence would suggest that the accounts originated in Athlone town. However, there are other considerations.

3 Harman Murtagh, *Irish historic towns atlas*, No. 6, Athlone (Dublin, 1994), p. 9. 4 Religious census of the diocese of Elphin, St Peter's parish (NAI, M 2466). 5 See OS,

The precise location of the household to which the accounts refer is difficult to pinpoint, but an analysis of the placenames in the account suggests strongly that the members of the household lived in or near the village of Knockcroghery in the parish of Killinvoy, county Roscommon.[5] Knockcroghery itself is mentioned six times when various items were purchased there. Some of these purchases were made at the fair of Knockcroghery but no specific dates are given. The accounts show that the household paid eight shillings as hearth roll money. This suggests a substantial house with four fireplaces, as two shillings was required to be paid for each hearth.[6] Four payments of £10 each, two per year, were recorded in the accounts as rent for a farm in the townland of Scregg to Mr Thomas Burke. The farm at Scregg is also mentioned as the source of much of the household income for the year 1733. The same sum of £2 8s. 6d. was paid in both 1733 and 1734 as quit rent. The entry for 1734 for quit rent suggests that this rent was due only on the land rented at Scregg. However, the surviving quit rent ledgers for county Roscommon start in 1742 and do not show an individual payment of £2 8s. 6d anywhere in that part of county Roscommon.[7] This suggests that the family involved with these accounts may have already left the area by 1742. If this were so, then the household may have relocated to St Peter's parish, Athlone, by the time the religious census of Elphin was taken in 1749. The other placenames mentioned in the accounts are mostly within a three-mile radius of Knockcroghery. Corbooley, Cornamart and Galey are all townlands adjacent to Knockcroghery townland, while Scregg, Lisdaulan, Ballagh, Rahara and St John's are to the south, and Portrunny, Keelogs, Ballymurray and Mote are to the north of Knockcroghery. The compiler of the accounts also records a number of visits to the towns of Roscommon and Athlone to purchase goods which probably were not available nearer home. He also attended fairs in Roscommon and Ballinasloe. He also sold various items in the nearby villages of Athleague and Castlecoote. On one occasion seeds were bought from Dublin, but through a third party, while chairs were purchased in 1733 at an auction in Clonbrock, county Galway. This purchase involved the considerable expenditure of £4 7s. 1d.

The items purchased over the two years covered were quite varied. The most commonly purchased item was food, of which there was a considerable variety, as can be seen from Table 1 below. The most commonly used meat in the house was probably chicken, although most entries in the accounts do not specify how many were bought at a time. The chickens cost 1d. each, according to a purchase of nine for 9d. in 1734. However, they were usually bought along with eggs. The cost of a turkey was 5d. Most of the poultry was purchased within a three-mile radius of Knockcroghery village. Beef and veal were the most popular of the red meats used, while there were only two purchases each of mutton and pork, and, surprisingly, no bacon was purchased. The beef was purchased from a number of

county Roscommon, sheet 42.   **6** K.H. Connell, *The population of Ireland 1750–1845* (Oxford, 1950), p. 6.   **7** NAI, Quit Rent Ledgers, county Roscommon.

Figure 2 Townlands mentioned frequently in the accounts.

locations, including the towns of Athlone and Roscommon. On two occasions the amount bought was described as a 'quarter', probably twenty-eight pounds in weight. One of those bought in Roscommon in 1734 cost 8s. 7d. As the money paid for beef was usually between 6s. and 8s., it would seem that it was normally bought in quarters. Fish was obviously bought in large quantities and there were frequent purchases, as many of the payments made were for 'fish at several times'. There appears to have been one main supplier. Oysters were also bought in large quantities. For example, the purchase of 300 for 1s. 1d. was recorded early in the accounts. The proximity of the river Shannon and Lough Ree probably accounts for the large quantity of fish consumed. Although, as will be seen later, the household had cows, large quantities of butter were bought in 1733 but none in 1734. On one occasion the purchase of nine pounds of butter at 3s. gives a price of 4d. per pound, while the purchase of one hundredweight of butter for £1 4s. 7d. gives a price of about 2½d. per pound.

Table 1 Food items purchased, 1733–4.

Items Purchased	No. of purchases 1733	No. of purchases 1744
Beef	5	6
Veal	4	3
Venison	1	2
Pork	1	1
Mutton	2	0
Chickens/Poultry	9	5
Turkey	2	1
Ducks	0	1
Wild fowl	0	1
Eggs	4	3
Fish	7	5
Oysters	7	5
Herrings	1	1
Apples	1	2
Coleyflower	0	1
Nutts	0	1
Currins	1	0
Salt	5	4
Peper	0	1
Mustard	1	1
Vinegere	1	0
Butter	8	0
Potatoes	1	0

This is an example of the advantage of buying in bulk. Potatoes were purchased once but this may have been for seed purposes. The quantity purchased was two barrels at a total cost of 11s. Most of the fruit purchased came from the St John's area where there was, and still is, an extensive wooded area.

A number of items were also bought in connection with the running of the household. These included items of delft and cutlery such as glasses, mugs, decanters, knives, forks, basins, pewter and wooden ware. With the exception of three purchases of glasses, these were once-off purchases. Candles and rushes were purchased – perhaps the latter were also used as a source of light for the house. Four purchases of soap and 'blew' were made, some by the sister of the writer. A number of items of clothing and footwear were also purchased, mostly in 1733, some of which appear to have been for the household servants. Items purchased included clothes, 'frize', shirts, 'breaches', a 'shammy' as well as brogues on three occasions, twice for 'old Mary' and once for 'Little Lackey'. These two were probably domestic servants, as they occur many times in the accounts.

Figure 3 Knockcroghery, county Roscommon looking from south to north soon after 19 June 1921 when Black and Tans burned most of the houses in the village.

It appears that the house was also undergoing some reconstruction or addition at the time the accounts were written. This is indicated by the purchase of a number of items needed for construction work. Indeed the first items purchased, in September 1733, were 'ribtrees', most likely a form of timber to be used in making a roof. It may have been this purchase, along with next three, which prompted the writer to start his accounts, as these were not regular purchases in the life of the household. Other items recorded which would be associated with house improvements included nails, hinges, locks and bolts, all of which were bought on more than one occasion. 'Tyles' were bought in 1733 at a cost of 19s. 7d. and again towards the end of 1734 he records '12 dozn tiles porch' at a cost of 10s. 8d. This suggests that tiles were used on the new porch that had been built. The notion that a new porch was added is also supported by the purchase of oak timber for a door and a 'street door', as well as hinges and glue in 1734. Payments to masons and to a 'glazier for the street door' also feature in the accounts and strongly support the notion that the house in question faced onto the street of some town or village, probably Knockcroghery. Another of the items bought in connection with this building work in 1734 was a 'hearth stone' costing 2s. 8½d., while carriage of the stone to the house cost a further 1s. 1d. Other purchases which may be linked to the house renovation, or at least to house maintenance, were 'gadds', bought in large quantities, which may have been used to secure thatch or for some similar purpose. Probably also used for similar purposes were the 'wattles and scallups' bought twice in 1733 and once the following year.

It would seem that this household was involved in farming and probably also in the malting or brewing business to a limited degree. Sheep were bought both years in small and large numbers. Forty sheep were purchased in 1733 and another forty in 1734 at the fair of Knockcroghery. These cost £11 15s. and £5 17s. 6d. respectively. This shows a decrease of 50 per cent in the price paid over the year. These were probably grazed on a farm rented at Scregg. It is not surprising, therefore, that a 'sheers' was bought in 1733; however, 12s. 8d. had to be paid to 'sheerers' the following year. Fat 'weadders', purchased individually, may have been killed and used as meat for the house. Pigs and cattle were also bought, but only two of each over the two years. However, an examination of the household income shows that cows and calves were also kept on the farm. Two horses were bought in 1734, one costing £1 17s. and the other, a plough horse, costing 18s. This suggests that some tillage was carried on, as is also suggested by the previously mentioned purchase of seed potatoes and cabbage plants. Other seed material was also purchased in the form of 'bear seed', oats and flax seed.

Iron and 'colters' were purchased for the making of a plough. In 1734 a number of smaller hardware items were purchased, all linked with farm work. These included a hatchet, a spade, a billhook and a reaping hook, as well as a 'slain' bought for Jon Olsogh. This latter purchase, coupled with the hiring of two horses at a cost of 7s. 4d. to bring home turf and a payment to the people of Corboley village for turf, seems to imply that the writer not only harvested his own turf, but also bought more. His requirements were considerable, given the four hearths referred to earlier and his other business activities.

The total expenditure recorded for the household in 1733 was £104 14s. and of this over 10 per cent or £10 14s. 7d. was expended on various occasions on the purchase of malt. Malt was barley or some other grain, which had been steeped in water, allowed to sprout and then dried in a kiln. It was used for brewing. In the same year £3 11s. was spent on 'hopps', almost 3½ per cent of total household expenditure. In that year also 9s. 4½d. was paid to a cooper for work, probably to make barrels to hold the beer that was being brewed. In all, over 14 per cent of the year's expenditure was on the purchase of materials and services for brewing. Despite all this brewing, beer was bought on one occasion from one of the local gentry for 6s. It is difficult to be certain whether this beer was sold or was consumed by the household. The second year of the accounts shows that over 10½ per cent of that year's expenditure related to brewing, including hops, malt, malting, and a payment to the cooper.

A number of services were also purchased over the two years. Some, like those of the cooper and mason, have been referred to already. Other services used and paid for included the work of joiners, smiths, glaziers, weavers, 'carmen', and gardeners a number of times. The farm work necessitated the use of a lot of labour from time to time and there are a number of entries where payment was made to groups of people for work. The people from each of the townlands of Ballagh, Corbooly and Cornamart were paid as a group. The two latter townlands are on the boundary with Scregg where the writer had a farm rented. There were also payments in 1733 of 11s. 8d. and in 1734 of 12s. 8d. to men for shearing sheep. One entry shows a payment of 1s. 1d. to a man named Old T. Muldowney for sowing wheat. There were also a number of servants, both indoor and outdoor, who had to be paid and some others who received payments or goods but may have been part of the family rather than servants.

The accounts contain receipts for the first year only, consisting of a mere eighteen entries, as opposed to 131 entries for expenses. All the receipts were said to be from the farm at Scregg and left the writer with a shortfall of £56 13s. 7d. The largest single item was £28 14s. 11d. received for wool and the same year more lambs' wool was exchanged with a merchant in Athlone for 'necessarys'. This accounted for over 50 per cent of total receipts that year. The rest of the income came principally from the sale of three cows, seven cowhides, three calfskins and twelve sheepskins. A sum of £2 3s. was received for a cow, which compares well with the prices of between £1 19s. and £2 3s. paid for cows in county Clare about the same time.[8] When buying a fat cow from Saml. Boat in 1734, the writer paid £2 6s. A cowhide made from 4s. to 6s. It is interesting to note that the writer tells us that some of these hides were sold as the result of cows dying. There was also a payment of £1 4s. for wheat, paid by his sister, Cathy. The writer of the accounts had four tenants from whom he received rent totalling £5 7s. 10d. One of those paying rent was a miller. These receipts confirm that the writer and his household were engaged in some farming and that sheep accounted for most of his farm income. The importance of sheep to the local economy can be gauged by the advertisement to sell a farm at Lisdallon, Killinvoy parish in a newspaper on 11 August 1739. There were 4,000 sheep on the farm at the time of the proposed sale.[9]

An examination of the names of the people with whom the writer of the account transacted his business gives us some idea of the interaction between the various social classes at the time. This analysis is helped by using the religious census of Elphin conducted in 1749 under the auspices of Edward Synge, Protestant bishop of Elphin.[10] The census covers all the parishes in the vicinity of Knockcroghery, giving names of heads of households, religious persuasion and occupations, as well as information on family size and numbers of servants. Many of those mentioned in the account can be identified from the census.

Business was conducted with a great variety of people, both Protestant and Catholic, some gentlemen farmers and some day labourers. Among the Protestants with whom business was transacted were Geo. Gardiner of Portrun,

8 Brian Ó Dálaigh, *Ennis in the eighteenth century* (Dublin, 1995), p. 49.   9 Moran Papers (NLI, MS 1543).   10 NAI, M 2466.

John Naughten of Galeybeg and the Siggins family, all farmers. Gardiner supplied the ribtrees, while John Naughten supplied iron on two occasions and hops on another. John Shiggins was paid for a road to the bog while a Mrs Shiggins, probably the wife of John Shiggins of Coolfoble, was paid for butter in 1734. Veal was purchased from 'young Gershon Boat' in 1733. He was probably Gershon Boat of Ballymurray, a Protestant butcher, listed in the census of 1749. Rachel Boat, from whom hops were purchased in 1733, was probably of the same family, as was the Saml. Boat listed as a Protestant malster living in Ballymurry in 1749. Tiles were purchased for the house on two occasions from William Corns, a Protestant potter, in Knockcroghery. The writer also seems to have been on good terms with the wealthier Protestants of the locality. On at least four occasions he paid gardeners and servant boys from the big houses to do work on his garden. These included a man from Capt. Lawder's house and the garden boy from Mote in 1733.[11] Mr Waller's gardener was used later in the same year. Robert Waller Esquire lived at Kilmore in St John's parish and had a very large household consisting of six young children, ten male servants and twelve female servants. The servant boy from Mote also brought veal, venison, nuts and apples to the writer at various times, but these were always paid for.

In 1734, the writer paid 6s. to Mr Jas. Sproule 'in exchange for beer'. Two persons named James Sproule were listed in Longfield, Rahara parish in 1749.[12] Both were Protestant gentlemen, a father and son, sharing a seventeenth-century towerhouse as their home. In 1749, this household had a total of eight servants. The father died in 1754 and his son died in 1757. In 1824, the then head of the Sproule family, also James Sproule, moved from Longfield to Athlone, mostly for economic reasons. He had found it impossible to continue at Longfield owing to his large extended family, 'followers and intruders' at the house and the burden of a large number of servants. After moving to Athlone he was able to reduce the number of his servants from twelve to five.[13] While the timing of the move by the Sproule family to Athlone probably had more to do with the hard economics of the early nineteenth century, some of the reasons for moving would be similar to those existing at the time the accounts were written and may explain why someone like the writer would move his household to the less expensive, more urbanized setting of Athlone. Others mentioned in the accounts who were most likely to have been Protestants included John Brogan, the merchant in Athlone, and John Potts.

Most of the other people who appear in the accounts were probably Catholics. Several of the names appear in the 1749 census listed as 'Papist'. For example, the census shows that, of the 172 households recorded in Killinvoy parish, 154 were headed by Papists, fourteen by Protestants and four by Quakers. It is not surprising, therefore, that with Catholics representing 90 per cent of the population their names appear most frequently in the accounts. The most

11 Mote Park, Ballymurry was the seat of Sir Edward Crofton, died 1745. **12** NAI, M 2466, Rahara parish. **13** Royal Irish Academy, Upton papers, no. 7.

unexpected name in the list is that of a priest, Fr Anthony Fflyn. The writer purchased forty sheep from Fr Fflyn in 1733 and the following year he purchased a similar number of sheep at Knockcroghery fair. It is possible that those purchased from Fr. Fflyn were bought at the fair also. It is interesting to see that a Catholic priest was involved in farming at this time and was involved in such a public way. Fr Fflyn was listed as parish priest of Kiltoom in1739 and 1748.[14] He is buried in the old cemetery there, where his tombstone inscription reads: 'Pray for ye soule of/ye reverent Father anthe/ny Flynn/mon..ed by da/niell Flnn nephew of/pater anthony Flynn'.[15] It is most likely that it was this Fr Anthony Fflyn who was recorded as Anthony Flinn, occupying 192 acres of land in Cornesier and Derry in Kiltoom parish, in the Quit Rent Ledger of 1742–7.[16] There must have been a considerable relaxation in the enforcement of the Penal Laws in the Roscommon area if Fr Fflyn felt free to conduct his farming business openly and not through a third party. Such an event would seem to have been impossible twenty years earlier when Gilbeert Ormsby of Tobervady in Athleague parish wrote to Dublin Castle on 12 March 1711–2 in the following terms:

> … I reckon that all our unhappiness and misfortune proceed from the priests to whom the greater men communicate their designs and they stir up the common people to execute them. Nor do I believe that we shall ever be safe or quite till a wolf's head and a priest's be at the same rate … [17]

In fact, according to the Report on the State of Popery in 1731, all the parishes around the Knockcroghery area had a priest, and in St John's parish there were three secular clergy and one 'resident' friar listed.[18]

The writer of the accounts had dealings with at least two Catholics, who were of the strong farmer rather than the labourer or small tenant farmer class. One of these was Bryan Kelly of Keelogues in the parish of Killinvoy. He was listed as a farmer in 1749, with two children over fourteen and one female servant in his household. It was from Keelogues that much of the fish purchased by the writer came, and there were at least seven purchases of fish from the Kellys. Hops, malt and a quart of brandy were purchased on three occasions from Bartole Hughes. This man is not listed in the census of 1749, but he was probably the Bartholomew Hughes who died in 1736 and is buried in Cam cemetery.[19] He had been involved in the leasing of land in 1731 in Cam parish.[20]

14 Hugh Fenning O.P., 'Clergy lists of Elphin 1731–1818' in *Collectanea Hibernica*, no. 38 (1996), p. 144; Hugh Fenning O.P., 'The diocese of Elphin 1747–1802: documents from Roman archives' in *Collectanea Hibernica* , no. 36/37 (1994–5), p. 162.   **15** Hazel A. Ryan, 'Kiltoom church and graveyard' in *county Roscommon Historical and Archaeological Society Journal*, vol vii (1998), p. 28.   **16** NAI, Quit Rent Ledgers, county Roscommon 1742–7, Athlone Barony.   **17** W.P. Burke, *The Irish priests in penal times, 1660–1760* (Waterford, 1914, reprint, Shannon, 1969), p. 440.   **18** 'Report on the State of Popery in Ireland 1731' in *Archivium Hibernicum*, iii (1914), pp. 139–40.   **19** William Gacquin, *Tombstone inscriptions Cam old cemetery* (1992), p. 24.   **20** RD, 67/534/47070.

Many of the people from whom services were purchased, like Tully the glazier in 1734, were also Catholic, as there was a Laughlin Tully, a Papist glazier, living in Monksland in St Peter's parish in 1749. Lyon, the smith, was probably the William Lians, a Papist smith, listed in Ballagh, Rahara in 1749. Daniel Mee, from whom oats were purchased, was probably the man of the same name listed as a Papist labourer in Clogherny, Killinvoy parish in 1749. The most numerous occupation listed in the religious census of 1749 for most of the diocese of Elphin was that of 'labourer'. In the parish of Killinvoy, labourers accounted for 67 per cent of the heads of households, while farmers accounted for less than 1 per cent or thirteen households. Of the thirteen farmers listed in Killinvoy in 1749, no less than nine of them were returned as Protestants or Quakers. This pattern can also be seen in the neighbouring parishes of Kiltoom and Cam where labourers represented 51 per cent of all the heads of households in those two parishes.[21] The high proportion of these labourers returned suggests strongly that this description was used to represent the peasant farmer class at that time.

Many of these people earned what money they could from local farmers and landlords. An example of this, from the household account being examined, was the payments made to individuals like Bryan Duffy as wages in 1744. He is probably the Bryan Duff listed as a Papist labourer in Corbooly in 1749. Duffy received 6s. for a 'qr wages' Similar payments were made to Bryan Dolan who received £1 4s. in 1734, probably his wages for a year, as it represents exactly four times the amount paid to Bryan Duffy for a quarter. This would give a very low daily rate of pay to a labourer of three farthings, assuming he worked all year round. Isaac Weld, in his statistical survey of county Roscommon, gives the daily rate of pay for a labourer in 1779 as six and a half pence.[22] One man, Roger Gorrick, received somewhat more when he was paid £2 for his work as a 'cowboy'. However, this is still less than 1½d. per day, assuming a full year's work. It is probable that Roger Gorrick was employed in looking after the cows on the farm, which were, as seen earlier, an important source of income for the writer. Roger Gorrick was recorded as selling a cow hide in 1733 for 4s. His wife also features twice in the accounts when she was paid for chickens and poultry. Another payment of £1 was made in 1733 to Brehony, the smith. Though this entry is difficult to read, it seems to be for 'a y[ea]rs salery'. Ambrose Roe was paid £1 in all to settle until May. Wage payments were also made to women in the accounts. Margaret Diskin was paid £1 in 1733 and Catherin Kenny was paid 11s. 7d. in 1734 'in full wages'. While these amounts are less than those paid to the men, and it is not possible to know what period of time was being paid for, the £1 paid to Margaret Diskin may represent a year's wage. If this were the case, then Margaret Diskin's wage was half of that paid to Roger Gorrick as cowboy. As well as a cowboy, the writer also employed

21 William Gacquin, *Roscommon before the famine: the parishes of Kiltoom and Cam, 1749–1845* (Dublin, 1996), p. 20.   22 Isaac Weld, *Statistical survey of county Roscommon* (Dublin, 1832), p. 637.

a shepherd, which is not surprising, given the money he earned from the sale of wool. The writer gave the shepherd money to purchase a shears, sheepwater, salt and tobacco. One purchase of tobacco cost 2s. 8½d. in 1734.

A number of people are repeatedly mentioned in the account and some of these are referred to by first name only, suggesting they may be relatives of the writer or permanent servants of the household. Reference has already been made to 'my sister, Cathy' but others given familiar names are Old Mary, Neddy, Little Lacky, Sally and Fanny. The first of these, Old Mary, received four payments in 1733, all small amounts, twice to get 'brogues', once to buy rushes and once for an unspecified purpose. In 1734, there was only one payment to Old Mary, of 1s. 1d. to buy rushes. It is most likely that these rushes were dipped in some form of oil or fat and used as tapers to supply light to the house at night. Both Fanny and Sally are mentioned only once each in 1733, when one was given money to buy chickens and the other money to buy 'blew'. These items were similar to those purchased by the writer's sister, Cathy, which included 'currins', poultry, butter, wooden ware and 'blew'. This suggests that both Fanny and Sally may have been family members also in the writer's care. There were two men whose Christian names only are given: Little Lacky who was given 1s. 1d. for brogues and 5s. 10½d. for 'frize' in 1733, and 4s. 4d. to buy more 'frize' in 1734. Another individual, referred to as Neddy, was mentioned once in 1733 and four times in 1734. Neddy was entrusted with the payment of money to others. In 1733, he paid 14s. 1d. to a carman. In 1734, he paid money for 'packing', bought a 'slain' for another labourer, and on two occasions he was paid money to go to fairs. These latter payments were substantial – one of 11s. 6d. to go to the fair of Ballinasloe. Allen Doyle was paid 9s. 6d. in wages in 1733, and in the same year he was, like Neddy, entrusted with the payment of money to others, in this case 5s. 7d. to pass on to Brehony. When John Potts was being paid for clothes in 1733, material to make breeches for Allen Doyle was specifically mentioned, which suggests he was at least one of the household servants. The most curious of these entries, one in each year, concerns a man called Geo. Campbell. He was given money to buy 'gadds' in 1733, and in the following year two shirts costing 8s. 5d. were purchased for him. Therefore, it would seem that he was in some way linked to the household. Perhaps he was the catalyst that brought the Campbell family of Kilberry in Scotland in contact with the writer of these accounts.

Two other names which occur frequently were Galloper and Cassady. The first of these, Galloper, was recorded seven times in the accounts. All of these entries had to do with the purchase of poultry or eggs and six of them were from the first year of the accounts. In total, 17s. 5½d. was expended on these items. Some of the references to Galloper suggest he may have been a servant, but the majority suggest he was an outsider. Cassady is never given a Christian name, but his residence is given as Galey, a townland in which at a later stage at least part of the village of Knockcrogherey was located. Despite this specific location in the accounts, there was no Cassady in Galey in the 1749 census returns. The items purchased from Cassady were all during the year 1733, and included butter on three occasions, also veal and a fat wether costing 11s. 6d. While most of the names in the accounts are from the general locality of Knockcroghery, there is one name which was mentioned twice and seems to have no local link. This is the name Perro, which was entered without a forename. One of the purchases from Perro was of a plough horse, costing 18s. 6d, and the second was a payment for carriage of 6s. 3d. These particular expenses suggest that Perro may have been a carman and, consequently, not from the locality. This theory is supported by the fact that both transactions were entered close together in the year 1734.

Of the four people who paid rent to the writer little information is available. Ed Purcell may be one of a family who lived in Knockcroghery in 1749 of the same name. T. Muldowney remains unidentified but he is probably son of Old T. Muldowney mentioned in the accounts and a relative of Connor Muldowney from whom soap was purchased on one occasion. Neither the miller nor Connor Kelly can be identified from the 1749 census material.

These accounts and the religious census of the diocese of Elphin of 1749 give a good indication of life in the village of Knockcroghery in the second quarter of the eighteenth century. One difficulty in using the census is that it is not possible to be certain of the boundaries of the townlands, due to the absence of any map with the census. The first OS map, dated 1837, defines the area of Knockcroghery townland as just over 217 acres. The census tells us that there were thirty-one households in Knockcroghery, with a variety of occupations, as can be seen from Table 2.[23] Of the thirty-one households, all but seven had children. Using a multiplier of 4.33 derived from work on the population of other parishes in the area this would give a population of 134 for Knockcroghery.[24] Thirteen of the houses had servants in 1749. As well as the usual list of labourers, innholders, merchants and craftsmen, such as tailors, weavers and smiths, the village of Knockcroghery had two occupations probably unique to that part of county Roscommon. The village had two potters and a pipemaker. Pipe-making is known to have been carried out in Waterford as far back as 1641.[25] Thomas Buckley, one of four Protestant house-holders, was a pipemaker and is the first man recorded as such in Knockcroghery, which later built up a considerable reputation as a pipemaking centre.

Table 2 Occupations in Knockcroghery in 1749.

Labourer	14	Farmer	1
Innholder	2	Mason	1
Tailor	2	Wigmaker	1
Weaver	2	Merchant	1
Potter	2	Pipemaker	1
Widow	2	Miller	1
		Smith	1

23 NAI, M 2466, parish of Killinvoy.   **24** Gacquin, *Roscommon before the famine*, p. 13.
25 Reg Jackson, Philomena Jackson and Roger Price, *Ireland and the Bristol clay pipe trade*

Tobacco smoking had become well established in Roscommon by the early eighteenth century, as evidenced by the accounts. The writer purchased tobacco on three occasions. On two occasions it was bought with another commodity and on the other occasion it cost 2s. 8 ½d. but the amount purchased was not specified. Isaac Weld gave a good account of the pipemaking industry in 1832, which suggested that it was by then widespread. The industry was started by an unnamed individual who was skilled in pipemaking and settled in the area. The clay for the pipes was found locally at first and in 1832 there were eight kilns producing from 100 to 500 gross of pipes a week. These were sold by pedlars in the surrounding districts for 1s. per gross, a reduction from the 2s. 6d. obtained in earlier years.[26] One of the principal uses of the Knockcroghery clay pipe was for wakes. This industry continued until the early twentieth century, when the village and its pipe-making enterprises were burned as a reprisal by the Black and Tans on 19 June 1921.[27] A local tile manufacturing industry probably drew on the same source for clay, initially at least, and is most likely represented by the potters in the census of 1749. There were two potters in Knockcroghery in 1749: William Corns, a Protestant, and Teigh Bracken, a Papist. The writer of the accounts bought 'tyles' from William Corns and his partner Mahon. By 1749, Mahon had either left Knockcroghery or died and his place was taken by Teigh Bracken.

The village of Knockcroghery is mentioned seven times in the account and was probably the location of several more of the transactions recorded in the accounts. Three of those references are to the fair of Knockcroghery. A patent to hold a fair in the village was granted to Collo O'Kelly on 1 January 1613. The day of the fair was to be the feast of St Luke the Evangelist (18 October). A second patent was granted on 20 December 1675 to Colonel John Kelly to hold one fair on an unspecified day.[28] The fair green was, and still is, located at the northern end of the village. By the early nineteenth century there were three fairs annually, on 26 May, 21 August and 25 October. The most important was that held on 25 October each year, and later on the following day as well. In later years this was always referred to locally as the 'old fair'. Several newspaper accounts report that it was next only to Ballinasloe in importance as a sheep fair. An indication of its size can be had from the report on the 1841 fair, when 7,865 sheep were sold and a further 6,820 remained unsold.[29] The earliest references to the trade carried on at the fair are contained in the accounts under study in this article. The writer bought forty sheep at the fair in 1734, as well as two 'truckle carrs', and in 1733 he bought 400 'gadds'. Apart from these, there are few eighteenth-century references to the fair. One of these is a newspaper advertisement for the fair to be held on 25 and 26 October 1767.[30] A deed memorial dated 19 April 1788 records the lease of the customs of the fair of

(Bristol, 1983), p. 38.   **26** Weld, *Statistical survey of county Roscommon*, pp. 508–15.   **27** Joe Norton, 'Knockcroghery, an Irish pipe making centre' in *Society for clay pipe research newsletter*, no. 11 (July 1986), p. 2.   **28** *Royal comm. fairs and markets, 1852–3*, p. 106.   **29** NLI, Moran Papers, MS. 1544, p. 480.   **30** NLI, Moran Papers, MS. 1543, p. 299.

Knockcroghery by Charles Tyler, a merchant of Athlone, to Nehemiah Sandys of Sandfield, Knockcroghery from 1 May 1788 for sixty-one years, at a yearly rent of £50. The lease had previously been held by George Alexander.[31] From 1828 onwards, with the arrival of the *Roscommon Journal* newspaper and other local papers, there are annual references to the October fair. In 1863, the nearby town of Roscommon started a fair on 23 October. This fair was abandoned in 1865, following pressure from the owner of the tolls of the fair at Knockcroghery.[32] By the mid-nineteenth century the tolls of the fair were owned by William Roper and in 1854 he made a return of the value of the tolls for the years 1852 to 1854. The report is to be found as a letter in William Roper's hand to a Jno. Montgomery among the Valuation Office House Books for Knockcroghery and is dated 4 September 1855. A summary of the value of the tolls is given in Table 3.[33] From this report the best return from the fair was just over £31 in 1854, which is a considerable reduction on the £50 a year earned by Charles Tyler when he leased the customs of the fair in 1788.

Table 3 Profits of Knockcroghery fair, 1852–4.

1852	1853	1854
May fair loss 1s. 6d.	May fair loss 7s. 9d.	May fair 18s. 6d.
Aug.fair 13s. 2d.	Aug. fair loss 2s. 7d.	Aug. fair £1 1s. 7d.
Oct fair £26 5s. 4d.	Oct. fair £18 5s. 0d.	Oct. fair £29 2s. 6d.
Nett gain £26 17s. 0d.	Nett gain £17 14s. 8d.	Nett gain £31 2s. 7d.

It is clear from this return that the October fair was the most valuable in terms of income for Mr Roper and that the other fairs, particularly the May fair, were not worth holding. The Valuation Office House Books tell us that William Roper had succeeded his father Edward as the owner of the fair and held the fair green in fee. He employed eight men for each fair at a cost of 1s. 6d. each or a total cost to him of 12s. The fair continued to be important to the local economy and gained a new lease of life with the opening of the rail line to Roscommon on 13 February 1860 and the building of a railway station in Knockcroghery village.[34] However, the changing pattern of agriculture in the last quarter of the twentieth century has led to the demise of the fair.

In conclusion, it can be said that these accounts certainly originated in south Roscommon and in all probability were written in or near the village of Knockcroghery. They present us with a unique glimpse of the life of a rural household in the second quarter of the eighteenth century. One striking feature of the accounts is that they refer to many items which would still have been part of the everyday life of a rural household until about thirty years ago. From the

31 RD, 397/19/262247. **32** *Roscommon Messenger*, 28 October 1865. **33** NAI, VO house books, county Roscommon, S. 3228. **34** Fergus Mulligan, *One hundred and fifty years of Irish railways* (Belfast, 1983), p. 74.

names of the people with whom the writer had dealings it is clear that there was co-operation between the various social and religious groups where the necessities of life were involved. The colloquial pronunciation of many surnames in south Roscommon today seems not to have changed from the time the accounts were compiled. Indeed, further study could be done on the language used in the accounts. While Irish was undoubtedly the language of many of the people with whom the writer of the accounts did his business, there were no references to it in the accounts except as part of peoples names such as Ambrose Roe or Bryan Ban's son.

APPENDIX

ARGYLL AND BUTE COUNCIL ARCHIVE

CAMPBELL OF KILBERRY PAPERS

REF.DR/14/1/5

Page 1

Sepr. 1th 1733	An accont of what money I laid out for the use of my co-partners in [this] house		
Impris	To Geo Gardiner[35] for ribtrees	18s.	11d.
	To the nailer[36] of Roscomon for nails	9s.	8d.
	To Tyles to Corns[37] & Mahon of Knockry	19s.	7d.
	To Edmond Kane[38] for work	7s.	11d.
	To the shepherd to buy salt & tobacco	2s.	8½d.
	To Wattles & Scallups from St. Johns	9s.	10d.
	To Corr the mercht. at Roscom for hinges	6s.	5d.
	To Wm. Clerk[39] joyner for work	£1 8s.	10d.
	To the chimney sweeper	1s.	1d.
	To Apples from St. Johns	4s.	0d.
	To the locksmith at Athlone for two locks	8s.	8d.
	To Ned Purcell[40] for Beefe	8s.	3½d.
	To Rachel Boat[41] for Hopps	13s.	6d.
	To Wm. Burke[42] Mason for work	8s.	5½d.

35 George Gardiner was listed as a Protestant farmer in Portron, Portron parish, in 1749, with nine children and eight servants.   36 There was only one nailer listed in 1749 in Roscommon parish. He was Denis Guff, a Protestant living in Abbytown and having five servants.   37 William Corns, Protestant potter, in Knockcroghery, Killinvoy parish, in 1749, with two children.   38 There was a Michael Keone a Papist cooper in Cornemart in 1749   39 This surname was listed in Knockonyconner, St John's parish in 1749. 40 There were two of this name in 1749; Robert Purcill, Papist labourer, in Kellybrook, St John's parish and Luke Purcill, Papist labourer, in Knockcroghery, Killinvoy parish. 41 There were two of his surname in Ballymurry in 1749, both Protestants.   42 In 1749 there was a Patrick Burke, labourer, in Lissdallun, Killinvoy parish; Edmond Burk and Walter Burk in Kilmore, St John's parish, both labourers; and a Bridget Burk, a spinner,

To Brogues for little Lacky	1s.	1d.
To Mr. Wltr. Kelly for two pair of principles	13s.	1d.
To Bartole Hughes[43] for Malt	£1 15s.	0d.
To Do. for Hopps	10s.	0d.
To Gallopper[44] to buy Cockrills	2s.	8½d.
To the mercht Lyon[45] at Rahara for Salt	1s.	8d.
To my sistr Catty to buy Currins & c ...	6s.	6d.
To Allen Doyle[46] to buy fresh Butter	3s.	3d.
To my sistr Catty for fresh Butter	3s.	3d.
To Cassady[47] at Galey for Butter	5s.	10d.
To a Barrell of Salt	10s.	10d.
To Gallopper for Butter Chickins & Eggs	7s.	9d.
To the Sieve man for two new Bottoms		10d.
To the oyster man for 300 oysters	1s.	1d.
To a woman from Ballagh[48] for 2 Turkeys		10d.
To the Collector of Quitt rent	£2 8s.	6d.
To ffish at severale times	8s.	7d.
To Turkeys bought from Mullan[49]	5s.	10d.
To 400 Gadds bought Knockry fair	1s.	6d.
To a Qr hundred of Soap from Athlone	6s.	6d.
To one hundred of Butter	£1 4s.	7d.
To the Butcher Rushel[50] for veal	2s.	4d.
To Gallopper for Chickins and Eggs	1s.	4d.
To Bryan Kelly's son[51] for ffish	2s.	2d.
To Frize? of Laky	5s.	10½d.
To old Mary for Brogues	1s.	7½d.
To 5tt Hopps to Bartole Hughes	10s.	0d.
To 10 tt Hopps one Quart of Brandy to Do £1	1s.	8d.
To 6tt of Candles to Do	1s.	6d.

all Papists.   **43** Bartholomew Hughes died 1736 aged 47 and was buried in Cam cemetery. He leased a townland in 1731 in Cam parish for £39 stg. per annum. His son lived in Farneykelly (Carrick townland) in 1749.   **44** This name occurred many times in the document, it is probably the modern name Gallagher. No one of that name lived in the Knockcroghery in 1749. It could also be a nickname.   **45** There were three of this name in Rahara parish in 1749 but none was listed as a merchant, one William Lians was listed as a smith.   **46** There was nobody of this name in the Knockcroghery area but there was a John Dowell (an old form of Doyle in county Roscommon), a Papist labourer, in Knockcroghery in 1749.   **47** There was no Cassady in Galey in 1749. **48** A townland in Rahara parish.   **49** The name Mullin was to be found in Kilcosh, Kilmane parish, Kellybrook, St John's parish and in Corbooly, Killenvoy parish in 1749. **50** There was a Mable Russell, a Papist widow with four children in Carrownamada, St John's parish in 1749.   **51** There was a Bryan Kelly, a Papist farmer with two children over 14 and one servant in 1749, in Keelogues in Killinvoy parish. Some of the fish purchased was recorded as being from Keelogues.

To the Shepherd for Sheep water	2s.	11d.
To Mr. Thos Burke for rent of Scregg	£10	0s.	0d.
To Phillipps Egan[52] to buy blew	1s.	1d.
To Glasses and Muggs & c ...	13s.	6d.
To ffish at 2 severale times	2s.	9½d.
To Herrings	1s.	1d.
To oysters	1s.	3d.
To Cassady for a fatt Weather	11s.	6d.
To Hugh Purcele for seeds	8s.	5d.
To 2 piggs from Lisdallon	1s.	1d.
To John Olsogh[53] for 200 cabage plants		4d.
To Cassady for veal and butter	7s.	4½d.
To 1ott of hopps to Bartole Hughes	15s.	10d.

Page 2 *left hand side*

To the Cooper for work	2s.	9d.
To 400 of oysters	1s.	4d.
To Cassady for Butter	1s.	6d.
To young Gershon Boate[54] for veal	1s.	6d.
To a Barrell of Salt	10s.	10d.
To the ffisherman at sevel times	4s.	10d.
To Roger Gorrick's wife[55] for chickins		6½d.
To a Qr. of hundred of soap	6s.	6d.
To a Side of Pork from Ballagh	4s.	3d.
To my sistr Catty to buy blew		6½d.
To John Potts[56] for Cloaths Shammy Breeches and makeing for Allen Doyle	£2 17s.	11d.
To 9 yds & ½ of Packing	4s.	9d.
To Gallopper to buy Poulterey	2s.	8d.
To old Mary	1s.	8d.
To Mr. Devenish for a fatt wedder	8s.	8d.
To 2 Barrells of potatoes from McLauglin[57]	11s.	0d.
To Oysters	1s.	1d.

52 This surname occurred eight times in the parishes around Killinvoy parish.   **53** This surname occurred twice in Ballagh, Rahara parish and twice in St John's parish in 1749. It was later anglicized as Knowledge.   **54** Gershon Boate listed as a Protestant butcher in Ballymurry in 1749 with two children under fourteen and one servant.   **55** This surname occurred three times in the locality: Elinor Gorrick, a widow and Patrick Gorrick, a labourer, in Knockdrimdonil, Kilmane parish and Denis Gorrick in Ballagh, Rahara parish, all were Papists.   **56** In St Peter's parish, Athlone there was a Mrs Jane Potts listed as a Protestant gentlewoman with seven children and five servants in the next house to Ed. and Loftus Glasse in 1749. She may have been the widow of John Potts. **57** There was a Dom'k McLaughlin, Papist innholder, in Knockcroghery village in 1749; also a John McLaughlin, a Quaker labourer, in Galy in 1749.

To Beef and Mutton from Athon	11*s.*	8½*d.*
To Far Anthony Fflyn[58] for 40 Wedders	£11 15*s.*	0*d.*
To Mullane for one sheep	2*s.*	6*d.*
To Eggs		4½*d.*
To two fflasks of byle to Ed Corr[59]	3*s.*	4*d.*
To Cassady for nine pound of butter	3*s.*	0*d.*
To Mutton from Knockry	2*s.*	6*d.*
To Brehony the Smith for a yar? salery	£1 0*s.*	0*d.*
To pickle oysters	1*s.*	1*d.*
To old Mary for brougs		6½*d.*
To Gorrick's wife to buy Poultry	2*s.*	2*d.*
To Tiege Kelly[60] to buy Steel	1*s.*	1*d.*
To Hives from Ballagh	1*s.*	3*d.*
To one hundred 32tt of Iron	£1 8*s.*	10*d.*
To Fresh beef from Athlone	5*s.*	7*d.*
To Gadds		7*d.*
To the Sherers	11*s.*	8*d.*
To Coals	£1 2*s.*	5*d.*
To Capt. Lawders man for work in gardn.	2*s.*	8½*d.*
To the Garden boy at Mote	1*s.*	1*d.*
To Fox the Joyner for work	10*s.*	9*d.*
To the Shephd to buy Sheers	1*s.*	4*d.*
To the Hearth Collectr.	8*s.*	0*d.*
To the Cooper for Hoops	2*s.*	8½*d.*
To Moran[61] the Cooper for work	3*s.*	10*d.*
To Galeopper for Poultry		10*d.*
To Lyon the Smith[62] for work and brand	13*s.*	7*d.*
To John Potts for the park locks	5*s.*	0*d.*
To Ed Corr's Bill for Tarr & c ...	£1 0*s.*	6*d.*
To Chairs at the Cant of Clonbrock[63]	£4 7*s.*	1*d.*
To 15 Barrells of Malt at 7 per Bl	£5 5*s.*	0*d.*
To Jemmy Kelly's bill for & Malt	£3 14*s.*	7*d.*

58 Fr Anthony Fflyn was a Catholic priest. He was parish priest of Kiltoom, Elphin diocese in 1748 and it was probably he who is listed in the Quit Rent Ledger of 1742–47 occupying 192 acres in Kiltoom. He is buried in Kiltoom Old Cemetery but the date of death cannot now be read from the tombstone due to erosion. The tombstone was erected by his nephew Danl Flyn and shows a priest with the chalice raised over his head. **59** A number of this name were listed in Athleague village in 1749. **60** Two people of this name were listed in 1749, one in Corbooly and one in Lissdallun, both Papist labourers. **61** There was a Dan Moran, a Papist labourer, in Lissdallon in 1749. **62** William Lians was listed as a Papist smith in Ballagh, Rahara parish in 1749. **63** Clonbrock, in the parish of Ahascragh, county Galway was the seat of the Dillon family, Lords Clonbrock.

To the oysterman for oysters	1s.	1d.
To Wattles and Scallopps from St. Johns	10s.	11½d.
To the fisher man	1s.	7½d.
To Beefe from Ballimurry	5s.	9½d.
To Fanny to buy Chickings	2s.	8½d.

Page 2 *right hand side*

To a Barrell of Salt		10s.	10d.
To Mr. Wallers[64] Gardner			6d.
To Mr. Thos Burk for rent of Scregg	£10	0s.	0d.
To Margt Diskin's wages	£1	0s.	0d.
To Reigny the Weaver		2s.	2d.
To the Bucher at Portreny for a Qr Beef		6s.	6d.
To the Oysterman		1s.	1d.
To ffish from Bryan bans[65] son		2s.	0d.
To Gallopper for Chickins & Eggs		1s.	1d.
To a Qr of hundred of Soap		6s.	6d.
To ffish		2s.	2d.
To Ed Corr for vinegare		4s.	0d.
To Sistr Catty for blew			6d.
To Mustard		1s.	3d.
To the Serv of Mote who brought veal and venison		1s.	1d.
To Geo Cammele[66] to buy Gadds		1s.	4d.
To Old Mary to buy Rushes		1s.	1d.
To Neddy to pay Wool Carmen		14s.	1d.
To the Carmen in full of Carriage		8s.	1d.
To Allen Doyle in part of wages		9s.	6d.
To allowed for Allen Doyle to Brehny		5s.	7d.
Laid as underneath p?ticulars? this year			
10 ?? Endshare out ? the …	£104	14s.	4d.

Sepr. 1th 1733 Reced for the use of the house out of
the farm of Scregg the following pticlrs

Impris	Recd for a cow sold to McLoughlin	£2	3s.	0d.
	Recd from Russele the Butcher for Cowhide		6s.	6d.
2d.	Cow hide exchanged for Tallow	£0	0s.	0d.
3d.	Cow hide sold to Corr[67] of Athleague		7s.	0d.
	12 Sheep skins sold to Tiege Kelly		18s.	0d.

---

64 Robert Waller was listed in 1749 as a Protestant esquire, in Killmore, St John's parish with six children under fourteen, ten male servants and twelve female servants. **65** This was probably the Bryan Kelly's son mentioned in footnote no. 51. **66** Perhaps this is a corruption of the name Campbell. **67** There were four of this surname in Athleague village in 1749 One of these was James Corr, Papist butcher.

1 Cow hide [that] Dyed & 2 Calve Skinns		7s.	4d.
1 Cow hide that dyed sold by P Egan		4s.	0d.
Recd for Cullim	£2	15s.	4d.
1 Cow hide & 1 calve Skinn [that] dyed to Corr		5s.	5d.
1 Cow hide that Dyed sold by R Gorrick		4s.	0d.
Recd from Ed Purcell for rent	£2	8s.	0d.
Recd from T Muldowney for rent		16s.	0d.
Recd from Neddy for cows sold at Roscomn	£5	3s.	0d.
Recd from Sistr for wheat	£1	4s.	0d.
Recd for Daggin		15s.	4d.
Recd from Connor Keley[68] for rent		7s.	0d.
Recd from the miller in full of rent bal	£1	16s.	10d.
Recd from John Potts for Wool	£28	14s.	4d.
the Lambs wool for necessarys for the house to Brogan[69] the Mercht Athlone	£0	0s.	0d.
Tottale of what I reced this yr	£48	14s.	11d.
Remains due to me on the Family this year … errorr excepted	£56	13s.	7d.

Page 3

Sepr.1 th 1734 An Accot of money I laid out this
year for the use of the house & Family
is as follows

Impris	To Edmond Keighran for Sheepwater		3s.	3d.
	To the Pewterr in Exchange		13s.	0d.
	To the egg woman Chickings & Eggs		2s.	4d.
	To a Qr of Beef from Roscomon		8s.	7d.
	To Bryan Duffy[70] in full of a Qr Wages		6s.	0d.
	To Hopps to James Kelly		15s.	0d.
	To Tiege Kelly for 2 Bullucks		13s.	0d.
	To Pat Galeavene & Ward for Malt	£1	5s.	10d.
	To Perro for a plow horse		18s.	6d.
	To Apples from St Johns		7s.	7d.
	To the Butcher of Portrenny for beef and Tallow		9s.	10d.
	To Jas Kelly for 5 lt of hopps		7s.	6d.
	To old Mary to buy rushes		1s.	1d.
	To the Shephd to buy Salt		1s.	8d.
	To Dennis Olsogh his Bull (?) for work		4s.	4d.
	To a hachet & Spade bought at Knockry		4s.	2d.

---

68 There was a Connor Kelly listed as a Papist farmer in Carnagh, St John's parish with eight children and two servants in 1749. **69** No Brogan was listed for the west side of Athlone in 1749. **70** There was a Bryan Duff listed as a Papist labourer in Corbooly in 1749.

To paid for 70 fresh herrings		2s.	0d.
To Six Turkeys and Ducks at Ballagh		2s.	6d.
To the Sieveman		1s.	1d.
To the Boy at Mote for nutts & App[les]		1s.	1d.
To my Sistr Catty to buy Chickins &		3s.	3d.
To Wattles & Scallopps from St. Johns		8s.	11d.
To Gallopper for Chickins & Eggs		1s.	1d.
To Carrol the Mason for work		5s.	6d.
To 6 Barrells of Bear seed	£2	0s.	0d.
To Ed Keighran for a horse	£1	17s.	0d.
To Wild Fowl from John Potts		2s.	4½d.
To the Oyster man		1s.	1d.
To Timothy Diskin for Malting		4s.	4d.
To Old T. Muldowney for sowing wheat		1s.	1d.
To Contingent		5s.	10d.
To Mr Jas Sproul[71] in exchange for bear		6s.	0d.
To a hatchet & Billhook		4s.	4d.
To the people of Corboley for 27 Caps Turf	£2	14s.	0d.
for sending home 12 Clamps	£1	4s.	0d.
To Mustard		1s.	1d.
To a Fatt Cow from Saml Boat[72]	£2	6s.	0d.
To Lacky for frize		4s.	4d.
To Danl Mee[73] for two Barls of Oats		7s.	8d.
To Mr. John Naghten[74] for Iron for the plow		6s.	3d.
To Quigly[75] for one Barl of Oats		3s.	10d.
To Darby Maddin for a hearth stone		2s.	8½d.
To Carriage of sd stone		1s.	1d.
To John Naghten for Cotters & Parts?		2s.	8½d.
To Sally to buy Blew			11d.
To Carroll the Mason for work		2s.	2d.
To a Sm Lyon for beef from Athlone		5s.	6d.
To ffish from Athlone		2s.	2d.
To Mr Thos Burk Scregg rent	£10	0s.	0d.
To the Shephd for Tobacco		2s.	8½d.
To Bryan Banes son for fish		1s.	10d.

---

71 There were two people of this name listed in Longfield, Rahara parish in 1749. Both were Protestant gentlemen sharing the one house, a seventeenth century towerhouse. The household had eight servants.   **72** Samuel Boate was listed as a Protestant malster in Ballymurry, Kilmean parish in 1749.   **73** Daniel Mee was listed in Clogherny, Killinvoy parish in 1749 as a Papist labourer with three children.   **74** John Naghton was listed in Galeybeg in St John's parish in 1749 as a Protestant farmer with nine children and six servants.   **75** This surname occurred a number of times in the vicinity of Knockcroghery in 1749.

To Salt		1s.	8d.
To 5 Quarts of Peap ? & Carriage Athlone		3s.	1d.
To the Collector for Scregg	£2	8s.	6d.

Page 4 *left hand side*

To the Nelor at Roscomon		4s.	7½d.
To a side of pork		2s.	2d.
To Jas Doyle for Malting		13s.	9d.
To Carriage of Trunks to Red Hill		4s.	4d.
To Tiege Kelly to buy beef at Athlone		8s.	8d.
To Danl Mee & Own Brehony[76] 2 Blls Oats		7s.	10d.
To 20 Quarts of Salt		1s.	8d.
To Moran to buy Hoops		2s.	2d.
To Saltpeter			4½d.
more to Moran to buy Keeler Hoops		2s.	8½d.
To Eggs			3d.
To nine Chickins			9d.
To 2 Shirtts for Geo Campbele		8s.	5d.
To Sistr Catty to buy Wooden ware		5s.	11½d.
To Carriage of the Flax seed		6s.	6d.
To Soap from Connor Muldowney		3s.	4d.
To Moran the Cooper for work		4s.	9d.
To Mrs Shiggins[77] for Butter		2s.	8½d.
To 12 Breams from Kelly		1s.	0d.
To Ambrose Roe[78]		14s.	0d.
more to Ambrose Roe in full till May		6s.	0d.
To Jas Kelly in full for Hopps	£3	17s.	0d.
To Catherin Kenny in full wages		11s.	7d.
To Sistr Catty for Chickins and poultry		1s.	8d.
To Tully the Glazier[79]		7s.	8d.
To Roger Gorrick his wages as Cowboy	£2	0s.	0d.
To Neddy to buy Packing		11s.	6d.
To Neddy to buy a Slain for Jon Olsogh		1s.	1d.
To Pickle Oysters		1s.	1d.
To the Iron Monger a 100 of Iron	£1	2s.	0d.

76 The surname Brehony occurred in Lisdallon and Killinravagh, Killinvoy parish in 1749.   **77** There were two Siggins listed in 1749: John Sigins in Coolfobole, Kilmane parish and Thomas Siggins, Galy, Killinvoy parish, both Protestant farmers. Both locations are close to Knockcroghery village.   **78** The second name here is the Gaelic 'Rua' meaning red. There was an Ambrose Creahan listed in Barnapregghan in 1749 as a Papist labourer. This is probably the person in the account as Ambrose was not a frequently used first name.   **79** There was a Laughlin Tully listed as a Papist glazier in Monksland, St Peter's parish in 1749 with one child and three servants.

To the Sheerers	12s.	8d.
To Oysters	1s.	1d.
To the boy at Mote for venison	1s.	1d.
To Perro for Carriage of Trunks from Red Hill	6s.	3d.
To Biddy Toy for knives & forks	18s.	6d.
To a Qr of veal from Roscomon	2s.	2d.
To Bryan Dolane his wages	£1 4s.	0d.
To Bryan Dolan to buy a reaping hook		8d.
To 3 pair of Turff Basketts	2s.	0d.
To 6 pike ffish		6½d.
To 2 Trukle Carrs at Knockry fair	16s.	0d.
To Neddy for Chargn to [the] Men to [the] fair	2s.	8½d.
To boy at Mote for Coleyflowers venison		6½d.
To Oysters at 4 severale times	4s.	4d.
To a Qr of veal from Athlone	2s.	2d.
To Garden seeds from Dublin [per] J. Dillon[80]	10s.	7d.
To Apples from Castlecoot	15s.	0d.
To Neddy to fair of Balinsloe	11s.	6d.
To the Nelor for the Street door & Glue	7s.	4½d.
To Beef veal Glasses potts Basons		
pepper & ... from John Brogan	£1 19s.	11d.
To John Shiggins for a road to [the] bogg	£1 3s.	0d.
To drawing the turff to [the] bogg side	£1 2s.	6d.
To Laughlin Donnelly[81] for work	14s.	6d.
To 40 Sheep at Knockry fair	£5 17s.	6d.
To a piece of Oak for the Street door	7s.	0d.

Page 4 *right hand side*

To Oysters at several times	3s.	3d.
To the Lyon for hinges & Mending park lock	6s.	10d.
To Hilliard for hinges lock & bolts for		
the Street door	£1 5s.	6d.
To Hanly[82] at Roscon. for 6tt hopps	12s.	0d.
To a Qr of Beef from Roscomn.	8s.	0d.
To Gallavane for horse hire for [the] Turff	2s.	6d.
To Jon. Ward[83] for horse hire for [the] Turff	4s.	10d.
To Mr John Naghten for hopps	£1 11s.	10d.
To Glasses and Decanters	11s.	6d.

80 There was a James Dillon listed as a Papist merchant in Athlone in 1749. **81** This surname occurred a number of times in St John's parish in 1749. **82** This was probably Hugh Hanly, a Papist distiller with eight servants and five children listed in Roscommon town in 1749. **83** This surname occurred a number of times in 1749 in the area but there was no John Ward listed.

To the Shephd. for Salt & Tobacco	3s.	6d.
To the Neilor at Roscomom	4s.	10d.
To 2 stone of Iron	7s.	1d.
To Thos. Burke for Scregg rent £10	0s.	0d.
To Cornes for 12 Dozn of Tiles Porch	10s.	8d.
To the Glazier for [the] Street door	2s.	6d.
To Ed Kane for work	6s.	0d.
To Fish from Keelog's	2s.	2d.
To the people of Ballagh for work £2	8s.	4d.
To the people of Corboley for work £1	6s.	5d.
To the people of Cornemart for work	16s.	7d.

The great Munster horse-fair of Cahirmee, county Cork

DENIS A. CRONIN

INTRODUCTION

The livestock fair was once the major forum for trading the surplus animals generated by commercial agriculture. Of the hundreds of fairs which were formerly held throughout the country (over 150 in county Cork alone), only a small number have survived the rise of the livestock marts. Those which do survive – like the 'Auld Lammas Fair' of Ballycastle in county Antrim or Puck Fair in Killorglin in county Kerry – do so as much for social or touristic as for commercial purposes. Those which continue to have an economic function, like the fair of Ballinasloe in county Galway, are often horse fairs, at the lower end of the market which is not catered for by the prestigious thoroughbred sales or horse shows. They were once part of a circuit attended annually by leading horse dealers. Cahirmee fair, held in Buttevant, county Cork on the twelfth of July each year, is one of these surviving fairs. A celebrated horse fair for at least two centuries it continues to have a role as a local and regional marketplace for horses.

Because of its antiquity Cahirmee has a fascination which is not associated with fairs of more recent origin. It is a traditional fair, believed locally to date back to pre-Christian times, and in that respect it differs from many other fairs, which are traceable to specific grants of patent in the seventeenth or eighteenth centuries. It is not intended here to speculate much on the possible ancient origins of the fair in this study. This task is best left to those more familiar with its folklore and legendary associations.[1] The purpose of this study is to examine and outline what primary documentary sources reveal about Cahirmee fair and to discuss its role as a local and regional marketplace.

ORIGINS AND OWNERSHIP

Cahirmee fair gets its name from a townland called Cahermee (*c.*276 acres) in the civil parish of Cahirduggan, about two miles west of Doneraile in north-east county Cork.[2] The fair was held in a field in this townland for at least 160 years

---

1 I am grateful to Mr John O'Connell of Buttevant for a fascinating account of the local traditions about the origins and associations of Cahirmee. **2** The spelling of Cahirmee varies: Cahermee is the official spelling of the townland name but Cahirmee is more

(and probably much longer) until it was moved to the town of Buttevant in 1920.[3] Situated in a countryside which has a long association with horses and horse-breeding, Cahirmee was well placed geographically to host not alone a local but a regional horse fair. Indeed it is possible to argue that Cahirmee's central location in south Munster was a major asset in its rise to prominence. Its location in north-east county Cork meant it was accessible from many of the principal horse rearing centres of Munster, like the limestone valleys of county Cork, and the 'Golden Vale' of counties Limerick and Tipperary (Figure 1). Although direct access to the fair field was via an old post road between Doneraile and Buttevant, the main road from Limerick to Cork passed through Buttevant, only a few miles from Cahirmee. The coming of the railways from the 1840s made Cahirmee even more accessible, because Buttevant became a stop on the main line from Dublin to Cork.

The history of organized horse-racing in the area is a long one. Sir John Percival of Kanturk recorded in his diary on 1 October 1685 that 'this day [I] went (to see the race at Ballibeg Course)', very close to Cahirmee.[4] Lands in the vicinity of Buttevant, Fermoy and, above all, Mallow, have provided the sites of race-meetings at one time or another for at least two centuries. Indeed it is claimed that, in 1752, the first steeplechase was run across country between the steeples of Buttevant and Doneraile, a distance of four and a half miles.[5] There is also a strong tradition of foxhunting in the district, with the local Duhallow Hunt said to have its origins in a hunt club founded in the eighteenth century.[6]

The oldest documentary records of organized trading in the locality of Cahirmee can be traced back to the Anglo-Norman borough-foundations of the thirteenth century. The lords of these new boroughs usually sought a licence from the crown to hold a weekly market and, in the case of the more important settlements, a yearly fair. In 1234, David de Barry was granted the right to hold a Saturday market and a yearly fair in Buttevant 'on the Eve and Feast of St Luke and six following days' (that is, 17–24 October).[7] But no documentary evidence has been found with which to date the foundation of the fair of Cahirmee itself, despite at least one determined search of the records during the nineteenth century.[8] Its origins are obscure, one account stating that it has been held 'since

commonly used for the fair. In this study the traditional spelling of 'Cahirmee' will be used for both townland and fair. **3** *Cork Examiner* (hereafter cited as *CE*), 13 July 1920 and 13 July 1921; C.J.F. McCarthy, 'An antiquary's notebook 6 – the fair of Cahirmee' in *Cork Historical and Archaeological Society Journal*, lxxxix (1986), p. 126. **4** Historical Manuscripts Commission, *Egmont diary*, iii, 352. **5** For examples of racemeetings see *CE*, 11 and 15 October 1841; M.P. Linehan, *My heart remembers how: being the story of Muscraidhe O'Donegan* (Dublin, 1944), p. 236. **6** Linehan, *My heart remembers how*, p. 234; On 3 Nov. 1823 *The Constitution, or Cork Morning Post* listed eight Duhallow hunts taking place in the Mallow and Doneraile areas during November. **7** *Royal comm. fairs and markets, 1852–3, appendix*, pp. 157, 209. **8** In 1830, the proprietor of the tolls of Cahirmee testified to a parliamentary committee that a search he had ordered in the Rolls Office for evidence of a grant was unsuccessful. See *Sel. comm. tolls and customs*,

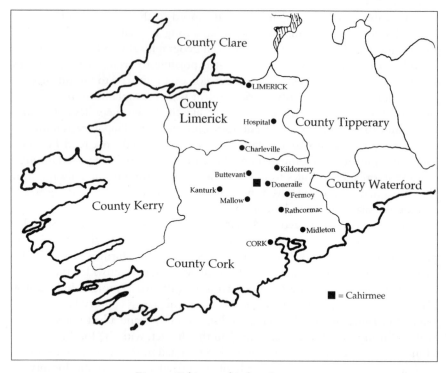

Figure 1 Cahirmee fair, location map.

the memory of man runneth not' and another claiming that it was granted a charter by King Charles I.[9]

It is possible, as local tradition asserts, that Cahirmee fair originated in the tribal gatherings of Celtic Ireland. One theory suggests is that it is descended from an ancient fair, *Aonach Cholmáin*, which apparently took place in this locality. A number of local placename associations indicate that Cahirmee was an important site in the ancient territory of the *Fir Maighe* (Fermoy) and archaeological evidence of considerable settlement on Cahirmee hill and vicinity makes this possibility worth considering. Perhaps the townland name itself refers to a stronghold or settlement associated with the local hegemony of the *Fir Maighe*.[10] The original fair may have been held on 1 July, only transferring to 12 July after eleven days were added to the calendar in 1752.

However, despite these possible ancient associations, the name of Cahirmee itself does not appear as a separate land unit until the eighteenth century. No

1834, p. 236; Mr John O'Connell of Buttevant maintains that a copy of a charter survives in the possession of the family of the last proprietors of Cahirmee fair.   **9** McCarthy, 'An antiquary's notebook', p. 126; *CE*, 13 July 1910.   **10** Linehan, *My heart remembers how*, p. 13. The association with the *Fir Maighe* is strengthened by the fact that Cahirmee is part of the barony of Fermoy.

such placename appears in the Books of Survey and Distribution for county Cork, in which a record of land ownership in the civil parish of Caherduggan in the seventeenth century is to be found. Following the outbreak of rebellion in 1641, possession of much of Caherduggan was in dispute between the old proprietors, the Roche family (mainly 'Redmond Roch, Irish Papist'), and the Grove family, who had recently settled there.[11] Both families lost out in the subsequent confiscations and Sir Peter Courthop[e] is recorded as owner of most of the parish, including the denominations of 'Caherdugan', Ballymee and Curraghikerry, after the restoration of Charles II in 1660.[12] Ownership of the fair field can be traced through the Courthope connection, making it likely that the townland of Cahirmee was then part of one of the above-mentioned denominations.

Alan Brodrick, the first Viscount Midleton, seems to have come into possession of Courthope land in Caherduggan through his second marriage to Sir Peter Courthope's daughter, Lucy, in 1693. His will, dated 19 April 1726, mentions several lands in north Cork, including a denomination called 'North Crogh Ikerry als. North Curragh Ikerry als. Glynn in B[arony]. Fermoy'.[13] A nineteenth-century deed records that Mary, Viscountess Midleton, let 299 acres of Caherduggan called the North East farm ... 'and part of Cahirmee with the fair and tolls thereof' to Henry Wrixon in 1750.[14] By 1830, the entire townland of Cahirmee, including the fair field and its tolls, was stated, 'under a late purchase', to be part of the estate of Lord Doneraile.[15]

The successive head landlords of Cahirmee do not seem to have been directly involved in operating the fair. By the middle of the eighteenth century, the fair field and its tolls were in the possession of tenants holding renewable leases of three lives. The main tenants of Cahirmee were the Freeman family. In 1755, Henry Wrixon leased to John Freeman 'that part of Cahirmee and Ballymee below the High Road leading from Cahirmee Ford to the town of Doneraile ... containing 101 acres plantation measure' for three lives renewable forever.[16] Freeman, who married Elinor Crofts of Churchtown about 1735, can also be identified as an early proprietor of the fair. When he died in 1776, his widow took over the rights to the fair and inserted the name of her son-in-law, James Hewson, into the lease in his place.[17] Thus the Hewsons in turn became

11 According to the list of deponents given in Nicholas Canny, 'The 1641 depositions as a source for the writing of social history: county Cork as a case study' in Patrick O'Flanagan and Cornelius Buttimer (eds), *Cork: history and society* (Dublin, 1993), p. 287, William Groves Esq. was living in 'Cardowgan' in 1641. The claims of the Grove family to Cahirduggan are discussed in detail by Col. James Grove White in his monumental survey of north east Cork, *Historical and topographical notes etc. on Buttevant, Castletownroche, Doneraile, Mallow, and places in their vicinity* (4 vols, Cork 1905–25), ii, 9–14.   12 Books of Survey and Distribution , county Cork (NAI, Ms. 2s. 2. 6; in microfilm at NLI, pos.3767), ff. 150, 151.   13 P. Beryl Eustace (ed.), *Registry of Deeds, Dublin, abstracts of wills*, vol. i (Dublin, 1956), p. 167.   14 RD, 704/314/482650.   15 *Sel. comm. tolls and customs, 1834*, p. 236.   16 NAI, Landed Estates Court rentals, vol. 59, no.8.   17 RD, 356/13/237728; Grove White,

proprietors of the fair, with Mrs Freeman passing on her own right to the fair to her three grandchildren, Lillias, Catherine and Alice Hewson.[18] Alice Hewson's right passed to John O'Mahony of Mallow after their marriage in 1809 and Lillias (or Lellia) Hewson's right passed to John Kearney of Cork, who came to live in Cahirmee on becoming her husband.[19] In a schedule of the tolls of Cahirmee, dated 1 July 1818, John Mahony, John Kearney and Robert Hewson were named as joint proprietors of the fair.[20] In time, probably in the late 1860s, following the marriage of John Kearney's grand-daughter Margaret to Michael Carroll of Park, the rights to the fair passed to the Carroll family, which continued to draw income from them until the fair moved to Buttevant in the 1920s.[21]

There is a record of a patent granted to a William Hull in 1771 for four additional fairs each year at Cahirmee, on 8 May, 6 October, 7 November and 8 December.[22] This grant seems to have been a speculative venture undertaken to cash in on the fame of the existing fair, while the dates chosen may have been part of an attempt to take business from other local fairs, like Mallow (11 May), Doneraile (12 November) and Buttevant (14 October and 20 November). Although these four additional fairs still existed on paper at the end of the eighteenth century (they were advertised along with the July fair in *Watson's Almanac* of 1798) they never succeeded in practice. While the difficulty of competing with well-established local fairs contributed to the failure of these additional fairs, the crucial factor was the cost of using the extensive fair ground at Cahirmee to host ordinary fairs. Only the great traditional fair attracted the big crowds that made it pay and by the 1830s Cahirmee had reverted to being a July fair only.[23]

CAHIRMEE IN 1830

A detailed account of how Cahirmee fair was managed in the years immediately before 1830 survives in the minutes of the report of a parliamentary select committee. On 8 June 1830, John Mahony of Mallow was questioned before the committee about the operation of the fair at Cahirmee.[24] Mahony stated that he was joint proprietor with another of the tolls of the fair under a lease dating back to 1769.[25] Although he did not hold the entire townland of Cahirmee, he and his partner had control of its fair ground.[26]

Historical and topographical notes, ii, 18–19. **18** RD, 763/548/518284. **19** RD, 634/380/436436; RD, 763/548/518284; Grove White, *Historical and topographical notes*, ii, 18. **20** *Account of schedule of customs, tolls and duties delivered to the clerks of the peace of counties, cities and towns in Ireland*, H.C. 1823 (458), xvi, 165. **21** Grove White, *Historical and topographical notes*, ii, 19. **22** *Royal comm. fairs and markets*, 1852–3, appendix, p. 151. It is possible that Hull was proprietor of the fair at the time. Alternatively, he may have held other lands in Cahirmee and may have tried to set up in opposition to the existing fair. **23** *Watson's Almanac*, 1798; *Sel. comm. tolls and customs*, 1834, p. 234; Lewis, *Dictionary*, i, 240. **24** *Sel. comm. tolls and customs*, 1834, pp. 233–41. **25** *Sel. comm. tolls and customs*, 1834, pp. 233, 238. **26** *Sel. comm. tolls and customs*, 1834, p. 236. Mahony stated that 'connectives'

According to a survey completed a few months before this evidence was taken, the site of the fairground measured 23 acres, 3 roods and 4 perches.[27] Mahony and his partners had enclosed it well, with a five-foot wall on one side, a four-foot wall on another side and with secure hedges and fencing on the other two sides.[28] The fair took place entirely within this fairground on 12 and 13 July each year and yielded him a gross income of between £47 and £60. It was the best attended fair in the locality, more popular, for instance, than the nearby fairs at Buttevant or Kildorrery. This can be seen by comparing the charges which the proprietors of each fair could levy. The toll on animals did not vary much from fair to fair, reflecting a need to encourage sellers of livestock sellers to attend. Thus, for example, the toll on horses sold at Cahirmee was 13*d*. and at Kildorrery was 10*d*. However, charges to sellers of other goods and services varied a great deal and give a clearer indication of the popularity of the respective fairs. Mahony was able to levy a charge of 10*s*. on tent holders at Cahirmee fair, whereas the charge on tents erected at Kildorrery and Buttevant was 6*s*. and 3*s*. 91*d* respectively.[29] Pedlars or dealers with high stands had to pay 3*s*. 9*d*. at Cahirmee but were charged only 1*s*. 1*d*. at Kildorrery.[30]

A toll board was erected at the entrance to the fair after it had become a legal requirement in 1818 (Figure 2). According to law, Mahony was not entitled to collect tolls because he did not possess a patent for the fair. However, he claimed the 'prescriptive' right that was allowed in cases where a fair could be deemed to have been held 'beyond the memory of man'. To ensure full collection of the tolls, Mahony employed about forty workers on the fair days, 'chosen from the best conducted of the lower order of the community, from the labouring class of best character'.[31] They cost him about £4 in wages for the two days, an average daily wage of 1*s*. per man.

The tollmen collected four kinds of toll. The first category was termed 'cattle', and included all livestock which was sold, whether horses, cows, sheep or pigs. All animals, sold or unsold, had to be driven by their owners or drovers through one of three customs-gaps on their way out of the fair-ground, 'whereupon custom is demanded upon all cattle without distinction'.[32] Each

---

of his held a principal part of the townland under a separate lease. The chief 'connective' appears to have been his brother-in-law, John Kearney, who is listed in the tithe applotment book for Cahirduggan as holder of about 69 Irish acres in Cahirmee on 9 Jan. 1828. Mahony appears in the tithe list only as one of the two commissioners who calculated the value of the tithe composition. He probably represented the interests of the occupiers. See NAI, Tithe Applotment Books, no. 6E/8 (mf. 12).   **27** According to a much later local account 'The fair field was 20 acres in extent and the galloping field 18½ acres. Three times around the galloping field was one mile' (See McCarthy, 'An antiquary's notebook', p. 126). This figure confirms the 38 acres 2 perches and 19 roods recorded in Griffith's *Valuation* for the land which hosted the fair.   **28** *Sel. comm. tolls and customs, 1834*, p. 234.   **29** *Sel. comm. tolls and customs, 1834*, p. 238.   **30** *Schedule of customs and tolls, 1823*, pp. 165, 168.   **31** *Sel. comm. tolls and customs, 1834*, p. 234.   **32** *Sel. comm. tolls and customs, 1834*, p. 233.

CAHIRMEE:

Schedule of Tolls and Customs levied at the Fair of Cahirmee, in the Barony of Fermoy, and County of Cork, as established by Prescription and immemorial Usage.

For and upon every beast sold the Toll following; viz.

	s.	d.
Every horse, mare, gelding or mule - - - - - - -	1	1
Every bullock, cow, bull or heifer - - - - - - -	—	6
Every yearling ditto, or calf - - - - - - - -	—	4
Every sheep, lamb, ram or goat - - - - - - -	—	1
Every pig - - - - - - - - - - -	—	3
Every sucking pig - - - - - - - - -	—	1½
For and upon every tent or booth in which goods, wares, merchandize or refreshments should be exposed for sale - - - - - -	10	—
Pedlars' or dealers' high stands, each - - - - - - -	3	9½
Pedlars' or dealers' flat stands - - - - - - - -	1	8
Every car load of wool, coopers' or turners' ware, or timber, manufactured or unmanufactured; earthenware, fruit or any goods whatsoever, that may be exposed to sale, the same being deemed to be a car load - -	3	9½
For and upon each horse load of frieze or flannel - - - - -	3	9½
For and upon each small piece of ditto - - - - - - -	—	10
Every shoemakers', broguemakers', glovers', hatters', or breeches-makers' stand - - - - - - - - - - -	2	6
Every butcher's stall or pot - - - - - - - - -	3	9½
Every hawker through the fair - - - - - - - -	—	10
Every small hawker - - - - - - - - -	—	6
For and upon all goods, wares or merchandize not particularly stated herein, the same being exposed to sale upon a flat stand - - -	1	8
For and upon each horse or mule or other beast found wandering or grazing upon the fair ground - - - - - - - -	—	10

Robert Hewson, Proprietor, and others.

Figure 2 Schedule of tolls and customs at Cahirmee, 1830.

gap was manned by a toll collector and his assistants, armed with sticks to prevent the driving out of cattle without payment. Any man trying to avoid this toll by claiming to have unsold animals was required to swear an oath to that effect on a book, or on a folded piece of paper (often a rolled up schedule of the tolls). The looseness of this requirement worried the members of the select committee because oaths at fairs were illegal. Even though 'that form of calling upon the attestation of the Divinity' was not gone through, they believed that such oaths provided a temptation to engage in frequent acts of perjury in order to evade the toll and thus encouraged a sense of moral laxity which might later extend to more serious oaths.[33] Mahony's solution to the problem, when questioned by the committee, was to charge a toll on all animals as they entered the fairground. This could be set at two-thirds the rate then current, to allow for the one-third of animals entering the ground that he estimated were not sold. He was unwilling, however, to agree with the committee that the rate should be reduced any further, despite conceding that his security costs at the customs-gaps would be lowered under a new system.[34]

33 *Sel. comm. tolls and customs, 1834*, p. 234.   **34** *Sel. comm. tolls and customs, 1834*, pp. 234–40.

The second charge levied was 'stallage' on owners of stalls or stands with goods displayed for sale at the fair. As well as 'stallage', an additional charge of 'pickage' was charged on tent-holders for turning over ground 'for the purpose of raising seats to accommodate persons who frequent them to take refreshments.'[35] The fourth toll was levied on hawkers and petty dealers or peddlers, that is, individuals who carried goods for sale upon their backs. This toll was 10*d.* on hawkers and 6*d.* on 'small hawkers', the distinction between them being somewhat arbitrary and at the discretion of the toll-collector.

The methods employed in collecting these various tolls caused some anxiety to the committee and Mahony was closely questioned about them. He stated that hundreds swore each year that they had animals unsold, and that these declarations had a solemn status. He accepted that disputes arose about the charges but was adamant that they did not lead to violence. He admitted also that altercations sometimes broke out over the other tolls, especially about the size of loads for stallage or over the distinction between 'hawkers' and 'small hawkers' but maintained that these disputes did not lead to any significant violence. As proprietor of the fair he gave much of his own time during the day to 'adjusting any differences that might take place, and in seeing that no altercation of any consequence ensues.'[36]

It is possible to estimate the extent of Cahirmee fair in the late 1820s from the gross income which Mahony reported it gave him, under the various tolls set out in Figure 2. He reported that the fair earned a maximum of £60 for him, broken down into £30 from tents, £20 from 'cattle' tolls, and £10 from the tolls for stallage and pickage (presumably this category included hawkers also, as their total payments are not reckoned separately). This means that in a good year there were up to sixty tents (at 10*s.* per tent) at Cahirmee. If Mahony's figures for cattle tolls are accepted, a good estimate of the number of animals offered for sale can be made. He stated that for every pound collected there were 'between 70 and 80 beasts sold ... 4 horses, 18 cows, 30 pigs and 25 sheep ... in which is included the small kind or young stock of each species'.[37] On the basis of Mahony's estimate of the quantities of each animal sold and adding one-third for those not sold, something like 120 horses, 540 cows, 900 pigs and 750 sheep could be offered for sale on a busy day at the fair of Cahirmee in the late 1820s.

A newspaper report of the 1842 fair describes the varied nature of its business at this time:

> Cahirmee Fair, on Tuesday, was well supplied with stock of all descriptions. Beef and mutton averaged similar prices to those obtained at Hospittle Fair [Hospital, county Limerick]. Store cattle in good demand, the

35 *Sel. comm. tolls and customs, 1834*, p. 237; see also the 'Schedule of tolls and customs levied at the fair of Cahirmee' in *Schedule of tolls and customs at markets and fairs in Ireland*, H.C. 1830 (204), xxvi, p. 470.   **36** *Sel. comm. tolls and customs, 1834*, p. 240.   **37** *Sel. comm. tolls and customs, 1834*, p. 236.

purchasers being graziers from the eastern counties, and parties for shipment. Store sheep in abundance and in great demand, prices ranging from 20s. to 30s. Store lambs sold at about 20s. each. A brisk demand for pigs, which sold at about 40s. per cwt. The purchasers for the latter were, with few exceptions, from Cork and Clonmel. There were few hunters in the market, but a large lot of colts, many of which sold at good prices up to 40 guineas for four year olds. An English buyer bought nine. There were some good colts, matches, for harness, at 60 and 80 guineas.[38]

'THE PRINCIPAL HORSE FAIR OF MUNSTER'

Although John Mahony's statistics and contemporary newspaper reports indicate that the sale of horses was by no means the only business conducted at the fair in the nineteenth century, it was this trade that made Cahirmee different from other local and regional fairs. It certainly seems to have been an important horse fair by the late eighteenth century, although it does not appear among the fairs listed in the directories until 1798.[39] Local tradition maintains that both 'Marengo' and 'Copenhagen', the respective mounts of Napoleon and the duke of Wellington at Waterloo, were purchased at Cahirmee. While these claims are not supported by available documentary evidence, they suggest that a thriving market in horses for military purposes existed there at the time of the Napoleonic wars and and probably had done for many years before that.[40] Cahirmee fair was certainly synonymous with horse trading throughout the nineteenth century: it was described by Mahony in 1830 as having been at one time 'the principal horse fair of Munster,' by Samuel Lewis in 1837 as being 'one of the largest horse fairs in the south of Ireland' and by Francis Guy in 1875 as 'a fair for horses'.[41]

Most newspaper accounts of the fair emphasized its role as a horse fair also, discussing this trade in more detail than that in any other livestock. For instance, in 1846 it was stated that 'celebrated as it has been for the large number of horses usually offered for sale, there was not within the last thirty years so large a fair as that of Monday. Horses for general use that is, for harness and saddle were in brisk demand and fetched large prices, several of them having changed owners at £120 each.'[42] Civilian horse dealers regularly came from England and Scotland to the fair, and military buyers were also regular attenders.[43] Despite its apparent popularity however, the value placed on the fair to the then proprietor of its tolls, John Kearney, was only £30 in 1850.[44]

The fair increasingly specialized in horses, with considerable success, during the latter half of the nineteenth century. An important contributory factor to the

38 *CE,* 15 July 1842.   **39** *Watson's Almanac, 1798.*   **40** See the short piece by C.J.F. MacCarthy on this topic in *Mallow Field Club Journal,* no. 4 (1986), pp. 107–8.   **41** *Sel. comm. tolls and customs, 1834,* p. 238; Lewis, *Dictionary,* i, 240; Francis Guy, *county and city of Cork directory, 1875–6,* p. 134.   **42** *CE,* 15 July 1846.   **43** *CE,* 14 July 1852.   **44** Griffith's

expansion of the trade in horses was the coming of the railway. Buttevant became a station on the line from Dublin to Cork in the late 1840s and was soon accessible by rail from all parts of Munster and beyond. This helped not only to increase the number of horses coming to the fair but also to bring buyers from further afield. Over 2,000 horses, as well as large numbers of cattle, fat sheep and lambs, were reported to have entered the fair field in 1870, which was also the year that a second field was opened by its new owner Mr Carroll, 'for the galloping and trial of horses'. Despite a reported decline in attendance on that occasion due to the effect of emigration- and 'an absence of that merrymaking which was one of the characteristics of Cahirmee of old,' the fair continued to attract the more prosperous horse lover. The attendance that year included the marquis of Waterford, earl of Shannon, Lord Coventry, Lord Fermoy, Lord W. Bentinck, Sir H. de Burghe and Sir John Arnott.[45] The depression year of 1880 had little effect on the popularity of the fair among the gentry and strong farmers. 'Distress may pinch the poor and lowly ... but the class of persons who have contributed, and still contribute to give Cahirmee the great name it enjoys, are not affected one jot by those periodic and (to many) disastrous visits' wrote the correspondent of the *Cork Examiner*.[46]

An analysis of two reports of Cahirmee fair near the end of its heyday at Cahirmee indicates the range of geographical origins of its patrons. In 1910, both the *Cork Examiner* and *Cork Free Press* reported that Cahirmee had come into its own again after some years of decline. At least 6,000 horses were reported to be present and the attendance was thought to have been the best for fifteen years. All the principal Irish dealers were present, as well as a large number of buyers from all parts of England, including:

> Messrs. Greer of Doncaster; Howard of Harlow; Gaskell, of Poulton; Nutt, of Petersborough; Perry, of London; Rock, of Kemble Junction; Young, of Carlisle; Richardson, of Leeds; Rush, of Carlisle; Weston, of Eastbourne; Hawes, of Leicester; Oliver Dixon, of Reading; James, of Bristol.[47]

Also present was an 'unusually large muster of continental buyers. They comprised Herr Bauman, Hanover; Herren Rosenberg, Muenster, Westphalia, Germany; Signor Marcha, Italy; Herr Lobb, Switzerland; Mons. Fiorruzi, Brussels; Mons. Royier, Paris and Mons. Matthieu, Brussels.'[48]

The sellers of horses were largely from the Munster area, often from counties Cork and Limerick and often indeed from within a close radius of Cahirmee itself. But not all came from Munster. Some sellers came from as far away as Armagh and one intriguing series of sales in 1905 was engaged in by Mr John Bourke of Westport House, Middleton, county Armagh who 'disposed of 20 troopers at prices ranging from £30 to £40 and six van horses from £40 to

Valuation for Cahirmee townland.   **45** *CE*, 13 July 1870.   **46** *CE*, 13 July 1880.
47 *CE*, 13 July 1910; *Cork Free Press*, 13 July 1910.   **48** *CE*, 13 July 1910.

Figure 3 Cahirmee fair field before 1920.

£60 to Mr J. McKenna, Armagh' and '10 harness horses from £30 to £50 to Mr
Thomas Horne, Armagh'.[49]

'A REAL IRISH FAIR'

Part of the attraction of Cahirmee, as of any other fair, was the opportunity it
gave to the local people to meet each other. All kinds of social networks
operated: town met country, landowner and land agent met tenant, farmers hired
labourers and, of course, buyers met sellers. Fairs were important meeting places
in rural Ireland and people attended them with the expectation of meeting
relatives and friends, and also of transacting business. Two entries from the diary
of James Grove White, the son of a landowner in Tipperary and north Cork,
illustrate the important social function of fairs:

49 *CE*, 13 July 1905.

July 12 [1821]. I went to Cahermee fair; saw John Seward, who gave me a letter to read from my Mother from Guernsey dated the 20th June ...

Jan. 6 [1822]. I went to Doneraile, on my way called at the Fair [of] Ahercross. Saw Roger Bourke, he told me that Fitzgerald's wife promised to call on him with the lease of Glenagoul & give it up to him.[50]

At Cahirmee, the networks seem to have been socially and geographically wider than at most local fairs because of its regional importance as a horse fair. The attendance at Cahirmee at its height in the late nineteenth century included horse lovers from all ranks in society, from the earl of Shannon to the itinerant tinsmith, and ranged geographically from Italy to Doneraile. The large variety of people attending must have given Cahirmee a cosmopolitan feel that added greatly to its charm.

Young and old alike looked to the fair as a highlight of the year. Houses in the vicinity were freshly painted in preparation for the fair. In the minds of children it was associated with the coming of their summer holidays from school. Refreshment tents were an important feature, 'wherein those who liked may indulge the baser appetites'.[51] Many other entertainments were also available, including old fairground staples like the 'roulette ball in its erratic gyrations', the three-card trick and 'the bottle to be broken (but which seldom was) in that evergreen pastime "timber maggie"'.[52] The presence of travelling players like 'Johnny Gooseberry' or 'Mr Laurence McEvoy' who could 'tear "passion to tatters" through six tragedies in an hour for the delectation of rustics' was a popular feature of fairs like Cahirmee and their absence was deemed worthy of comment by correspondents.[53] Several local doctors and veterinary surgeons were in regular attendance in case of accidents

In the middle of all this activity the 'Baron' of the fair, assisted by his employees, was to be found circulating around the fair, sometimes '[astride] his grey charger and [sporting] his three cornered hat'.[54] To help keep order, a large number of police (up to fifty on one occasion) was present. However, newspaper reports generally emphasised that police intervention was little needed at Cahirmee. In 1845, perhaps mindful of a recent outbreak of violence at a fair in Ballinahassig near Cork city, a large military force was reportedly kept on call to supplement the police but did not need to be used. The *Cork Examiner* reported that, far from being violent, 'there could not have been less than fifty thousand people present, but not a drunken man was seen'.[55]

50 Anna-Maria Hajba, 'James Grove White's memorandum book, part 1' in *Mallow Field Club Journal*, no.16 (1998), pp. 98, 101. The fair at 'Ahercross' refers to Aghacross near Kildorrery, about ten miles from Cahirmee. 51 *CE*, 14 July 1875. 52 *CE*, 13 July 1880. 53 *CE*, 14 July 1885. 54 *CE*, 14 July 1885. 55 *CE*, 15 July 1845.

Innovations for the benefit of patrons were sometimes reported. For instance, in 1880, it was reported that Mr. Carroll introduced a cloakroom and office for the receipt of telegrams.[56] In 1910, 'there were some innovations, one of which was a portable coffee-stall which did a roaring trade all day long'.[57] By contrast, at the same fair, the number of liquor stalls was reported to be down from the usual forty or more to fifteen, which was blamed on the 'crushing taxation of Mr John Redmond's Budget'.[58]

Cahirmee fair has long been an important meeting place for members of the travelling community and many of the reports of the fair noted the presence of travellers. In 1870, a newspaper correspondent remarked that 'a party of gypsies were encamped near the roadway leading to the field, and were very largely patronized by the visitors to the fair' while the report of the fair in 1885 commented on the 'tipsy shouts and noisy revellings, which the nomadic race of tinkers and their following indulge in, interspersed as these are with several fistic encounters' as one of the elements which made Cahirmee 'a real Irish fair'.[59]

One chronicler of the heyday of Cahirmee related an unusual, probably apocryphal, story told to him by an old groom which idealizes the intermingling of the disparate social classes who visited the fair. The groom recalled how he saw a 'red-haired young girl, of the travellin' class ... with a voice on her like a linnet and her proud ways' take the fancy of an American millionaire attending the fair. Three years later he came across her in Leicestershire 'seated on a chestnut mare, dressed like a lady', married to the American and claiming to belong 'to some old county family.'[60]

THE END AT CAHIRMEE

During the last decade of the nineteenth century and the first decade of the twentieth the viability of the fair at its traditional site was seriously threatened by horse-trading in and around Buttevant on the days leading up to the fair. Eventually this practice seems to have expanded to include the designated fair days also. Sellers and buyers (many of them foreigners who spent several days in Ireland) had more time to search each other out, and were saved both the inconvenience of travelling out to the fair field and the price of the tolls. As proprietors of the fair, the Carroll family attempted by means of court injunctions to stop the street-trading but met with little success for well over ten years. Supporters of the fair argued on at least one occasion that the unlicensed trade threatened not alone the existence of Cahirmee fair but the health of the region's horse breeding industry itself:

56 *CE*, 13 July 1880.   **57** *Cork Free Press*, 13 July, 1910.   **58** *Cork Free Press*, 13 July, 1910.
59 *CE*, 13 July 1870; *CE*, 14 July 1885.   **60** *The Cork County Chronicle*, 13 July 1935.

The preservation of this fair, which must be recognised as a national institution for farmers who cannot afford to travel to shows to dispose of their property, has become a very serious question. If they have not a mart where they can secure paying prices they must cease horse breeding, and if selling on the streets of Buttevant is allowed to continue on the days of the fair, foreign dealers, who naturally raise the market, must recognise the futility of attending Cahirmee with the knowledge that there is nothing there that they require. The quality of a horse can not be tested on a public street.[61]

The fair field continued to attract traders during this time, albeit in lesser numbers than before, but by 1905 it was believed that sales on the street outstripped those at the official fair.[62] An American visitor, touring Ireland by motor car in 1907, witnessed the hurly burly of the fair on the streets:

Buttevant is indulging in a horse fair where David Harums congregate from all the land roundabout. As our car rolls through the streets we are regarded as legitimate prey and have horses of all ages, sizes, and colours, – 'Sound? Glory be to God, as sound as yer honour,' shoved in front of us.[63]

The proprietors and their supporters continued to oppose the unlicensed sales and criticized the failure of the police to stamp them out. They even hired a photographer on one occasion to provide the authorities with pictorial evidence of their failure to prevent trading in Buttevant.[64]

In 1910, the Carrolls appear to have successfully restricted trading outside of Cahirmee. Through the use of court injunctions and by negotiating with dealers and local shopkeepers, they persuaded the vast majority to refrain from dealing until they went out to the fair field.[65] Only two instances of dealing outside the fair were reported that year and proceedings were to be brought in both cases.[66] According to the *Cork Examiner's* correspondent, the fair had recovered its old prestige:

The Field was practically filled at eight o'clock, an unusually early hour; and when the last arrivals had passed the gate not less than 6,500 animals were on view. Not for 15 years was the attendance anything like so great, and if the support of sellers was thus encouraging, the support of buyers was also good. All the principal Irish dealers from the four provinces were represented.

The correspondent went on to list the principal British and continental buyers (including buyers from Germany, Italy, Switzerland, Belgium and France) who were in attendance.[67]

61 *CE*, 15 July 1900. **62** *CE*, 13 July 1905. **63** Michael Myers Shoemaker, *Wanderings in Ireland* (New York, 1908), pp. 130–1. **64** *CE*, 13 July 1905. **65** *CE*, 13 July 1910; *Cork Free Press*, 13 July 1910. Mrs. Carroll's son, Anthony, of Rathealy, Fermoy, who was appointed Crown Solicitor for county Cork's East Riding in 1905, probably led the family's legal campaign. See Grove White, *Historical and topographical notes*, ii, 19. **66** *CE*, 13 July 1910. **67** *CE*, 13 July 1910.

This accommodation between all parties was reported to have given Cahirmee fair 'a new lease of life' and the fair of 1914, no doubt helped by the suppliers of livestock to the European armies, was said to have been very successful.[68]

But the advent of war in September 1914 caused an immediate reduction in demand for horses of various kinds and a consequent decline in the fair. In 1915, no continental and very few English buyers turned up at Cahirmee. Irish dealers were present but their attention was largely confined to heavy draught horses for Government purposes. Even more ominous for the small breeders of county Cork was the absence of buyers for hunters. The fox-hunting class had gone to war and to near destruction and, although servants and hounds were retained in hopes of better times, 'hunting in the real sense of the word [had] really ceased'.[69] Thomas Carroll, 'Baron' of Cahirmee, was reportedly very fortunate in 1915 to have found a purchaser at £150 for a hunter that 'in ordinary times at Ballsbridge would probably have been a £400 horse.'[70] The fair never fully recovered from the effects of the Great War. The demand for hunters never returned to its former heights. Farmers who had switched to producing draught horses found that the demand for working horses began to fall after the war, due to competition from cars, lorries and tractors.

When the war ended, a new crisis, the struggle for independence, affected the fair. Trade was disrupted and there were shortages of good quality horses for the overseas market. Some local feeling opinion against the Carroll family, who were regarded as part of the *ancien régime* and who reportedly let the fair field and its environs to the British military based in Buttevant, 'for polo matches or other purposes'.[71] In the weeks before the fair of 1920, rumours circulated locally that the IRA would enforce a ban on the fair. Yet, when the end came for Cahirmee, it may have been more by accident than design:

> The rumours had of course come to the ears of the Volunteers, who decided definitely and officially that not alone would they not interfere in the matter, but they strongly recommended all members of the organization that in their individual capacities they ought not interfere with the fair. They even went further, for they had actually made arrangements for the policing of the field and the roads leading thereto, with a view to preserving order, and so that nothing untoward should occur. In adopting this attitude the Volunteers recognized that any interference with Cahirmee would deal a severe blow which they considered outweighed any local political feeling over the letting of the fairfield for the purpose of polo-playing or any other reason.[72]

68 *CE*, 13 July 1915.   69 *CE*, 13 July 1915.   70 *CE*, 13 July 1915.   71 *Cork Constitution*, 13 July 1920.   72 *CE*, 13 July 1920; *Cork Constitution*, 13 July 1920. The reports are almost identical and were clearly written by the same correspondent. They differ in only one significant respect: in the staunchly nationalist *Cork Examiner* the local irregulars are described as 'Volunteers' but in the (staunchly unionist) *Cork Constitution* they are called 'Sinn Feiners'.

Events on the day of the fair seem to have led to confusion. Early arrivals at the fair field found the gates closed and, thinking that the rumours were true, returned to Buttevant, causing any others they met to turn back. The fair, much diminished from its glory days, was held on the streets of Buttevant that day and continued there on the second day. The following year, very few horses went to the old fair ground and the fair was again largely conducted in Buttevant. It was never again to return to Cahirmee in any real way.

A sense of loss pervaded the report of the fair in 1921. It had only been saved from total collapse by the recent calling of a truce in the War of Independence. Without the truce it was felt that the authorities would have prevented the fair being held in the town (presumably because of the risk of an attack on the garrison there), while much local opinion would have opposed a return to the old site. Buyers and locals felt Cahirmee fair had lost much of its old importance and was now 'merely an ordinary horse fair'.[73] Thirty years before, the Great Southern and Western Railway Company had brought in 200 wagons of horses to Buttevant annually and in one year handed over to the London and North Western Railway alone over 1,000 horses. In 1921, the railways brought only fourteen wagons to Buttevant from all parts of Munster, and fifty wagons were enough to take away all that was bought. The *Cork Examiner's* correspondent noted several factors that caused the decline in the fair. European buyers were still absent, as they had bought 'for war purposes and having had their war, they do not need troopers – at least for the present'.[74] Only a dozen English buyers came and there were fewer Irish dealers present. There were fewer breeders and less hunting and so the quality of the horses available was poor. Finally he noted that 'the displacement of the carriage horse by the motor, and the draught horse by the lorry' also contributed to the decline.[75] Any hopes that the Carrolls may have had of restoring Cahirmee as the site of the fair in 1922 were complicated by a controversy over Anthony Carroll's involvement in an eviction near Rathcormac, county Cork.[76] This led to a further boycott of Cahirmee and to the effective end of the fair there.

CAHIRMEE IN BUTTEVANT

Remarkably, however, the sense of gloom about the decline of Cahirmee fair did not last long and the fair recovered its equilibrium within a few years of its move to Buttevant. In 1924, a correspondent of the *Cork Examiner* admitted that, despite a decline in the extent of the fair, the move from Cahirmee to Buttevant was not 'altogether regarded by a fairly large bulk of buyers in an unfavourable light' due to 'the cutting off of the journey in reaching the old venue'.[77] By 1925, the correspondent was more ebullient, reporting that 'there

73 *CE*, 13 July 1921.   **74** *CE*, 13 July 1921.   **75** *CE*, 13 July 1921.   **76** Correspondence from John O'Connell of Buttevant, 16 Feb. 2000.   **77** *CE*, 14 July 1924.

Figure 4 Traveller women and children at decorated caravan, Buttevant,
county Cork (photo: courtesy of NLI, Elinor Wiltshire collection).

was a very high attendance of buyers and horses ... and business was excep-
tionally brisk'.[78] In 1930, the fair was in many ways as colourful and busy as ever.
Business began as early as the tenth of July, with vendors and buyers travelling long
distances from all parts of Munster, and, by the twelfth, the streets of Buttevant were
full of activity.[79]

The importance of the fair to the travelling community was not affected by
the new venue and travellers continued to flock to Buttevant. Newspaper
reports which referred to their presence tended to emphasize stereotypical views
of travellers. The *Cork Examiner* reported in 1925 that 'an altercation took place
at Buttevant between some tinkers who were on their way to Cahirmee fair.
There were a number of fistic encounters in which men and women took part,
sticks and stones being freely used.'[80] In 1930, it reported:

> For several days past, the countryside around, and the confines of Buttevant,
> have been infested with roving bands of humble horse dealers, gypsy vans
> and encampments, tinkers and hawkers etc. These are old associations with
> 'Cahirmee' which are little diminished.[81]

78 *CE*, 15 July 1925. **79** *CE*, 14 July 1930. **80** *CE* 15 July 1925. **81** *CE*, 14 July
1930. The language of these reports sometimes betrays a subconscious hostility, like the

As late as the 1950s and 1960s newspaper references to travellers continued to alternate between disapproval and patronizing colour pieces. Nevertheless, the presence of travellers was largely accepted as an integral part of the Cahirmee experience and was officially recognized by its organisers. In 1951, the *Cork Examiner* reported that a 'much coveted cup is awarded to the smartest nomad turnout. All the caravans were newly painted in the most vivid shades, lending a veritable blaze of colour to the scene.'[82]

Despite the ending of its glory days at Cahirmee, the fair transferred successfully to the streets of Buttevant. It remained enough of a showcase for the region's bloodstock to continue attracting the main Irish and British dealers. In 1946, Buttevant was full of visitors from all parts of Ireland and from Britain, many of whom had to stay in the nearby towns of Mallow and Charleville.[83] The fair of 1951 was described as 'the largest ever' and the collection of horses as 'unique and magnificent'.[84] Hunters were in greatest demand but working horses, ponies and even some donkeys were also available. A silver tankard was presented in 1962 by the famous horse trainer M.V. O'Brien, to be awarded annually for 'the animal most likely to make a hunter'.[85] The traditional attraction of Cahirmee fair continued to bring regular British buyers to Buttevant. As recently as 1971, Cheltenham Gold Cup winning rider Tony Grantham of Ashurst in Sussex was reported to have interrupted a holiday in Clare to buy a pony for his daughter at the fair. He was following in the footsteps of his father, who had attended the fair regularly for fifty years.[86]

Amusements continued to be an important feature of the fair. These included the usual fairground amusements, dances and, in the early 1950s, a 'monster carnival'.[87] A local festival was built around the fair, with one innovation in 1962 being the crowning of Miss Betty O'Callaghan of Rathclare, Buttevant as the first Faery Queen of the Cahirmee Fair Festival, 'which was performed by Mrs Marie O'Flaherty, Munster Mannequin Agency, Cork, who held a fashion show previously in the local cinema.'[88]

CONCLUSION

Cahirmee fair still lives on today, its name a reminder of its origins. Though smaller now than it once was, it remains a working fair and is still attended by those who have horses to buy and sell. It attracts locals and tourists alike, although Buttevant is now as likely to be jammed with cars as with horses. Members of the travelling community, 'recognized nowadays by their modern caravans rather than by the traditional pony and cart and tent', still attend in

use of the word 'infested' above. **82** *CE*, 13 July 1951. **83** *CE*, 13 July 1946. **84** *CE*, 13 July 1951. **85** *CE*, 13 July 1962. **86** *CE*, 13 July 1971. **87** *CE*, 13 July 1946, 13 July 1951. **88** *CE*, 13 July 1962. The title of 'Faery Queen' refers to the Buttevant connection with Edmund Spenser's poem, written at nearby Kilcolman Castle.

large numbers and continue a tradition of celebrating weddings while visiting Buttevant.[89]

It may be appropriate to end by quoting the words, written as long ago as 1910, of a newspaper correspondent who, though conscious of the encroachment of modernity, hoped for a long life for Cahirmee and its horse trade. 'Motor progress, and aeroplaning nothwithstanding, it would still seem that the horse has got his uses, and it will be many a long day before the noble quadruped is in danger of being ranked with the dodo.'[90]

It is a tribute to the longevity of Cahirmee fair, to the robust tradition which it embodies, and the continuing role of horse breeding in the local and regional economy that these words still hold true today.

---

89 *CE*, 13 July 1971, 13 July 1981.   **90** *Cork Free Press*, 13 July 1910.

'Slaughtered like wild beasts'.
Massacre at Castlepollard fair, 1831

PAUL CONNELL

I

The parish of Castlepollard in county Westmeath lies north-east of Mullingar and shares its boundaries with the parishes of Collinstown, Coole and a portion of the diocese of Ardagh. The present parish is an amalgamation of three ancient parishes – Rathgraff, Lickbla and Foyran – all of whom originally belonged to the abbey of Fore. In 1834 there were 6931 Catholics and 532 non-Catholics in the parish of Castlepollard.[1] According to the 1831 census there were 291 houses and 314 families in the town of Castlepollard with a total of 3612 inhabitants.[2] Today the population of the town is approximately 800.

The town of Castlepollard and its surrounding countryside has been associated with the Pollard family since the sixteenth century. A family of great antiquity in Devonshire, England, the Pollards began their association with Ireland when Captain Nicholas Pollard, the founder of the Irish branch, accompanied Walter, earl of Essex to Ireland in the reign of Elizabeth I. In return for military services rendered, Nicholas was given a grant of the castle and lands of Mayne (now known as Coole) in county Westmeath. His son, Nicholas, born in 1567, built the castle of Rathyoung, which he called Castlepollard.[3]

This Nicholas was succeeded by his son Walter and it was he who surrendered his lands to the king for the purpose of having them erected into a manor. This was done by letters patent dated 26 Charles II (1675), and the lands were given the name of Castlepollard. Walter also received a patent for holding fairs and a weekly market, along with an order from the lord lieutenant and council for building a church at Castlepollard.[4] Walter's great grandson, William Pollard, was granted a second patent by George III to hold two other fairs at Castlepollard.[5]

The 1852–3 report of the commissioners appointed to inquire into the state of fairs and markets in Ireland dates these patents to 16 January, 26 Charles II (1675) and 15 November, 5 George III (1764). According to the report, the two fairs granted by Charles II were to be held on 10–11 May, and 29–30 September. The

---

1 Revd Anthony Cogan, *The diocese of Meath, ancient and modern* (3 vols, Dublin, 1867; reprinted, Dublin, 1992), ii, 400.   2 *Population of the counties in Ireland, 1831*, H.C. 1833 (254), xxxix, I.   3 John Charles Lyons, *The Grand Juries of Westmeath – from the year 1727 to the year 1853, with an historical appendix* (2 vols, Ledestown, 1853), ii, 259.   4 Ibid. 5 *Report comm. fairs and markets*, 1852–3. p. 114.

fairs granted under the patent of George III were to be held on 10 December
and 1 August.[6] The report also states that the four fair days were now held on 21
May, 1 August, 10 October, and 10 December. The May and October dates are
roughly in line with the original patent, once allowance is made for the calendar
change of 1751, which effectively added eleven days to previous dates. According
to Lewis in his *Topographical Dictionary*, fairs for livestock were held at Castlepollard
every Wednesday in conjunction with the petty sessions.[7] These fairs were
obviously the weekly markets mentioned in the original patent. The taking out
of a patent for fairs and markets was done by landlords to safeguard their property and ensure that no rival could lay claim to such franchises. The ownership
of the markets and fairs thus became related to the manorial system and ensured
that attempts to develop such facilities for towns depended on the initiative, or
at least the good will, of the local landlord.[8]

The fair day in Castlepollard was similar in type and function to other fairs
held throughout the country. It served a variety of functions in addition to
providing a location for the purchase and sale of livestock. The fair was an
opportunity to buy products not available locally, so it was attended by vendors
offering a wide variety of goods. Bills were paid, credits established and other
business transacted. Entertainment was provided by travelling musicians and
other wandering showmen. It was well-attended and drew people from considerable distances. For this reason, fairs could often be fractious affairs as people
of different political and religious persuasions met in one place. Old rivalries
were renewed and faction fighting was often a characteristic of fairs.

We know something of what brought people together at Castlepollard from
the evidence given at the inquest into the incident which occurred at the fair
on 23 May 1831. Catherine Connolly had a tent at the fair and was selling
bread. Also giving evidence were Matthew Carlisle, a dyer, James Malone, a
nailor, and Michael Gill, who was at the fair 'selling a slip of a pig'. Owen Casey
also gave evidence, saying he was a dealer from Sligo.[9] Gerald Dease, the local
magistrate, in his evidence said that at one point he accompanied the Chief
Constable, Peter Blake, to a showman's exhibition

> which seemed to attract a great number of persons ... conceiving the show
> might be an enducement to the people to delay, witness recommended Mr.
> Blake to desire the showman to shut up in good time.[10]

Also examined was Patrick Keogh, a servant and assistant 'to Miss Brown who
travels with a public exhibition'.[11] Fair day in Castlepollard therefore, was like
many others throughout the country.

6 Ibid.   7 Samuel Lewis, *Topographical dictionary of Ireland, with historical and statistical
descriptions* (2 vols, London, 1837), ii, 499.   8 W.H. Crawford, 'Development of the county
Mayo economy, 1700–1850', in R. Gillespie and G. Moran (eds), *A various country: essays in
Mayo history* (Westport, 1987), p. 70.   9 *Freeman's Journal*, 30 May 1831.   10 Ibid.   11 Ibid.

II

The fair of 23 May 1831 however, proved to be very different for all the wrong reasons. There is a great deal of evidence from various sources that fair days throughout the country were occasions for faction fighting and general disturbance, due to the great numbers of people gathered and the free flow of alcohol. This is why the local magistrate and a large force of police were usually present at fairs. Their task was to ensure that peace and order were preserved. Normally, any difficulties that arose were dealt with and serious miscreants were sent for trial to the next assizes. But this particular fair day in Castlepollard was to end with nine people dead and several others wounded. The ensuing outcry was to have implications not just for the police and the law, but also for the Liberal government, which at this time was trying to develop a working relationship with the newly elected Daniel O'Connell M.P. It was, after all, O'Connell and his thirty supporters who had given the government its majority in a critical division exactly three months before the 'Castlepollard Affray', as it soon became known.[12]

What happened at Castlepollard on that fair day?[13] Despite the opposing views on the matter after the event, the essential facts are not in doubt.[14] During the course of the fair, at about two o'clock, a number of men were drinking in James Fagan's public house. A jug was broken and a dispute started over who should pay for the damage. The row spilled out into the street and eventually Sergeant Mills and three other unarmed policemen arrived on the scene and arrested one of the men involved. However, as soon as he was arrested a crowd gathered around them and rescued the prisoner. As they were retiring to barracks, the Chief Constable, Peter Blake, who by now had come upon the scene, was hit by a stone and almost knocked down. Following the intervention of the local magistrate, Gerald Dease, matters quietened down until some time between six and seven o'clock in the evening. By this time Dease had left the town, having thought that the situation no longer needed his presence. Before he left, he advised Blake that he and his men should remain in the area until twelve o'clock that night.

By six o'clock the majority of people had left for home but a number remained and became involved in a fight in the town square. At this point, Chief Constable Blake led twenty-four fully armed men into the square. Having marched towards the fight and waited some minutes, they began to retire to barracks once

12 J.C. Beckett, *The Making of Modern Ireland 1603–1923* (London, 1966), p. 308.   13 The author gratefully acknowledges the assistance given him by Mícéal Conlon. See also, Mícéal Conlon, *The Castlepollard Massacre*, an occasional paper produced for the Westmeath Archaeological and History Society, May 1981; Sabina Davitt, *Fr John Burke and the Castlepollard Massacre*, an unpublished project presented to the Department of Modern History, St Patrick's College, Maynooth, in partial fulfillment of the requirements for the award of the College Diploma in Local History, 1997.   14 *Freeman's Journal*, 26 May 1831, 30 May 1831, 25 July 1831, 29 July 1831. *Westmeath Journal*, 26 May 1831, 28 May 1831, 4 August 1831.

Figure 1 Map of Castlepollard, showing the constabulary barracks,
the Market House and Fagan's public house.

again. There was some hissing from the crowd and a number of stones were thrown at the police. Blake and his men then wheeled around and fired a number of times into the crowd, killing nine people and wounding another eight. Two of the dead were women – Mary Neill, aged thirty, and Mary Kiernan, aged fifty. The other seven were Patrick Dignum, Patrick McDermott, John Slevin, James Fagan, Patrick McCormack, Patrick McDonagh and Bryan Mahon. One of the injured, Patrick Ledwith, died later of his wounds on 9 June. According to the account in the *Freeman's Journal*, Dignum was a native of Longford, and one of the others, possibly Patrick Mc Donagh, was a forty-five year old cattle jobber from Leitrim.[15] Evidence was given at the subsequent trial by one of the witnesses that Patrick McDermott was a young 'cripple boy'.[16] Another victim may have died subsequently. The local parish priest, Fr John Burke, mentioned in a letter that a total of eleven people were killed.[17]

III

Reaction to the events at Castlepollard fair was not long in coming. Predictably, the attitude taken depended on the political orientation of the commentator. The *Freeman's Journal* demanded justice for those killed and injured. Under a heading – 'The Police – Nine Persons Killed and Seven Mortally Wounded' – it went on

> In what country do we live? Is there to be any mercy for the lives of the people of Ireland? Or for the slightest causes, which in England are severely punished by the constables' staff, are they to be slaughtered like wild beasts? … Lord Anglesey surely will bring the murderers to instant trial.[18]

It quoted two reports from eyewitnesses to the event. The first was very clear in his mind about what happened

> It is well you were not here on yesterday to witness the slaughter of the poor innocent men, women and children, who fell victims to the blood thirsty peelers – I will not call them police … I saw the riot at an end when the peelers, without any provocation than a few stones having been thrown by a few deluded persons, commenced firing at every person that came in their way.[19]

The *Westmeath Journal*, as might be expected from the local establishment paper, took a slightly different angle. In its report on 26 May it stated that several

15 *Freeman's Journal*, 30 May 1831.   16 *Westmeath Journal*, 28 July 1831.   17 James Woods, *The Annals of Westmeath* (Dublin, 1907), p. 287. Fr Burke in fact lost ten parishioners. Patrick Dignum and Bryan Mahon were from Coole parish, and Patrick McCormack was from Collinstown parish.   18 *Freeman's Journal*, 26 May 1831.   19 Ibid.

riotous proceedings had taken place at the fair during the day. Called out in the evening to preserve the peace, Mr Blake, the Chief Constable, had begged and entreated the 'deluded people' to desist but to no avail, even when the Riot Act was read.

> Some fiendish wretch cried out 'Make another Clare of it, boys' alluding of course to the murder of five policemen there, and then an onset of such a character ensued that the police were obliged to fire and to continue to do so for some minutes, and soon after the mob ran away.

It concluded its report by remarking that

> Amidst the feeling of regret at such a dreadful catastrophe, it must be pleasing to every good man to acknowledge the very great deal of forbearance and humanity evinced by the police, in endeavouring to avoid a conflict. Their conduct has been lauded by every person with whom we have spoken and, we believe, not a second opinion exists on the matter.[20]

It is difficult to gauge the reaction of the Dublin authorities to the event because the correspondence relating to it is missing from the State Papers. That they took it seriously is not in doubt however. The *Freeman's Journal* assured its readers that the local magistrates had forwarded a report to Dublin Castle which requested a full investigation of the affair.[21] More to the point, the Solicitor General, Philip Cecil Crampton, was sent to Castlepollard to inquire into the affair. He arrived in Castlepollard accompanied by Major James Tandy, Acting Inspector General, on Thursday 26 May. His brief was to investigate the circumstances and report to the government. He took unsworn testimony from several witnesses. These same witnesses also gave sworn testimony at the inquest which had already begun, presided over by the coroner. Crampton asked for the assistance of the local magistrates and the local Catholic clergy with his inquiry and he allowed them to question the witnesses. At the conclusion of his investigation, he remarked that he was impressed at how peaceable the neighbourhood was. He had expected it to be otherwise, given the circumstances, and he thanked the local Catholic clergy for their assistance with his investigation. Fr Patrick O'Donoghue, the parish priest of Mountnugent, and as such one of the local priests, replied that the people were quiet because of the assurances given to them by the local magistrate, Mr Gerald Dease, and Fr John Burke, the parish priest, that justice would be done by the government of the country. Crampton in reply stated that 'nothing would be left undone to sift the matter to the bottom, and administer strict and impartial justice.'[22] Along with the magistrates

---

20 *Westmeath Journal*, 26 May 1831.   **21** *Freeman's Journal*, 26 May 1831.   **22** *Freeman's Journal*, 30 May 1831.

and some of the local gentry Crampton raised money for the relief of the bereaved families.[23]

The *Westmeath Journal* welcomed the arrival of the Solicitor General, remarking that he had remained almost two days 'inquiring most minutely into all the facts of the case'. It noted however that he must have seen

> the violence with which the priests and their party collected and magnified, if they did not do more, every circumstance that could directly or indirectly lead to the conviction of the Police ... we cannot but notice the great excitement in this county caused by this sad occurrence ... while those persons bow their heads in mute submission to midnight atrocities and the bloody murders of Captain Rock, and every other ubiquitous ruffian.[24]

The reaction of the investigators to the events in Castlepollard can be gauged from a letter written by Major Tandy to Lord Stanley, the Chief Secretary on 2 June 1831

> With reference to the unfortunate occurrence at Castlepollard in the county of Westmeath on the 23rd, I take the liberty with great respect to submit for the consideration and decision of His Excellency the Lord Lieutenant, that the Constabulary Police be cautioned to remain *within* their barracks at places where Fairs are holding (abstaining from all participation in, or interference with, the amusements or disputes of the assembled people) until called out personally by a Magistrate under whose orders they should act; the Constables or Sub Constables not loading their arms until directed to do so by the Magistrate through the medium of the Chief Constable (if present).

Tandy further recommended that the Police should not be permitted to attend at a fair where there was no barracks unless they received a written request from a magistrate to so do. Finally, he wrote

> I would also beg to suggest that when the Magistrate retires the Chief or other constables should in no instance remain behind. ... My recommendation does not go to interfere with the regular performance of the other duties of the Constabulary who, in the event of their lives being actually endangered by the violence of a mob, or being assailed whilst on patrol or escort duty ... might be justified in firing on the assailants in their own defence but they should be instructed invariably to forbear using their arms until reduced to the last extremity when remonstrance and intimidation prove unavailing.[25]

23 Ibid.   **24** *Westmeath Journal*, 1 June 1831.   **25** NAI, CSORP 1831, Carton No. 1831/1525.

IV

The inquest into the killings, conducted by the county Coroner, Hugh Dixon, began on Tuesday 24 May and lasted four days, with a very large number of witnesses being called. The relatives of the dead were represented at the inquest by a Dublin solicitor, John Coffey. The coroner impanelled a jury, the majority of whom were local people, and they spent the first day viewing the bodies of the dead.[26] At the outset, Colonel Osborne, the head of the local constabulary, said that he thought the police involved should not be treated as civilians. The coroner, however, rejected this approach and replied that 'he did not see how any difference could exist with regard to the means of accomplishing the ends of justice, no matter whether the accused was a peer or a peasant'.[27]

The various witnesses who gave evidence described what they saw on the day and where they were at the time. A large number of them were able to identify the policemen who had fired at those who were killed. Many were also of the opinion that there was no rioting at the time the police fired on the crowd. Matthew Crosbie of Castlepollard saw John Slevin falling and saw no rioting or stones being thrown at the police. John Malone saw Sergeant Mears 'level his piece and fire at Slevin'. Mary Malone said she knew Patrick McCormack and had a conversation with him shortly before Chief Constable Blake gave the order to fire. He fell immediately after the first volley. She saw no riot or stones being thrown. Catherine Reilly took cover after the firing began and Mary Neill fell dead on top of her. Patrick Kennedy knew Patrick McDermott to be a young cripple with no use of his hand. He was shot at Kennedy's side despite there being no riot at the time.[28]

Arthur Bush, the son of the lord chief justice of Ireland, who was in Castlepollard for the May fly-fishing, also gave evidence. He said that he saw a fight, and sticks waving, and heard a great deal of shouting. He witnessed the police emerging from their barracks, and 'the people he observed at this time pressed very much on the police'. Stones were thrown at the police and he 'took particular notice of a large one'. In general his evidence gave the impression that the police were pushed into firing at the crowd. The local magistrate, Gerald Dease, gave evidence but he was not present when the firing occurred. More worrying for the police was the evidence given by Edward Brady of Cummerstown, who said that Chief Constable Blake had cried out in a loud voice 'to fire and not to spare either man, woman or child.' On the other hand, Michael Nugent swore that he saw a policeman take down Patrick Ledwith and that the same policeman was about to fire on James Dermody, who was crying over a dead body, when Blake prevented him from shooting.[29]

26 Edward Fox (foreman), John Hunter, William Mc Cormack, Charles Dopping, Andrew Fagan, Patt Smith, William Egan, Michael Fagan, James Fagan, William Sharwood, John Fagan and Patrick Fagan.   **27** *Freeman's Journal*, 30 May 1831.   **28** Ibid. **29** Ibid.

At the conclusion of the evidence the coroner told the jury that there was no controversy with regard to the facts. What they had to decide was whether there was anything to justify the police in firing and whether they were entitled to do so in the circumstances. They were entitled to defend themselves in a riot situation but was there sufficient violence on the part of the crowd? After three hours, the jury returned with a verdict. Patrick Dignum died from a gunshot wound inflicted by Sergeant Mills. John Slevin and Mary Kiernan met their deaths in the same way from shots fired by Sergeant Mears and John Todd. All the others died from gunshot wounds inflicted by a party of eighteen police with Chief Constable Blake at their head.[30] Following the verdict the police were lodged in Mullingar gaol.[31]

V

The *Westmeath Journal* was not impressed at this turn of events. In its view the jury had been biased

> Of the jury who were to decide upon what was to be a party case, TEN were Roman Catholics, of those ten five or six were nearly related and one of them had been once or twice in the custody of the police on a charge of felony.[32]

An application for bail on behalf of the policemen was made subsequently at the Court of King's Bench. The application was heard on 13 June 1831. The two judges, Burton and Vandeleur, remarked that the inquest jury had expressed no opinion as to whether there was murder, homicide or justified homicide. They decided that Chief Constable Blake and the four others who had been identified, Sergeants Mears and Mills and Constables Todd and Hall, should remain in prison, but that the other policemen should be freed on bail.[33]

Meanwhile, the people of Castlepollard had not been idle. Their reaction to the possible bailing of some of the policemen was shown at a meeting in the town held on 7 June. A memorial was adopted and addressed to the lord lieutenant, the marquis of Anglesey. It attributed the peaceful atmosphere in the district to

> the prompt and satisfactory measures adopted by your Excellency, in order to afford to the offended laws, and to the afflicted relatives, of those who fell victims to that sanguinary attack, in which so many innocent lives were sacrificed, that impartial justice which can only maintain the one and appease the others.[34]

---

30 The original newspaper accounts give a figure of twenty-four police.   **31** Ibid.
32 *Westmeath Journal*, 1 June 1831.   **33** *Freeman's Journal*, 14 June 1831.   **34** Certified copy of NAI, CSORP 1831 in the possession of Micéal Conlon, Castlepollard.

Figure 2 Castlepollard Square, from an early twentieth-century postcard.

They were happier with the presence of the military in the town than with the by now hated police, but they had heard

> With astonishment that it is the intention, of many of the magistrates of this county, to apply to the Lord Chief Justice of the King's Bench, in order to have the police, who are identified and committed to prison, liberated on bail before the approaching Assizes, and deplore that such a measure should be for a moment under the consideration of those who are sworn to uphold the laws of the Country.[35]

Collections were taken up in the local chapels to provide a legal fund to hire a lawyer to act on behalf of the relatives of the dead and injured at the trial.[36] The *Westmeath Journal* claimed it had

> authenticated reports of seditious and inflammatory harangues, propounded from the altars ... Priest Burke did use such language to his parishioners as was deemed dangerous, seditious and inflammatory, and was called to Dublin Castle on the subject, and as usual in these conciliatory times, was sent back to his mission of peace, on promising to be good in future.[37]

The reference to 'these conciliatory times' is an interesting comment. The newspaper obviously believed that the government was trying to act cautiously in order not to antagonize O'Connell and his supporters in parliament. That Fr John Burke was actively involved in seeking justice for those bereaved is not in doubt. He signed the memorial protesting at the bail application on behalf of the police. He also wrote to Daniel O'Connell asking him to persuade the government to allow the lawyer acting for the relatives to conduct the prosecution at the upcoming trial.[38] On 16 June Burke was present at a meeting of priests, witnesses, and lawyers in Castlepollard, organised to prepare for the trial.[39]

O'Connell brought up the question of who would prosecute at the trial in a debate in the House of Commons on 11 July. He said he had

> been favoured with communication from the Revd Mr Burke who had care of the peasantry in that district, stating that the utmost dissatisfaction would be produced if the government refused to allow them to conduct their case by their own counsel.[40]

Replying for the government, Lord Althorp stated that the government had a difficult decision to make. It could prosecute the case without the assistance of

---

(Unfortunately the author could not trace the original in the National Archives). **35** Ibid.   **36** *Westmeath Journal*, 7 July 1831.   **37** Ibid.   **38** *Freeman's Journal*, 11 July 1831.   **39** *Westmeath Journal*, 21 July 1831.   **40** Hansard, 3rd series, IV, 11 July 1831, 1059 and following.

the relatives of the deceased, or leave the matter entirely in the hands of the relatives, or join with the relatives in the prosecution. O'Connell objected to the Attorney General being involved on the grounds that he had been 'partisan' before his appointment. Colonel Rochfort, M.P. for Westmeath, objected that Fr Burke was not one to quote in the matter, as 'the reverend gentleman had not contributed to allay the excitement since the unfortunate transaction.' Lord Stanley, Chief Secretary for Ireland, then intimated to the House that the government would allow the counsel for the relatives to challenge.[41] In the end the prosecution at the trial was undertaken by the Serjeant at Law for Ireland, Edward Pennefather, assisted by four others barristers. The relatives were represented by T. Wallace and J.C. Brady. The Crown Solicitor was P. Geale, while solicitor for the next of kin was John Coffey.[42]

VI

Before the police could be tried they had to be sent for trial by the Grand Jury. It was sworn in on Saturday, 23 July and included many of the local gentry. The judge, the Hon Baron Smith, addressed them about the task ahead of them. He warned them that no party feeling should cloud their judgement and that they should decide the matter on the evidence alone. There had been 'a disastrous and too copious effusion of human blood' but the lives of several human beings depended on their deliberations. In this case, ministers of the law were accused of abusing their powers. If they had done so, they deserved the penal consequences. If, on the other hand, they had acted properly, they were entitled to the protection of the law. The Grand Jury should find only against the policemen who had actually fired shots. If these policemen had acted in self-defence, they had no case to answer. If they had done so out of vengeance, they should be sent for trial, charged with murder. However, if they had acted in the heat of the moment, the charge should be manslaughter.

Interestingly, he went on to say that some people held that the police should not be armed, as was the case in England. His reply to this was simple

> Let the people cease to post threatening notices, to burn houses and to plunder arms; let illegal oaths, insurrectionary violence, and combination cease; and then, for the bayonet the law may substitute the staff.

He agreed there was always a danger that the police would use arms rashly. The way to guard against this danger was to keep the police firmly under control and to inflict exemplary punishment on those who transgressed. He was very pleased that the Crown was prosecuting the case. When police had been shot the Crown prosecuted, and in order to be impartial it was important that

41 Ibid.   42 *Freeman's Journal,* 25 July 1831.

they also did so in cases like this. The fact that the counsel for the relatives of the deceased was assisting the prosecution was also welcome, as it would give added vigour to the case. However, he had heard epithets like 'atrocious' and 'a massacre' used about the affair, perhaps justly, perhaps not, but they were certainly premature until the evidence was assessed. The jury should have no opinion on the matter, the evidence ought to be let speak for itself.

The Grand Jury began its deliberations the following Monday and, having heard from a large number of witnesses, they decided to indict the police for manslaughter rather than murder. The following morning, Baron Smith expressed his satisfaction with their decision. Because of their findings there would be 'no star chamber proceedings' and the evidence would now be heard by all in open court.[43] Jury selection for the trial began at ten minutes to one and went on until 2.30 p.m. There were 400 on the panel, of whom 132 were present. After sixty challenges on the part of the Crown and twenty-two challenges on the part of the defendants the jury was impanelled. Unlike the inquest jury, which was made up of local people, this jury was more diverse, and several of its members were from a gentry background.[44]

Twelve of the policemen, including Chief Constable Peter Blake, were then formally charged with the manslaughter of Patrick McDermott on 23 May 1831. They all pleaded not guilty. Five other policemen were discharged, as the Grand Jury had decided they had no case to answer. Samuel Hall, however, was indicted for the murder of Patrick Ledwith, as evidence had been sworn that he had deliberately targeted Ledwith. This indictment was put on hold and Hall did not go on trial until 16 July 1832.[45]

The prosecution case was opened by Serjeant Pennefather. He first of all asked the jury to put aside all prejudice. Their task, he said, was either to find the defendants guilty of manslaughter or to acquit them on the grounds of self-defence. He assured them that the Crown was not being vindictive in bringing the prosecution and went on to state the facts of the case as he saw them. In conclusion, he told the jury that they should acquit if they found the police could not have stopped the riot without firing those fatal shots.[46]

The first witness called for the Crown was the local magistrate Gerald Dease. He repeated the evidence he had given at the inquest and emphasized that when he left the town at five o'clock all seemed quiet. He said he told Chief Constable Blake that it would be better not to call out his men from barracks unless there was a necessity to do so. Blake had replied 'and very urgent necessity'. After the shootings he had an opportunity to talk to Blake and he said to him on that occasion, 'Mr Blake, this is dreadful carnage'. Blake had replied

43 *Freeman's Journal*, 15 July 1831.   44 Charles Arabian, Robert Matthews, John Thompson, Richard Levinge, Tennison Lyons, John Black, Christopher Adamson, Robert Jameson, Peter Smith, John Smith, Aungier Black and Peter Grace.   45 *Westmeath Journal*, 26 July 1832. Tried before the Hon. Judge Jebb he was acquitted on the charge of murdering Patrick Ledwith on 23 May 1831.   46 *Freeman's Journal*, 28 July 1831,

yes said he and I wonder it has not been more, for I examined the pouches of the men and found they had fired 58 rounds of ball cartridge.[47]

Thomas Nugent gave evidence that, after the incident earlier in the day where the crowd had freed a prisoner from the police, Constable Lennon had pointed at bruises in the door of the barracks and said

> Mr. Nugent, look at this ... they deserve balls in place of them, and shall get them before night ... they would give them bullets instead of stones.[48]

Edward McCarthy gave evidence that there had been a bad fight before the police emerged from their barracks. When they came out a few stones were thrown. Blake had struck up the guns with his sword as if to prevent the police firing. But when they fired, they did so in the direction in which the people were retreating. Henry James O' Neill also gave evidence. He said that he went to Chief Constable Blake after the firing began and appealed to him to order his men to cease firing.

> For God's sake Sir, desist firing, don't you see the people are running in all directions, the people were running in all directions; he took no notice but ordered his men to fire, and four of the police fired and fell back, and four more came forward again; witness then begged again of Mr. Blake to desist, and he said why do you interfere? I do so from motives of humanity; he then made no reply but in a few moments ordered the men to retire.[49]

Thomas Devine said he had shouted at Chief Constable Blake that he was committing a slaughter but to no avail. Under cross-examination he said the people were by no means circled in around the police. James Kennedy said that the police continued firing even while the people were running away. He heard Blake tell the men to fire on, and not to spare man, woman or child. Other witnesses gave testimony also as to the paucity of stones fired at the police. James Malone said he saw a party of police fire shots and identified Sergeant Mears as one of them. Frank Creamer said it was Mears who had shot John Slevin.[50]

It was midnight by the time the Crown's case was finished. Everyone expected Baron Smith to adjourn until the morning but, to everyone's surprise, he insisted that he would not adjourn and asked the defence to put its case. 'It is quite evident I do not consult my own personal convenience.'[51] The defence began its case with evidence from Arthur Bush, son of the lord chief justice. His evidence was similar to that which he gave at the inquest: he insisted that he saw a shower of stones thrown and he felt Chief Constable Blake had been justified in the action taken as it was a riotous situation. John Shaw Hamilton corroborated everything Bush had said. The police had only fired after a second shower of stones was thrown. What he meant by a shower of stones was thirty or forty large ones coming in the space of five seconds. They had come from all parts of the crowd. William Clemens gave evidence that he felt the police were in danger and therefore justified in their action. The people had continued to throw stones after the firing began. Two other witnesses, John Hood and William Leslie, agreed that a great number of stones were thrown.[52]

A number of witnesses then gave evidence that Sergeant Mears was in the barracks during the firing and could not have participated. Jane Ray said she had gone to the barracks and, while there, she helped Mears put his wife and children across the wall of the barracks into the Pollard demesne. Henry Blake, brother of the Chief Constable, said he was in the barracks at the time and he assisted Mears in getting his wife and children over the wall. James Riggs also agreed with this version of events. The defence case concluded at 5 a.m., after several character witnesses were called for Chief Constable Blake and some of the other policemen.

Despite the fact that the court had been sitting all night, Baron Smith proceeded to spend an hour and a quarter charging the jury and then ordered them to retire to consider their verdict. To quote the *Westmeath Journal*:

> At this hour the court presented a scene as unusual as it was ludicrous; the sun had already risen with splendour, and yet the remains of unsnuffed tallow candles shed their sickly glare around, while barristers of both grades and all ages, grand jurors, constabulary chiefs, squires and squireens, etc, afforded in all directions auricular and occular demonstration of their inability to resist the leaden influence of the sleepy God.[53]

After three-quarters of an hour the foreman of the jury came into court and said they were unanimous in acquitting Sergeant Mears but there was no likelihood of them agreeing about the others. Baron Smith ordered the jury to be sequestered and adjourned proceedings until two in the afternoon. At half past three the jury came into court and said they wished to acquit Mears but could still not agree on the others. Baron Smith made a number of points to them. In law every doubt was a grounds for acquittal. If the police were so hemmed in then they may have been justified in firing. But they also had to consider whether they were justified in continuing to fire. If resistance by the people was continuous during the firing then they should acquit. The jury retired again and at twenty minutes to six emerged and handed in a verdict of acquittal for all the prisoners.[54] The *Freeman's Journal* reported the general rumour that while the jury was divided on a verdict, nine were for acquitting and three were for a verdict of guilty.[55]

52 *Freeman's Journal*, 28 July 1831, *Westmeath Journal*, 4 August 1831.   53 *Westmeath Journal*, 4 August 1831.   54 *Freeman's Journal*, 29 July 1831, *Westmeath Journal*, 4 August 1831.   55 *Freeman's Journal*, 29 July 1831.

Before discharging the defendants Baron Smith addressed them. The case had been a momentous one. The jury had deliberated for eleven hours. The spilling of blood had been very great; innocent people had died; indeed he could not say that any of the dead were not innocent. But the jury had found that the act of firing was justified, even if the result was deplorable. Addressing Chief Constable Blake, he said that a person of his rank should see the great necessity of avoiding any rash acts which might have penal consequences for himself and the men under his command. He hoped he would profit by the lesson the trial had taught him. The people distrusted the law. He believed that it was up to everyone in authority, by the way they conducted themselves, to prove that this distrust was ill founded. 'Kindly show them that the law is their best protector', he advised. He was aware that the police were unpopular with the local people because of what had happened. However, it was not surprising that some individuals in so large a force had transgressed. Therefore it was all the more important to prove the worth of the police to the ordinary people. Smith then concluded by saying:

> Though I think the verdict to be what is commonly called a merciful one, (for yet I will not shrink from uttering my sentiments) I think it a verdict the propriety of which is not liable to censure.[56]

VII

As can be imagined, the local people were not happy at the outcome of the trial. The newspapers reported that the result had 'grievously disappointed the great mass of the people here, yet a sullen quiet and tranquility prevail'.[57] The reaction of the parish priest, Fr John Burke, is clear from a letter he sent on 18 August in reply to a request from Dublin Castle to assist in taking the census.

> You want the census of my parish. All the information I can give you is, that its population was reduced, on the last shooting day, eleven in number, and that we have laws which forbid me to characterizse that deed as it deserves. The Government which is supported at an enormous expense for the purpose, or under the pretence (which you know is the same thing) of protecting each man's rights inviolable, calls upon me to help number the rest of my flock, without alluding, in the smallest degree, to those eleven I have lost. Does the government think that I could so soon forget them, or that I can ever forget them? ... send your Orange messengers and enumerators to those to whom they are welcome ... I am too affected by the loss of my parishioners.[58]

56 Ibid.   **57** *Freeman's Journal*, 30 July 1831, *Westmeath Journal*, 4 August 1831.
58 Woods, *Annals of Westmeath*, pp. 286–7.

Considering the terrible loss of life that occurred, the reaction of Fr Burke and the local people is understandable. They would have seen the outcome as a whitewash and a travesty of justice. Given the hopes he had expressed with regard to the government providing justice for the people, Fr Burke was especially bitter, as the above letter indicates. The granting of Catholic Emancipation, coupled with the informal alliance between the government and O'Connell, had generated a sense of a new beginning in the country. The Castlepollard killings put all of this under strain.

There is no doubt that the authorities in Dublin Castle, the local magistrates, the police, and everyone concerned with the administration of justice realized that a terrible injustice had been done. The police had lost control, and as a result, their actions had horrific consequences. The report of Inspector General Tandy, and indeed the comments of the judge, Baron Smith, indicate as much. He referred to the dead as 'innocent human beings' and his description of the verdict as 'a merciful one' speaks volumes. Chief Constable Blake could not have been happy with the thinly veiled dressing down he received from Smith at the end of the trial.

On the other hand, the view of the authorities must have been that they could not countenance the alternative. If the police had been found guilty and possibly sentenced to death as a result, it would have been in the words of Lord Denning at the Birmingham Six trial, 'an appalling vista'. How could the police be expected to keep order in future if they feared the consequences of firing their weapons? The truth of the matter was that the government was caught in a terrible dilemma. It had to be seen to be concerned about the incident, especially in light of its informal alliance with O'Connell. Yet, despite the realization that the police had made a terrible blunder, the government had to be seen to support the forces of law and order. The situation was not unlike the incident at Mitchelstown much later in the century, when Chief Secretary Balfour defended the police in public while scolding them in private. At the very least, the Castlepollard disaster must have been yet another reason for pushing forward the reform of policing in Ireland which was to lead to the emergence of the Royal Irish Constabulary.

Whatever about the dilemma faced by the government, the whole episode reinforced the sense of resentment felt by ordinary people against the actions of what they saw as an uncaring and alien government. Their feelings can be best summed up in the words of a poem which was published in the *Dublin Evening Mail* shortly after the trial.

> Come all you friends of Ireland, wherever you do be
> Come listen to the tale I tell, 'tis a doleful tragedy
> Come listen though through choking sighs and many a bitter tear
> I tell the murderous deeds of death at Castlepollard Fair.

In peace and quietness went on the business of the fair
Until the peelers were brought out to raise a riot there
Oh! then the work of death began, a woeful bitter fray
The fatherless and widows to lament the dreadful day.

They drew up round the market house, their chief he bade them fire
Whilst the astonished flying crowd on all sides did retire
'Twas human blood they wanted, their deadly aim they took
And Castlepollard streets with gore were running like a brook.

'Twould make a heart of stone to bleed and shake in fear and dread
To see the walls besmeared with brains, the channels running red
While men and women, old and young, lay dead or dying there
And shrieks and groans and muskets' clang rang on the startled air.

An inquest then was ordered and witnesses came there
Who proved to all the peelers done at Castlepollard Fair
These murderers then were sent to jail, a happy sight to see
But a sham trial was brought on, which quickly set them free.

May fiery red and burning Hell its torments now prepare
And vengeance black as night and death o'ertake them while they're there
And may the chief of devils take their chieftain in his care
And every imp his man possess that fired a musket there.[59]

APPENDIX

The following satirical piece relating to the picking of the jury for the
Castlepollard Trial was found by Micéal Conlon in the archives of Westmeath
County Library. Contemporary with the events, its origin is unknown.

The Secrets of the Sheriff's House

It is right to state, that the following memoranda was picked up near
Rochfortbridge – it fell from the pocket of the Reporter to the Secret Service
Committee, who was sent specially down for certain State reasons.

Scene – A room in Gallston House – the furniture of which reminds one of
Swift's

59 *Dublin Evening Mail*, 8 August 1831.

Oaken, broken, elbow chair,
A caudle cup, without an ear,
A shattered, battered ash bedstead,
A box of deal, without a lid, etc, etc.

The remainder of the old trumpery having been removed to London, for his wife's accommodation, by its very uxorious owner.

The Hon. Mr. Browne, High Sheriff, reading the *Evening Mail*, when he is interrupted by the entrance of the Sub Sheriff, Mr. Cuffe, Colonel Osborne, and Captain Thomson, Pay Clerk to the Constabulary.

Mr. Browne – I received your letter, Colonel, respecting the Jury to try those Police, who slew the men and women in Castlepollard.

Colonel – Oh! It is most important to have a Jury of *our own sort* to try those loyal poor fellows, who done their duty so nobly.

Mr. Browne – I am a soldier and am unacquainted with those matters. I would not be a party to such a transaction as that of packing a Jury – but my Brother has insisted on it, and I must comply.

Captain Thomson – Mr. Cuffe will inform you, that there is nothing more easy or more common, in *this county* particularly; at each Assizes I have had a Policeman or two to defend, and I have managed it with *Mr. Cuffe*, to have twelve men of the sort now much wanted, to acquit my Papist slayers, and I have always, on my solemn oath -*(laughing)* – given the men excellent characters, for sobriety, morality, peaceable and passive dispositions. I have sworn – (*again laughing*) – they were the most mild and merciful men living.

Mr. Cuffe – I have brought a list of Jurors, of the *right sort*, out of which it matters not what twelve are taken, they will be sure to acquit the prisoners.

Mr. Browne – Then read the names, Mr. Cuffe, if you please.

Mr. Cuffe reads –

Sir Richard Levine, Baronet.

Colonel – True blue – approved.

James Gibbons, Junior.

Colonel – strike him off, he is too fond of praying.

John Charles Lyons.

Thomson – he won't do – he is both sides of a gutter gentleman – I know his heart is with us, but being a pretended Liberal, I reject him.

Joseph Morgan Daly.

Colonel – Right!

Francis Pratt Smyth.

Colonel – Capital!

Thomas Fane Uniake.

Colonel – After my own heart.

William Robinson.

Thomson – His heart is black, but he is too thick headed – I should like a better.

Percy Fitzgerald Nugent.

Mr. Browne – Is he not a Papist?

Colonel – No matter – he may be a Papist in Chapel, but he is a staunch Protestant in Court – put him on – he is the second best we got yet.

Thomson – He is with us – though apprised of the circumstances, he never came to Castlepollard until the last day of the Inquest – *My Cousin of Buckingham to wit*.

Henry Tiger Smith.

Colonel – The fellow has something of a conscience – strike him off!

Bull and Mouth Smith.

Colonel – He is courting popularity – he won't do.

William Dutton Pollard.

Colonel – Damn the fellow, he is too obstinate, and means too well.

Thomson – He was too impartial during the Inquest.

Hugh Morgan Tuite.

Colonel – G- damn you, Cuffe, do you want to hang them all!

William Meares Kelly.

Colonel – Any money for twelve of his sort.

Cuthbert Fetherston, Mosstown.

Colonel – Equivocal!

William Fetherston, Carrick.

Colonel – Devil blow the better!

Henry Daniel.

Colonel – His name is a host.

Fitzherbert Batty.

Colonel – A mere ninny – I should like a better.

Richard Hugh Levinge.

Thomson – He will do, if he thinks our side the strongest.

Colonel – Tell him he shall get the contract for supplying the gaol with potatoes and meal, and you may depend your life on him.

Tennison Lyons.

Thomson – It all depends on the humour he is in, he has disappointed me often.

William Reilly.

Colonel – Treasurer to the Brunswick Club – I'll answer for him.

James Langstaff.

Colonel – Don't know the fellow.

Thomson – I do well – Blake wishes of all men to have him on.

Edward Briscoe and his brother William Briscoe.

Colonel – Now, by St Paul, all goes bravely on.

Cuffe – I think, Gentlemen, you may leave the rest to Thomson, the Crown Solicitor, and myself. I will add some more ultra strong Protestants to the Panel, and conclude with a few of what are called Orange Papists, who are as good as the best of them.

The party were retiring – the High Sheriff to fish for the remainder of the week, day and night, with his Brother, the indefatigable Sporting Parson, and the Colonel and county to finish what they so nobly begun – when in walks the Coroner himself, head and pluck, who upon being upbraided by Thomson, for not attending, vociferated, '*I done my bit in Castlepollard, and though I did, I am ready to do more.*'

Thomson – Just what we all knew you would do, Hugh, my boy.

Changing images of Donnybrook fair

SÉAMAS Ó MAITIÚ

INTRODUCTION: THE USE OF VISUAL SOURCES

It is only recently that visual sources have been used as tools to investigate and to interpret Irish history.[1] While images are as valuable a source as text for the historian, they have suffered from particular neglect. The reasons for this are many, the main one being the claim that not enough visual material exists. Kevin O'Neill points out that this is only partly true. He argues that although the Renaissance and its artistic legacy largely bypassed Ireland a substantial amount of material nevertheless exists which has been largely ignored.[2]

A notable example of the use of visual material can be seen in the close study made by W.H. Crawford of a large painting by Joseph Peacock entitled *The patron, or festival of St. Kevin at the Seven Churches, Glendalough, county Wicklow 1813*, which is in the Ulster Museum.[3] Having made a study of Donnybrook Fair and being aware of at least a dozen visual representations of the event, the present author was prompted by Crawford's work to make a closer scrutiny of them.[4]

More than twenty depictions of Donnybrook Fair have been identified (see appendix). This makes the fair one of the most popular Irish gatherings depicted in art. This is not surprising, as Donnybrook was the best known Irish fair. Its proximity to Dublin together with the fact that it was held in late August, a popular time for tours of Ireland, meant that it was much visited by tourists to the capital.

DONNYBROOK FAIR

Donnybrook Fair was established by patent of King John in 1204. It was held at various times of the year until 26 August was finally established as the date of its commencement. It became the chief carnival of the citizens of Dublin and was

1 Brian P. Kennedy and Raymond Gillespie (eds), *Ireland: art into history* (Dublin, 1994) and Adele M. Dalsimer (ed.), *Visualising Ireland: national identity and the pictorial tradition* (Boston, 1993) are two works that break much new ground in this regard.   2 Kevin O'Neill, 'Art and artfulness in colonial Ireland' in Adele M. Dalsimer (ed.), *Visualising Ireland*, p. 55.   3 W.H. Crawford, 'The patron or festival of St Kevin at the Seven Churches, Glendalough, county Wicklow 1813' in *Ulster Folklife*, vol. 32 (1989), pp. 37–47. 4 Séamas Ó Maitiú, *The humours of Donnybrook: Dublin's famous fair and its suppression* (Dublin, 1995).

a byword for revelry and riotous behaviour.[5] The fair was held on the green adjacent to the ancient graveyard of Donnybrook. Numerous attempts were made to suppress it and newspapers called for its demise year after year. Serious efforts were made by the city's lord mayor in 1819 and 1824 to curtail or suppress the fair as a result of pressure from respectable petitioners. While this curbed its excesses for a while, the annual debauchery was soon restored. In 1837, Lord Mayor William Hodges restricted the fair to one week, excluding the Sabbath. The reformers failed to suppress the fair entirely, as the local Madden family then held the fair's royal charter which could not be interfered with.

However, the spread of temperance and evangelicalism married to rising middle-class respectability and the creation of a centralized police force boded ill for the annual festivities. The spread of middle-class housing to the environs of the fair brought matters to a head in the 1850s. Spearheaded by the local Roman Catholic clergy, a campaign was started to purchase the patent from an elderly member of the Madden family to whom it had passed. This was accomplished in 1855 and the fair was allowed to lapse.

EARLY ILLUSTRATIONS

The wealth of detail found in Peacock's portrayal of the 'patron' or pattern of Glendalough is largely missing from the depictions of Donnybrook. Nevertheless, much valuable information regarding the material culture of those who frequented the fair can be gleaned from them. The earliest representations of the fair are by Francis Wheatley (1747–1801). The son of a London tailor, Wheatley first visited Ireland in 1767. His second visit began in 1779 and lasted for four years. He had come to Ireland to escape his creditors and so was under some pressure to produce work which would earn him money. This need was to start Wheatley on a very productive period in his career. He was a versatile artist, willing to turn his hand to any medium. Portrait painting and large-group painting eventually proved a moderate earner and gave rise to such well-known paintings as *A view of College Green with a meeting of the Volunteers* and various portraits of members of the Irish House of Commons.[6]

However, Wheatley did not sell these works as readily as he expected and quickly turned to picturesque Irish scenes in ink and water-colour. Being based in Dublin, he found a colourful subject matter in the annual fairs held in the vicinity of the city, especially at Palmerstown and Donnybrook. Wheatley's biographer, Mary Webster, sees the influence of Wouvrmans in the figures depicted in these works, in which she believes Wheatley succeeded in delineating the character of the Irish peasantry. Wheatley found a strong market for these rustic

---

5 For a full account of the fair and its suppression see Ó Maitiú, *Humours of Donnybrook*.
6 James Kelly, 'Francis Wheatley: his Irish paintings 1778–83' in Dalsimer, *Visualising Ireland*; Patricia A. Butler, *Three hundred years of Irish watercolours* (London, 1997), p. 62.

Figure 1 Buying ale at Donnybrook Fair, near Dublin, 1782.
Francis Wheatley, ink and watercolour (National Gallery of Ireland).

scenes and disposed of them as soon as they were completed. His biographer suggested that he could have become wealthy as a result of this work but that his expensive tastes caused him to fall into debt again and he was forced to flee back to London.[7]

However, these works were so lucrative that Wheatley continued to create them from notes and sketches long after he had returned to England. As a result it is sometimes difficult to say whether Palmerstown or Donnybrook fair is depicted.[8] The two fairs were often linked as they fell on successive weeks. Palmerstown fair was held on 21 August and Donnybrook on 26 August and many of the pleasure-seekers of Dublin attended both fairs. In addition many of the traders who had set up on Palmerstown Fair Green struck tents and immediately headed for Donnybrook.

Wheatley's watercolours of Donnybrook Fair depict an uncrowded peaceful scene of people gathered around the tents. People are at rest and there is a distinct lack of the frenzy and excitement shown in later illustrations of the fair. The scenes are completely devoid of the stage Irishman element so prominent

7 James Gandon and Thomas Mulvany, *The life of James Gandon* (Dublin, 1846), p. 208.
8 Mary Webster, *Francis Wheatley* (London, 1970), p. 48.

in later pictures. They therefore can be regarded as more realistic than the later depictions.

The figures shown are engaged in leisurely activity. They are usually conversing, perhaps engaged in some business transaction. The tents depicted seem to be ale tents and in one picture a lady is drawing ale from a barrel for a man on horseback. Outside another, a table has been set up, complete with incongruous table-cloth, and a drink is being poured from a pitcher (Figure 1). These tents are quite primitive and unlike the elaborate pavilions set up by Dublin publicans at the fair in later years.

The later scenes of frantic indulgence, singing and dancing are missing, nor is there the bustle of buying and selling found in Peacock's portrayal of Glendalough. The pictures portray a rural idyll rather than the hustle and bustle usually associated with an Irish fair. Figures are stretched out asleep and in one a couple are love-making on the banks of the Dodder. The scenes are so unlike the later depictions of the fair that one has been misnamed *A gypsy encampment*. However, it is clearly part of the Donnybrook/Palmerstown Fair series, and an ale-sign surmounting a tent clearly marks it out as more than just an encampment.

The clothes of the individuals depicted are worth noting. In Figure 1, two of the women, in particular the one on the cart, are dressed in large cloaks. Numerous references to the fair at the end of the eighteenth century mention women in cloaks. Crimson cloaks seem to have been the commonest worn at this time. It was stated in 1799 that females 'of the red cloke tribe' had gone to Donnybrook with children in their arms and had 'drunk deep' at the fair. They were then unable to carry their children home and 'transferred the labour of child-bearing' to their husbands.[9] A report from the following year states that a group of women, described as 'Oonahs', returning tipsy from the fair at night were attacked like the Sabine women by ruffians who lay in wait for them and robbed them of their crimson cloaks.[10]

In Wheatley's picture all men wear hats. In the days before the mass-production of clothing items of attire were scarce and expensive and in the hurly-burly of the fair were often the target of thieves. Hats, universally worn by men, were a particular favourite, due to the ease with which they could be removed.

Primitive tents are the only structures found in the paintings of Wheatley. The tents, so common at Irish fairs, were described by Sir Jonah Barrington in his piece 'Receipt for a Donnybrook tent'. Barrington was an avid promoter of the stage-Irishman and he describes the erection of these tents with humour and exaggeration:

> Take eight or ten long wattles, or any indefinite number, according to the length you wish your tent to be (whether two yards or half a mile makes no difference as regards the architecture or construction). Wattles need not

9 *Freeman's Journal* (hereafter cited as *FJ*), 27 Aug. 1799.   **10** *FJ*, 26 Aug. 1800.

be provided by purchase or sale, but may be readily procured any dark night by cutting down a sufficient number of young trees in the demesne or plantation of any gentleman in the neighbourhood – a prescriptive privilege, or rather practice, time immemorial, throughout Ireland.

Having procured the said wattles one way or other, it is only necessary to stick them down in the sod in two rows, turning round the tops like a woodbine arbour in a lady's flower-garden, tying the two ends together with neat ropes of hay, which any gentleman's farmyard can (during the night-time, as afore-said) readily supply, – then fastening long wattles in like manner lengthways at top from end to the other to keep all tight together; and thus the 'wooden halls' of Donnybrook are ready for roofing in; and as the building materials cost nothing but danger, the expense is very trivial.[11]

Sir Jonah explains that a tent fifty feet long can be erected in this manner in about five minutes.

In a Wheatley water-colour entitled *Palmerstown Fair* the striped markings on the tent covering suggest that it was in fact made from a blanket.[12] Such an improvization is also alluded to by Barrington:

Every cabin, alehouse, and other habitation wherein quilts or bedclothes were used, or could be procured by civility or otherwise (except money, which was not current for such purposes), was ransacked for apparel wherewith to cover the wattles. The favourite covering was quilts, as long as they were forthcoming; and when not, old winnowing sheets, sacks ripped open, rugs, blankets, etc. etc. Everything, in fact was expended in the bed line (few neighbours using that accommodation during the fair – and recourse often had to women's apparel, as old petticoats, praskeens, etc. etc.[13]

He goes on to describe the quilts, which comprised scraps of all hues in the rainbow, cut into every shape and size, patched on each other and quilted together. He describes the signs and symbols surmounting the tents thus:

The covering being spread over the wattles as tightly and snugly as the materials would admit, all was secured by hay-ropes and pegs. When completed, a very tall wattle with a dirty birch-broom, the hairy end of an old sweeping-brush, a cast-off lantern of some watchman, rags of all colours made into streamers, and fixed at the top by way of sign, formed the invitation to drinking; – and when eating was likewise to be had, a rusty tin saucepan, or piece of a broken iron pot, was hung dangling in front, to crown the entrance and announce good cheer.[14]

11 Sir Jonah Barrington, *Personal sketches of his own times* (third edition, London, 1869), vol. ii, p. 329.   12 Webster, *Wheatley*, illustration., p. 49.   13 Barrington, *Sketches*, p. 330.
14 Ibid.

The symbols erected over the tents have been alluded to elsewhere.[15] The object hanging over the ale tent in Wheatley's picture is noteworthy. A similar object was also depicted by Peacock at Glendalough, which Crawford describes as a harrow. The use of such symbolism in a largely illiterate society is difficult for us to interpret. The check pattern of the harrow may hold a clue to its origin. The name 'Chequers' was a common name for inns in England and was advertised by a sign of a chequered board. In the 1920s there were at least two hundred and seventy such inns in England.[16] Flags are prominently displayed in pictures of Donnybrook, including a British Jack in a print published in the *Gentleman's & London Magazine* in September 1790.

This print (Figure 2), entitled *Donnybrook Fair* is a parody of Hogarth's *Southwark Fair*. While Wheatley uses the fair to portray a rural idyll very much in vogue in the art market of the day the object of this print is parody. The Irish work is anonymous and is inscribed 'Pat Hogarth Jun[ior]'. A comparison between Hogarth's print and its parody is instructive. Both artists revel in the confusion and chaos resulting from the pursuit of pleasure by all types and classes in a confined space, but the Irish scene is noticeably more chaotic and wild than the English.

Southwark Fair takes place in what is clearly an urban or semi-urban setting. The fair is held in the precincts of the church. Indeed rope walkers have their rope attached to the church tower, and there are many other buildings close by. The site of Donnybrook Fair appears to be entirely rural. Any manifestation of the built environment, such as churches or houses, is absent.

While Hogarth no doubt intended to portray the anarchic nature of such an event, in fact the overall impression of the English fair is one of organization. A great deal of preparation and logistical control is evident. The various entertainers and sellers are the product of a highly structured and complex society. Despite the complete contrast of setting between the urban Southwark and the rural Glendalough, they are alike in that in both a bewildering variety of objects are present. The objects on display in Glendalough are commodities for sale. The remote setting of Glendalough meant that the pattern fulfilled the function of the distribution of goods, not readily available to a mountainous people. On the other hand the items on display in Southwark are largely objects associated with organized leisure; prominently displayed are musicians, puppeteers, a peep-show, slack-rope walkers and numerous showmen with elaborate sets. Donnybrook Fair falls between two stools. It had by 1790 become a largely pleasure fair, so there are not many goods of a utilitarian nature for sale, most frequently mentioned are toys for children. However organized leisure has not reached it yet. This would come later.

In the representation of Donnybrook Fair, the scene, echoing Barrington, is one of tawdriness and utter chaos. Everything is make-shift – instead of the

15 Ó Maitiú, *Humours of Donnybrook*, pp. 17–19. **16** G.J. Monson-Fitzjohn, *Quaint signs of olde inns* (London, 1994), p. 45.

Figure 2 Donnybrook Fair (Gentleman's & London Magazine, Sept. 1790).
This is an Irish parody of Hogarth's *Southwark Fair.*

English wooden booths we have the familiar tents of rags. No attempt appears to have been made to allocate space to the different activities. Even traffic on the fair green was not controlled. The scene of turmoil and tumult was no exaggeration. In 1822, the poet Charles O'Flaherty records that a gentleman's foot ended up a pot of broth. He had, unwittingly, wandered to the rear of the tents and was lost in a labyrinth of kitchens. In his endeavour to extradite himself, he put his foot into one of these pots and was 'ballyragged and near mauled by a cooking wench'.[17] The whole area of the fair green and village was thronged for the week of the fair and this, combined with the narrowness of the village's main street, posed a danger to life and limb.

The vast crowd attending the fair was regularly reported in the Dublin press. In 1823, the correspondent from *The Warder,* having reached the entrance to the village, found various obstacles blocking his path and had to wait half an hour before any progress could be made. He somewhat dramatically claimed that he found himself jammed in a crowd of 'screaming infants, shouting females and dying steeds', the whole tangle presenting a perfect opportunity for a gang of pickpockets to ply its trade.[18] In 1833, his colleague from *Paddy Kelly's Budget,* a

17 Charles O'Flaherty, *Retrospection* (Dublin, 1824), pp. 83–4.   18 *The Warder,* 30 Aug. 1823.

humorous journal, found himself stopped at the entrance to the village by a look of 'thus far and no farther' on the faces of three horse policemen with drawn sabres opposite Carrigan's Rose Tavern. At length, by dint of kicking shins, elbowing ribs, and swearing like troopers, his party rounded a corner of the crooked main street and beheld the glorious, glittering scene of the fair green.[19] In 1841, John and Peter Madden, the owners of the patent to the fair, made a 'scientific calculation' of those entering the fair green on one day, the twenty-sixth of August, and it amounted to 74,792.[20] At this period the population of Dublin was about a quarter of a million.

The newspapers of the day revelled in descriptions of the modes of transport pressed into service to bring the huge crowds to the fair. An account of the road to Donnybrook on 'Walking Sunday' 1804 – the Sunday preceding 26 August, the designated fair day – provides a catalogue of vehicles employed:

> At an early hour in the morning, and during the entire day, the road from Dublin presented as motley a cavalcade as on any former or similar occasion. Coaches, chariots, landaus, jingles, gigs, cars of all kinds, barouches, curricles, noddies, hunting carts, dirt carts, drays, horses, colts, geldings, mules and asses followed in such rapid succession, that the pedestrians had hardly a space left to them.[21]

The jingle resembled a coach with the doors, upper sides and door removed and held six persons sitting face to face. It was a very high vehicle, held aloft on four large wheels and made a jingling sound while in motion, hence the name. The noddy, a Dublin favourite, was hardly more elegant. It was a low-roofed vehicle with high shafts which nodded as it went along. The driver sat so that 'the rump of his horse is at his mouth, and his rump at the mouth of the person in the chaise'. It was mainly the lower orders that nodded along in this strange vehicle: a contemporary proverb alluded to 'elegance and ease, like a shoeblack in a noddy'.[22]

A report of the fair in 1815 lists more eccentric vehicles. They included a coach drawn by four blood horses, a seat in a dustman's barouche, a sweep's tandem, a coalporter's landaulet, a Custom House cabriolet and a green-grocer's gig. A number of ladies rode out on a convoy of 'Jerusalem ponies'.[23]

The drawings of Wheatley depict a very ancient-looking cart or dray and the parody of Hogarth from the *Gentlemen's and London Magazine* shows a very elegant carriage moving through the fair green. This carriage has its counterpart in a landau drawn by four brown horses taking five well-dressed ladies to the Glendalough pattern. Numerous members of the gentry visited Donnybrook, many of them not alighting but observing the scene from the safety of their carriages. It is also noticeable both from Peacock's depiction of Glendalough and

19 *Paddy Kelly's Budget*, 4 Sept. 1833.   **20** *Saunder's Newsletter* (hereafter cited as SN), 27 Aug. 1841.   **21** *The Star*, 3 Sept. 1804.   **22** Kevin B. Nowlan (ed.), *Travel and transport in Ireland* (Dublin, 1993), pp. 51–2.   **23** *SN*, 28 Aug. 1815.

Wheatley's depiction of Donnybrook that many people did not dismount but had conversations on horseback.

In stark contrast to the quiet scenes of Wheatley, a picture by William Sadler, painted before 1788 (the artist died in that year), portrays a type of scene more typical of the common perceptions of the fair. The fair is viewed from afar but the whole panorama is one of a battle-field with what amounts to a forest of shillelaghs raised everywhere.

LATER DEPICTIONS

A gap of about three decades separates the Wheatley group of pictures from the next extant illustrations of the fair. In 1831, in honour of his appointment as the first lord lieutenant of the king's reign, the marquis of Anglesey presented to King William IV a bog oak tankard mounted in silver and elaborately carved after a design by Edward Lorenzo Percy of a view of Donnybrook Fair.[24] This tankard has not been traced so it is not known what its depiction of the fair was like, but the fact that a scene from Donnybrook Fair was chosen is indicative of the fact that it had come to represent the colour and vivaciousness of Irish life.

Two prints exist dating from 1830 and they depict a very different scene from that portrayed by Wheatley. One is by George Victor Du Noyer and the other by William Sadler. Du Noyer (1817–69) was born in Dublin, was a pupil of George Petrie, and worked as his assistant. He was employed in the Ordnance Survey of Ireland and for many years in the Geological Survey of Ireland. A number of his sketchbooks, which are full of interesting scenes of everyday life, are kept in the Royal Irish Academy. The print of Donnybrook Fair attributed to him (not reproduced here but found in Ó Maitiú, *The Humours of Donnybrook*) was made about 1880 from a drawing made by him 'on the spot' in 1830. This is his earliest dated work. If the dates are correct, the artist was only thirteen years old when he executed the drawing, a display of remarkable precociousness.[25]

In this lively picture we see for the first time the presence of menageries and theatre booths on the fair green. The arrival at Donnybrook of these organized shows from England has been pinpointed to the second decade of the nineteenth century.[26]

Huge pictures of the wild animals to be seen inside were painted on cloth and attached to the sides of wagons.[27] These visual enticements, together with the calls of showmen or the blare of musicians, were calculated to draw a crowd. An eye-witness, calling himself 'A stroller over Donnybrook Green', reminiscing

24 W. J. Lawrence 'The Story of Donnybrook Fair' in *The Lady of the House* (Christmas 1915), p. 26.   25 Adrian le Harival, 'Du Noyer the artist and antiquarian' in Fionnuala Croke (ed.), *George Victor Du Noyer, 1817–1869: hidden landscapes* (Dublin, 1995), p. 30. 26 Ó Maitiú, *Humours of Donnybrook*, p. 22.   27 This print is reproduced on the cover of Ó Maitiú, *Humours of Donnybrook*.

on the fair after its suppression, remembered these canvasses in particular – fierce lions and tigers, a diabolical-looking boa-constrictor and a tropical forest complete with 'Ourang Outang' and parrots. The reality inside was very different however:

> Mangy-looking, overgrown, tawny, and striped or brown cats, lying on their dirty boards, winked at us with their wicked eyes. Monkeys, whom not to see we should at any time gladly pay a trifling bribe, chattered for the visitors offerings and quarrelled among each other with as much spite and as much respect for themselves as individuals of the human race. The horrible-looking alligator springing at an Indian maid to devour her, body and sleeves, dwindled to an ugly drab-coloured lizard four feet long, and the boa-constrictor reposed at its ease in a folded blanket about the size of a two-year old eel.[28]

Polito's and Wombwell's menageries were frequent visitors to Donnybrook. Polito's was the most famous menagerie of its day in England. It started in 1758 and held sway until George Wombwell began his in 1805. It is a tribute to the importance of Donnybrook Fair that these great cumbersome shows added it to their itineraries and were prepared to undertake the hazardous sea journey to get there. Indeed Donnybrook proved to be a contributing factor to the decline of Polito's. In either 1835 or 1836 they lost almost their entire show in a shipwreck while crossing over to Ireland.

From the 1820s, Wombwell's menagerie was one of the most frequent of all the English shows to visit Donnybrook. George Wombwell first toured the English provinces with his large collection of wild beasts in 1807. As a young man he had collected wild animals from ships returning from the tropics arriving at London port. A well-known verse where the name of the local fair could be inserted in the last line ran as follows:

> Wombwell's wild beasts is come again
> Where works of nature's art are seen
> Lions, tigers, panthers, apes and bears
> Are all to be seen at Donnybrook Fair

On the left-hand side of Du Noyer's print is what appears to be a bewildered-looking countryman being consoled by a more knowing-looking individual, who could very well be in league with the woman who appears to be in charge of the gambling table. Countrymen, easily recognisable by their large frieze coats, were frequently recorded at the fair.

Apart from over-indulgence in the native and consorting with ladies of ill-repute, gambling was a common pastime engaged in at the fair. Well-known

28 *Dublin University Magazine*, Oct. 1861.

Figure 3 Donnybrook Fair, 1830. Drawing by William Sadler.

fairground tricks were to be found, such as the trick o' the loop, the three card trick, the thimble-rig and the wheel of fortune. Much of this activity was illegal. Apart from the relatively harmless gambling on the fair green, some more organized gangs hired houses in the vicinity of the fair and installed roulette tables. Touts were sent to the fair green and young men were enticed into these haunts. These houses were often raided by the police. Indeed, attempts to organize more serious gaming on the green itself often received the attention of the law. In 1842, a Simon Flaherty was arrested for organising an illegal lottery. He had erected a large sheet of paper on which were marked blanks and prizes, the outcome to be decided by the throw of a dice.[29]

A transformed fair can also be seen in Sadler's print (Figure 3). The British Jack of the 1790 depiction has been replaced by a flag bearing a harp and the inscription 'Erin go Bra' on one tent and the stars and stripes on another. A mounted member of the Dublin Metropolitan Police, identified by the force's initials, with sabre raised, can be seen wading into the crowd. Standing nearby and clearly enjoying the scene is a less diligent member of the force on foot. The police were a regular feature of the fair, usually called out by the lord mayor to strike the tents after the revelry had been deemed to have gone on long enough.

29 *SN*, 22 Aug. 1842.

The Dublin Metropolitan Police was re-organized in 1838. John Flint, a disgruntled ex-inspector of the old force, gives us an insight into the way the new police dealt with the fair in the first year of its operations. Flint states that the provisions of the act of the 2nd and 3rd of Victoria were strictly carried out in relation to tents but that they were suspended in relation to public houses in the vicinity. The tents were thus closed at six in the evening and a police sentinel placed at the entrance to the fair green. The effect of this arrangement was to drive the crowd from the tents to the 'foetid atmosphere of the public house, where time and opportunity was afforded them to get drunk in order that they might be taken into custody afterwards'.[30]

Flint was very suspicious as to the motives for this move. He states that he does not know why it was done but that at the conclusion of the fair that year a snuff box and a dinner were given by the publicans of the village to the police superintendent who made the arrangements. These arrangements, he claimed, only increased drunkenness and disorder. When the public houses were finally cleared, police, on horse and foot, with truncheons drawn, formed a line across the fair green and any individual capable of it was driven out of the village, while those that were not were dealt with otherwise.[31]

Sadler depicts what is meant to be an academic, who in 1830 would only have been from Trinity College, enjoying the robust activities of the fair. While the student body generally would not have been in college during fair week the presence of graduates and undergraduates from the college were often noted at the fair. In 1840, the *Irish Penny Journal* regaled its readers with a tale of three 'academic larkers', whom they called Dan Sweeny, Bob O'Gorman and Dick Hall, who together with a number of undergraduates went to the fair for a spree. They devised a ruse which involved dressing Dick (who although small and effeminate-looking was very strong), in female attire and anticipating the consequences which would ensue for any male who would dare molest the 'young lady'. The plan did not work out, however, and the three academics had to flee from a tent crying 'Trinity, Trinity' to seek help from the undergraduates scattered around the fair green. The adventure finished with a scrimmage between representatives of 'town and gown'.[32]

As the day wore on and night fell, song and dance took pride of place in the tents. The interior of two tents can be glimpsed in the anonymous print of 1830. In the tent on the left the revellers are seated at a bench and table, while the Shamrock Pavilion is adorned with a double-ringed candelabra hanging in the middle of the tent. Sir Jonah Barrington describes as follows the rather more primitive furniture of the tents he saw:

> As to furniture, down the centre, doors, old or new (whichever were most handy to be lifted), were stretched from one end to the other, resting on

30 John Flint, *The Dublin police and the police system* (Dublin, 1847), p. 43.   31 Ibid.
32 *Irish Penny Journal*, 22 Aug. 1840, 1833.

hillocks of clay dug from underneath, and so forming capital tables with an agreeable variety both as to breadth and elevation. Similar constructions for benches were placed along the sides, but not so steady as the table; so that when the liquor got the mastery of one convivial fellow, he would fall off ... [33]

As the convivial jug went round, the mirth of those drinking in tent and booth was most often expressed in song. In 1802, fiddlers were reported to be 'in great practice', and in almost every tent was to be heard 'the scraping of catgut and to be seen a Darby and Juggy footing it away in the highest warmth of pure love'.[34] Popular dances of the period are referred to in the reports. In the first quarter of the nineteenth century, it was said that quadrilles were universally popular, and that Irish women, to their honour, were rejecting the waltz. In 1820, it was reported that the 'enlivening planxty' was to be heard from every tent.[35]

Prospective dancers often paid a set price to a musician to play for them. A board, usually a door removed from its hinges for the week, was laid down at the lower end of each tent on which those who wished to foot it out could show their steps. At the end of the fair, when 'de boords' or 'the flure' were deserted, a balladeer reminisced:

> Could you see the now deserted 'flure',
> With indignation would your bosoms burn:
> No more we 'welt it' on the prostrate door;
> 'Pay for the boords', no more the fiddler cries;
> 'Rouse it your soul', no more poor Pat replies.

In 1845, the price of a dance was three pence. A young man named James McGrath, together with a young girl friend and another young man, approached a bald-headed fiddler named Owen Murphy and engaged him to play for them. When the dance was over, McGrath gave Murphy a six penny piece and asked for three pence change. The fiddler refused and held on to the sixpence. McGrath warned that he would smash the fiddle if he did not get his money. What happened next led to them contradicting each other in court. Murphy said that McGrath took the fiddle from him and smashed it across his knee. McGrath claimed that Murphy himself smashed the instrument.[36]

While dancers battered away on 'de boords', ballad singers could be heard wheezing out their ditties, mournful or merry, all over the fair green. The beggar on the extreme left of Du Noyer's picture appears to be a ballad singer. It was reported, however, in 1830 that such performers had a bad time of it. They grew hoarse despite all the mollifying powers of the 'mountain dew' and might as well have lit their pipes with their broadsheets for all the money they made from them. One had a new verse for an old song:

33 Barrington, *Sketches*, pp. 330–1.   34 *FJ*, 28 Aug. 1802.   35 *SN*, 30 August, 1820.
36 *SN*, 1 Sept. 1845.

Figure 4 Donnybrook Fair. Painting by Erskine Nicol, a Scotsman who
lived in Dublin from 1845 to 1849 (Tate Gallery, London).

Bryan O'Lynn had no watch to put on
So he scooped out a turnip to make him a one
He next put a cricket clean under the skin
Oh! they'll think its a-ticking, says Brian O'Lynn.[37]

The culmination of all these illustrations of the later fair is a large painting by
Erskine Nicol in the Tate Gallery in London (Figure 4). Nicol was a Scotsman
who visited Ireland between 1845 and 1849. His painting shows the commer-
cialized fair in all its glory. In the foreground, the now well-dressed figures are
engaged in similar pursuits to those in Wheatley's pictures, but the background
could not be more dissimilar. Elaborate show booths and showmen's caravans are
arranged in order, including the imposing Bell's American Circus, and at the
other side swinging boats and other amusements entertain the younger folk. The
utter chaos of 1790 is missing. Despite the vast throng the fair seems regulated
and peaceful.

Finally, the demise of the fair coincided with the development of photography. Tantalizingly, photographs were taken of the last legally constituted fair
in 1854. These were advertised in the Dublin newspapers but, unfortunately,
none of them survives. James Robinson made the announcement thus:

37 *SN*, 27 Aug. 1830.

Photographs of Donnybrook Fair! – James Robinson begs to announce that on yesterday morning he succeeded in taking eight beautiful photographs of this celebrated annual scene of amusement and fun, some of them taken instantaneously, and measuring 17 inches long by 12 broad. Impressions will be printed this day, and on sale at moderate prices ... 65 Grafton Street Dublin.[38]

While the numerous paintings and prints of the fair were undoubtedly subject to artistic licence, one might expect that a truer picture of the fair was available through the eye of the camera. However, one must still be careful. *A carte de visite*, a smaller forerunner of the postcard, was in circulation claiming to represent the fair.[39] It depicts a basket woman being arrested by a member of the Dublin Metropolitan Police on the fair green. However, even a cursory examination will show that the scene is a mock-up, concocted in a photographer's studio.

APPENDIX

KNOWN DEPICTIONS OF DONNYBROOK FAIR

(A number of works have been identified with the help of Walter George Strickland, *A dictionary of Irish artists*, 2 vols, Dublin, 1969 edition).

1782   Francis Wheatley, *Buying Ale at Donnybrook Fair*, ink and water-colour (National Gallery of Ireland, 3027)

1782   Francis Wheatley, *Bargaining at Donnybrook Fair, near Dublin*, ink and water-colour (National Gallery of Ireland, 3028)

1783   Francis Wheatley, '*Outside the Ale Tent at Donnybrook Fair*, ink and water-colour (National Gallery of Ireland, 2700) n.d. William Sadler (died 1788), *Donnybrook Fair*

1790   'Donnybrook Fair' in *Gentleman's & London Magazine*, Sept. 1790 – parody of Hogarth's *Southwark Fair* (1733)

1811   'Depiction of recruiting scene near Donnybrook Fair' in *Walker's Hibernian Magazine*, Aug. 1811

n.d.   Samuel Lover (1797–1868), *The Couple Beggar at Donnybrook*, reproduced in Ó Maitiú, *Humours of Donnybrook*, p. 27

n.d.   William Brocas, *Donnybrook Fair*, on display in the Department of Joseph Peacock, *Tent at Donnybrook Fair* (Strickland)

1830   William Sadler Junior, *Donnybrook Fair*, lithograph by W. Collins.

1830   drawing by Du Noyer, *c.*1880 (Alla Farrell collection).

38 *SN*, 26 Aug. 1854.   **39** In the private collection of Eddie Chandler, photography historian, Dublin.

1831   Bog oak mounted tankard in silver after a design by Edward Lorenzo
        Percy of a view of Donnybrook Fair
1833   'Donnybrook Fair'in *Dublin Penny Journal*, 16 Nov. 1833 [with many
        similar features to the Du Noyer print above].
1845–9 Erskine Nicol, *Donnybrook Fair*, oil painting (Tate Gallery, London).
1852   'Donnybrook Fair under the new Lord Lieutenant'in *Punch*. n.d. 'The
        Dance at Donnybrook' – from a print by J.M. Wilson (Strickland,
        reproduced in *The Lady of the House*, Christmas, 1915, p. 25.
c.1859 Robert Richard Scanlan, fl. 1826–64, painting *Donnybrook Fair*, exhibited
        1859 (Strickland).
n.d.   Samuel Watson (1818–67), large painting *Donnybrook Fair* (Strickland).
n.d.   Henry MacManus (*c*.1810–78), painting *Donnybrook Fair* (Strickland).
n.d.   Daniel Maclise, *Donnybrook Fair* (seen by the author on sale in Dublin
        antiques market).
c.1853 Print by Thomas Knox after an engraving by John Kirkwood Junior,
        Returning from Donnybrook Fair.

Belgard Castle possesses a carving over a fireplace of an Irish fair, said to be of
Donnybrook Fair by a daughter of Dr Evory Kennedy, the owner of the castle
in the nineteenth century.

The rise and demise of the Dublin cattle market, 1863–1973

LIAM CLARE

ESTABLISHMENT OF NEW CATTLE MARKET[1]

When the Dublin Cattle Market Company was publicly launched in November 1861, it was generally agreed that the city's existing cattle market facilities in Smithfield were thoroughly unsatisfactory. Indeed a royal commission in the 1830s had noted that 'the neglect of the [Smithfield] market by the corporation authorities, has been frequently made a subject of remonstrance, and though occasionally attended to, is still a cause for much complaint'.[2]

In 1664, a new paved market to be called Smithfield was established on Oxmantown Green, the location of Dublin's cattle and produce markets since 1541. Complaints, endemic from its earliest days, had intensified in the 1830s and 1840s. For example, in 1849, the country's land-owners and graziers, meeting at the great Ballinasloe October cattle fair, published 'A few reasons for the establishment of a new cattle market in Dublin in place of Smithfield'. They objected to its inconvenience and to the disgusting sanitary conditions. No improvement resulted, however.[3]

A royal commission to examine the state of fairs and markets in Ireland heard evidence in November 1852 of a closed shop and a salesmasters' monopoly in the so-called 'free market' of Smithfield. Mr Ganly, a new salesmaster, could not get 'one foot of ground' in the market until the lord mayor became involved. Then, having secured a foothold, he started charging half the regular commission. And

1 In addition to staff members of the institutions whose assistance has been acknowledged in the introduction to this book, I wish to thank the many people who assisted me in the preparation of this paper, particularly Mary Clark and Raymond MacCarthy of Dublin Corporation who made documentation available, and Tom Robinson, Theo. Robinson, Tim Gallagher, Larry Lenehan and Christy Geoghegan who met me to provide guidance and to supply information. Maire Kennedy and her staff in the Gilbert library, Mary Guckian in the Institute of Public Administration and Mary Doyle, Librarian, Department of Agriculture all helped me in my research and in addition Ms Doyle arranged for the supplying of the illustrations.   2 *Freeman's Journal* (hereafter cited as *FJ*), 16 November 1861; *Royal. comm. municipal corps., 1835, appendix to first report, the City of Dublin*, p. 219.   3 John T. Gilbert, *Calendar of the Ancient Records of Dublin* (Dublin, 1889), i, p. 441; Grainne Doran 'Smithfield Market – Past and Present' in *Dublin Historical Record*, vol 50, no. 2 (Autumn 1997), pp. 105–8; *Irish Times* (hereafter cited as *IT*), 7 May 1862; *FJ*, 21 March 1862; *IT*, 22 April 1862; *FJ*, 26 June 1862.

farmers seeking to exercise their right to sell directly to consumers, rather than through middlemen, had their animals hunted away by the drovers employed in the market. The city council had secured powers under the Dublin Improvement Act of 1849 to provide and regulate a new cattle market but had never invoked them. The commissioners noted that vested interests and established usage had vitiated the lord mayor's authority to improve matters: 'everyone [is] dissatisfied but no alteration is effected'.[4]

The new proposal envisaged establishing a metropolitan cattle market 'for the sale of cattle, horses, sheep, pigs, hides, skins ...' at Sheriff Street/East Road in the North Wall district, with a large paved and covered area, and a slaughter-house to facilitate the growth of the dead meat trade. The proposal was prepared by G.W. Hemans, a civil engineer, at the request of the duke of Leinster and Richard More O'Ferrall, M.P. for Kildare. The proposed location was influenced by its proximity to the port and to potential links with the rail network. Hemans emphasized the importance of the cross-channel cattle trade, and the vast increase in both export and local consumption since the construction of the railways. He forecast a continuing increase in trade. Smithfield and the new market could compete for available trade. The proposers estimated that 110,000 horned cattle, 230,000 sheep, and 162,000 pigs had reached the city in 1859, mainly for export.[5]

The city council decided to oppose the bill authorizing the new market, on the grounds that it would 'seriously injure' the Smithfield area. They would undertake to enlarge and improve the Smithfield market instead. The lord mayor chaired a protest meeting to condemn the bill and to organise a petition against it.[6] Meanwhile the promoters had employed a Conservative Registration Society canvasser to collect signatures in support of the bill, leading to allegations that the proposal was being made a political and a religious issue.[7]

The project generated great controversy. Two city councillors, Robert O'Brien and Peter Aungier, were cattle salesmasters, and Alderman John Reynolds, the leader of the opposition to the bill, had other cattle trade connections. The bill's supporters in council included Alderman James Martin, whose family owned property in the North Wall area, and Captain Knox, a shareholder in the new company. Knox also owned the *Irish Times* which strongly supported the proposal. It was equally strongly opposed by the *Freeman's Journal*, owned by another councillor, Dr John Gray. Conservatives generally supported the private enterprise approach while liberals and nationalists supported public control. The councillors of Arran Quay Ward, which included Smithfield, opposed the bill; at

---

4 *Royal comm. fairs and markets, mins, 1854–5*, pp. 110–11; Section 80 *et seq.* 12 & 13 Vict. (1849), Cap 97; *Royal comm. fairs and markets, 1852–3*, pp. 29, 31.   **5** *FJ*, 16 November 1861; G.W. Hemans, *Report on a proposed general cattle market for Dublin* (Dublin, 1860). **6** *IT*, 18 December 1861; *Dublin Builder* (hereafter cited as *DB*), 15 December 1861; *IT*, 24 February 1862; *FJ*, 14 March 1862; *FJ*, 15 March 1862; *FJ*, 27 March 1862.   **7** *FJ*, 22 March 1862; *Daily Express*, 21 March 1862; *IT*, 21 March 1862.

least one North Wall councillor supported it. The railway companies initially advocated the proposal strongly, but the important City of Dublin Steam Packet Company opposed it. All were looking after their own interests.[8]

The main arguments in favour of the new location were the conditions at Smithfield, 'a miserable, narrow, dirty and exposed area';[9] an area of only two acres, where tired cattle and footsore sheep were cruelly forced through crowded streets; a market wholly uncovered; an insanitary, unhealthy area; a spot where existing salesmasters monopolized the public market space to the exclusion of producers or other salesmen; a location requiring cattle for export to be driven down the north quays to the docks. In contrast, the new market would be spacious, fifteen to twenty acres in extent, with two acres initially, and five acres ultimately covered. It would be paved, drained and supplied with ample water. There would be free access for both producers and salesmasters from Smithfield, subject to payment of a small fee. Most of the cattle would arrive directly at the market by rail via the Midland Great Western Railway Company's (M.G.W.R.) proposed railhead at the docks, or via the Great Northern Railway, which between them served the most important grazing areas to the west and north of the city. A proposed underground rail link (under the Phoenix Park) would carry stock from the south and south-west. Only the cattle from the south-east would not have convenient access to the new market. The animals, when sold for export, would be close to the embarkation point. Alternatively, they could be slaughtered at the new, clean and convenient abattoir which would compete with the existing objectionable slaughterhouses. The market's quay-side location would attract more English buyers and lead to greater trade.[10]

Those opposing the proposal emphasized the convenience of Smithfield to the city and the potential threat to that area. They also stressed the interference by the promoters with the lord mayor's prerogative to control city markets, and Smithfield's proximity both to the existing railheads and to the local grazing areas, with as a consequence, minimal traffic congestion. The difficulties of driving cattle from Kingsbridge Station down the quays to the North Wall, or the herding of Wicklow-bred animals down Grafton Street and across Carlisle (now O'Connell) Bridge to the new market were emphasized. Opponents also claimed that the new site was damp and unhealthy and, unlike Smithfield, too remote from the grazing lands of Inchicore, Cabra and Glasnevin.[11]

These arguments were first tested before a select committee of the House of Commons. The promoters' witnesses included G.W. Hemans, who had produced the initial proposal, representatives of the railway companies, salesmen who had found Smithfield market unsatisfactory, and a large landowner who was also a

8 Various contemporary newspapers such as *IT*, 9 December 1861; *FJ*, 26 March 1862; *FJ*, 11 April 1862; *IT*, 22 April 1862; *FJ*, 18 June 1862; *FJ*, 26 June 1862; *FJ*, 19 July 1862; *FJ*, 25 November 1863.   **9** Hemans, *Cattle Market*, p. 9.   **10** Hemans, *Cattle Market*; *FJ*, 24 March 1862; *FJ*, 26 June 1862.   **11** *DB*, 1 July 1862; *FJ*, 9 December 1861; *FJ*, 26 March 1862; *FJ*, 4 June 1862; *FJ*, 18 June 1862.

railway company director and a subscriber to the Dublin Cattle Market Company. The corporation in turn produced a variety of witnesses – landowners, graziers, butchers, business interests and Parke Neville, the City Engineer – to put their case. They admitted the shortcomings at Smithfield, blaming their inactivity in tackling them on lack of funds and on their concentration on the new city water supply. They promised a major improvement there, if the bill for the North Wall market was rejected.[12]

The select committee approved the bill, leaving the city fathers in recriminatory mood. Alderman Reynolds, the council's leading witness, criticized the chairman and some members of the select committee for lack of courtesy, saying that they 'did not get fair play' from this 'exclusive English tribunal'.[13] Nevertheless Dr Gray, both at the city council, and through his newspaper, the *Freeman's Journal*, deplored the unfavourable impression given by the corporation's own formal petition, which he said implied ignorance, neglect and incapacity within the corporation with regard to conditions at Smithfield. It had proved the promoters' case. He strongly blamed the law agent who had drawn up the petition (even though the councillors themselves had adopted it). The case would be better presented at the coming House of Lords hearing.[14] Meanwhile, a challenge to the legality of the corporation spending public money on opposing the bill, was rejected by the courts, ending legal threats against individual councillors who would vote to authorise such expenditure.[15]

At the next stage, a hearing before a House of Lords select committee, the corporation sought the appointment of a royal commission to determine the most appropriate site for the market. The move was vehemently criticized as an attempt to by-pass the recent decision of the House of Commons select committee. At the Lords, too, the promoters of the new market criticised the monopoly and the physical conditions in Smithfield, and the alleged obstruction and lack of action by the corporation. In response, the corporation's witnesses stressed the convenience of Smithfield's location on the inland edge of the city for the large number of cattle regularly walked to the market, the absence of any firm proposal to link the Great Southern and Western Railway with the port, and the traffic congestion which would be generated by the proposed location.[16]

A proposal by the corporation to proceed immediately to relocate their own cattle market near Smithfield became public a few days before the House of Lords hearing in June 1862. They had conditionally agreed to take a site from the city coroner, Dr Kirwan, east of Prussia Street, but this move ran into difficulties and was abandoned.[17]

The Lords approved the bill on 28 July 1862, thereby authorizing the construction of the proposed new market, but neither guaranteeing its completion nor putting the old regime out of business. Having lost the parliamentary battle,

---

12 *FJ*, 20 March 1862 to 28 March 1862.   **13** *FJ*, 11 April 1862.   **14** *FJ*, 27 March 1862; *FJ*, 11 April 1862; *FJ*, 16 June 1862.   **15** *FJ*, 11 April 1862; *FJ*, 4 June 1862; *IT*, 2 May 1862.   **16** *FJ*, 18 June 1862 to 30 June 1862.   **17** *FJ*, 21 June 1862; *FJ*, 30 June 1862.

the corporation's alternative initiative was launched in earnest early in July, at a gathering in the home of a Smithfield salesmaster. This was attended by city councillors and 'gentlemen interested in the cattle trade'. The council would use their existing market powers to acquire either Richardson's fields or Jameson's lands near Smithfield. Thirty-nine of those present committed personally the £14,000 required by issuing mortgages, repayable by the corporation after twenty years at 6 per cent interest, to be met from the market tolls alone, without recourse to the rates.[18]

On 11 July, Thomas Richardson offered a site (now O'Devaney Gardens) to the corporation. The army authorities nearby objected, and in addition the title was considered defective. An alternative site, owned partly by Jamesons the distillers and partly by the Martin family, was secured. It had a large house suitable for conversion to a hotel. This site, officially No. 51/54 Prussia Street, bounded by Prussia Street, Aughrim Street and North Circular Road, became the Dublin Cattle Market.[19]

The financial arrangements were criticized as an 'illegal sham' originated by salesmasters and abetted by the corporation. The pledge that the market would not burden the rates ran into legal difficulties, which were eventually overcome by committing the city's general funds in support – thereby technically breaking the pledge – but balancing this by simultaneously securing from the lenders an undertaking to limit their demands for payment to the surplus on the tolls.[20]

The corporation, after years of torpor, was now moving rapidly. A tender was accepted from Mr Michael Meade of Great Brunswick Street, at £17,221. Work commenced in February 1863, and a month later the transformation of the site was manifest, with heaps of earthenware pipes, whinstone paving blocks and chiselled granite base courses scattered around where previously there had been cattle grazing among the elms and ashes of Jameson's fields. By June, a team of forty masons, twenty-four smiths, a number of stone-cutters and 130 labourers were working away, grading down the road level on the North Circular Road by three feet, erecting twelve gates, constructing masonry boundary walls of up to eighteen feet in height, assembling iron railings (which were to be transferred a century later to St Augustine's Park), paving the main roads of the market, laying channels, gratings and sewers, and setting pens in concrete. The former Jameson residence was rapidly being fitted out as a hotel and bar, ensuring that all would be in order for the formal opening on 24 November 1863.[21]

The formalities commenced with a procession of city councillors in their carriages from the Mansion House to the cattle market, which was bedecked

18 *FJ*, 30 June 1862; *FJ*, 3 March 1863; *FJ*, 7 April 1863; *FJ*, 12 July 1862; *DB*, 15 July 1862.   19 *FJ*, 19 July 1862; *FJ*, 18 September 1862; *DB*, 15 September 1863; *Dublin Evening Post* (hereafter cited as *DEP*), 13 June 1863.   20 *IT*, 15 July 1862; *IT*, 22 July 1862; *FJ*, 3 March 1863; *FJ*, 7 April 1863; *FJ*, 8 April 1863; *IT*, 7 April 1863; *IT*, 9 April 1863.   21 *Dublin Post*, 13 June 1863; *DB*, 1 April 1863; *DB*, 1 November 1863; *FJ*, 24 November 1863; *FJ*, 26 November, 1863.

with decorations, flags and banners. A band played the national anthem while the celebrities perambulated the bounds. At the main entrance the lord mayor was handed the key and declared the market open. That evening a banquet was held in the Cattle Market Hotel. Business was transferred from Smithfield to the new market two days later.[22]

Despite the principle of free availability of stands for casual sellers and new salesmasters, the initial allocation of pens caused the market's first public controversy. James Ganly, who had previously experienced difficulty in securing a space in Smithfield and who had later opposed the North Wall location (but was not among the financiers of the new market), objected publicly when the pens were allocated to salesmasters in order of size of their financial contributions. However he later expressed satisfaction with the allocation which he himself eventually received. Disputes over pens were to remain a continuing fact of life in the market.[23]

Meanwhile, having won the parliamentary battle, the Dublin Cattle Market Company was free to proceed with its North Wall proposals. The first meeting of the company, in September 1862, was a fairly upbeat affair, with news of half the capital already being secured and 'great progress' being made on the earthworks. The directors, although noting the corporation's alternative proposals and accepting that the city could not support two cattle markets, still expected their own company to be profitable, due to the backing of the railway companies. Before their next meeting in April 1863, however, the corporation's Prussia Street market was under construction, their own site-filling work had slowed down, and their engineer had recommended a reduction in the size of the scheme 'for the present'. The directors of the M.G.W.R. had recently reneged on an undertaking to support an investment in the new company, because the London and North Western Railway Company had also pulled out. No further progress had been made by the time of the directors' next report in March 1864, due to lack of funds. The corporation market was now open and any chance of the company raising further capital had gone. The company decided to go into liquidation.[24]

Why did the Prussia Street venture succeed while the North Wall project failed? Initially, the supporters of the latter scheme issued brave words about two cattle markets competing side by side. But they were at that time comparing the prospects of the state-of-the-art North Wall project and the obsolete Smithfield market. When the actual competition for North Wall took the form of a second up-to-date market at Prussia Street, supported by the existing salesmasters, the balance was tipped away from the entrepreneurs. The corporation had the powers, the finance, and the backing of the cattle trade to make their market a

22 *FJ*, 25 November 1863.   **23** *DB*, 1 February 1861; *DB*,15 July 1862; *FJ*, 21 November 1863 to 1 December 1863; *FJ*, 5 July 1904; Minutes of Dublin City Council (hereafter cited as Mins or *Mins*) (manuscript to 1880 and held in Dublin City Archives, then published), 5 January 1953; *Mins*, 2 February 1953.   **24** *FJ*, 17 September 1862; *IT*, 20 March 1863; *FJ*, 1 April 1863; *IT*, 1 April 1864; *FJ*, 14 May, 1864.

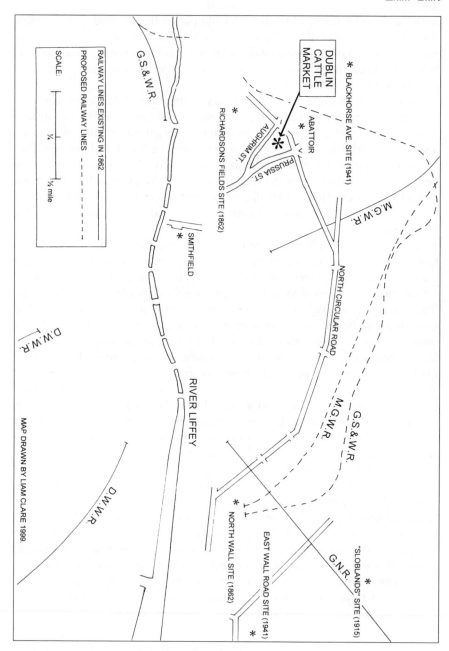

Figure 1 Location map – Dublin cattle market.

success, and when it moved with speed to acquire and develop the North Circular Road site, the financing commitments for the North Wall scheme began to unravel. Moreover, the corporation had won the battle for the peoples' support, and the location of Prussia Street was demonstrably more convenient for the salesmasters based at nearby Smithfield, for the city's butchers, for the cattle producers and the dealers who walked their cattle to the Dublin market.

THE NEW MARKET

The new market, officially named 'The Dublin Cattle Market', opened for trading on Thursday, 26 November 1863. The first market was attended by twenty-seven salesmasters and was described as large, 'with a full clearance, though trading was not as brisk as at the last market in "Old Smithfield"'.[25]

While it was intended to trade cattle, sheep, pigs, horses and goats, and agricultural carts and vehicles in the new market, the sales of milch cows, store cattle and pigs continued in Smithfield for the time being, due to the initial shortage of paved areas. The transfer of these smaller markets would cause major problems in the future.[26]

Graziers and dealers supplied stock to the salesmasters to sell by private treaty rather than by auction. The purchasers were the city butchers, cattle exporters, or British buyers purchasing for immediate slaughter. Few farmers took advantage of the 'open market' principle to sell personally. The salesmasters sold 'by hand', that is, the agreed opinion of vendor and purchaser, rather than by weight, deducted tolls and 'gifts' or 'luck pennies' as well as commission, and guaranteed payment to the seller. By-laws came into force on 3 August 1864 to regulate the market and fix tolls.[27]

Cattle were typically walked to the market from within a radius of twenty to thirty miles, or were delivered by train from further afield. Exports were walked from the market to the North Wall to join cattle bought elsewhere for shipping to Britain. The gates of the market opened at midnight (changed to 3.00. a.m. in 1926).[28]

Initially, 134 permanent cattle pens were supplemented by temporary pens brought up from Smithfield. By 1869, there were pens for 3,020 cattle and 10,200 sheep, plus temporary accommodation. Further accommodation was provided in 1872, 1873 and 1875, and from time to time in later years. Shelters were eventually provided for visitors to the market, but cattle sheds, despite constant demands, never materialized.[29]

25 Mins, 5 October 1863; Mins, 6 November 1863; *FJ*, 27 November 1863; Mins, 1 March 1864.   **26** *FJ*, 13 September 1864; *Annual Accounts of Dublin Corporation 1869 et seq* (hereafter cited as *Accounts*).   **27** *Royal commission market rights, mins, 1890–91*, vii, pp. 39 et seq; NAI, CSORP 17849/1864.   **28** *Mins*, 26 August 1926.   **29** *FJ*, 24 November 1863; Parke Neville, *Report on Public Works of the City* (Dublin, 1869); *Report to Dublin City*

Offices and advertising hoardings were built for letting to salesmen, seedsmen and other agricultural suppliers. Offices numbered at least twenty-one by 1869, and there were forty-two offices and five small shops in the market in 1878. The arrival of piped water from the new Vartry system in September 1867 ended the much-criticized filthy conditions underfoot.[30] The 'mansion' on the site, was converted to a hotel with first, second and third class taverns. The first lessee was soon replaced by Moses Dowd, whose daughter, Elizabeth (O') Dowd, was to run the premises as the Cattle Market Hotel (later the City Arms Hotel), for many years.[31]

The Prussia Street development envisaged the construction of an adjoining abattoir for the development of a dead meat market, with on-site slaughter of animals to replace the many private slaughterhouses, which were considered to be both morally objectionable and public health nuisances.[32] The history of the abattoir would require a separate monograph, but it is necessary to record here that, in 1867 and during the 1870s, proposals for an abattoir were opposed vehemently and overthrown politically by the slaughterhouse owners, by their clients the butchers, and by their apprentices. On 11 April 1882, the new municipal abattoir was finally opened but was boycotted by butchers for many years. Moreover, attempts to suppress the city's most objectionable shambles or slaughterhouses resulted in long-term legal difficulties.[33] The abattoir had a dead meat market with thirteen killing rooms – and a large paddock – on a ten acre site directly across the North Circular Road from the cattle market. Its fortunes were closely linked with the market, and it survived for only a couple of years after the demise of that facility.[34]

As noted earlier, the new cattle market and the 'Old Smithfield' market could legally co-exist, although the corporation intended to centralise sales at Prussia Street. But as soon as the sales of store animals had begun in the new market, grumbling about the tolls commenced. Eventually, in November 1866, the store cattle suppliers organised a walk-out from Prussia Street back to toll-free Smithfield. Although the corporation reacted by opening a special section for store cattle in the Dublin Cattle Market in 1868, with an introductory toll-free status, it failed to attract the store cattle salesmen, and the stores market remained in Smithfield.[35]

The cattle market had initially been financed by mortgaging its anticipated income to a group of financiers, mainly cattle salesmen. As early as 1869, the

Council (hereafter cited as *Rep*), *178 of 1878; Mins*, 29 November 1886; *Mins*, 25 July 1887. **30** *DEP*, 22 November 1866; *FJ*, 3 September 1867; Mins, 1 March 1864; Mins, 3 July 1865; Mins, 3 February 1869; *Rep 178 of 1878*.   **31** Mins, 5 October 1863; Mins, 1 March 1864; Mins, 3 July 1865; Mins, 23 October 1865.   **32** Hemans, *Cattle Market*, p. 17; *Rep 223 of 1879*.   **33** *Rep 223 of 1879; FJ*, 2 September 1879; *FJ*, 25 November 1879; *Farmers' Gazette* (hereafter cited as *FG*), 25 January 1896; *Royal comm. market rights, mins,1890–91*, p. 40 et.seq.   **34** *FJ*, 2 November 1880; *FJ*, 12 April 1882.   **35** *FJ*, 27 March 1862; *FJ*, 30 June 1862; *FG*, 26 October 1866; *DEP*, 22 November 1866; *DEP*, 29 November 1866; Mins, 6 July 1868.

market's income was sufficient not only to pay the interest on borrowing, but to make a loan repayment to the corporation's central Boro' Fund. Therefore, the initial promise to insulate ratepayers from financial risk seems to have been reasonably met. New financial arrangements were agreed in 1879. A sinking fund was established, and the original mortgages began to be repaid.[36]

CONSOLIDATION AND GROWTH

An outbreak of foot-and-mouth disease in February 1883, finally ended the 'Old Smithfield' cattle market. A general ban was put on the sale of cattle in Dublin, except under licence, or unless they were being sold in the Dublin Cattle Market for immediate slaughter. The corporation had at the outbreak of the disease, carried out major paving, water and drainage works in the cattle market – though not in Smithfield – to meet the disease control requirements of the Privy Council. Consequently, even when the outbreak ended, no licence was issued for Smithfield market, because of its insanitary condition.[37]

A public meeting of 'pig factors, salesmasters, dairymen, residents and others interested in resisting the removal of Old Smithfield Free Market' was called on 28 May 1883 to oppose the 'sudden arbitrary closing' of the old market. The next city council meeting considered two memorials or petitions, one from the Smithfield interests, the other from the residents near the cattle market, both protesting, but for their own different reasons, at the transfer of the pig market to Prussia Street. The council referred the petitioners to the Privy Council, which had forced the Smithfield closure.[38]

The pro-Smithfield lobbyists met with little success. A deputation to the Lord Lieutenant heard two reasons for refusing a trading licence for Smithfield, the lack of paving which inhibited disinfection, and the existence of a hay and straw market at Smithfield, which would result in various animal diseases being carried home on farmers' carts from an infected market.[39]

In 1884, the city council considered converting the paddock at the cattle market into a permanent pig market. After some years of deferred and reversed decisions because of local opposition – including a decision to return to Smithfield which foundered on the potential cost – the council was urged in 1889 by its newly-elected markets sub-committee to proceed with the 1884 proposal. This provoked opposition from Aughrim Street Catholic parish, whose church had been built on a portion of the paddock bought from the corporation. 'A large indignation meeting' of parishioners heard Very Reverend Joseph Burke P.P.,

36 *Rep 192 of 1879; Rep 27 of 1869.* **37** *FG*, various dates 1883; *Return for 1883, under 59th section of contagious diseases (animals) act 1878 as regards Ireland*, pp. 35–6, H.C. 1884 [C 3960], lxxiv, 79–80; *Weekly Freemans Journal* (hereafter cited as *WFJ*), 19 May 1883; *Rep 12 of 1883; FG*, 8 September 1883. **38** *WFJ*, 2 June 1883; *FJ*, 5 June 1883. **39** *Rep 12 of 1883; FG*, 20 September 1884.

Figure 2 General view of the market.

criticize the decision as 'inconsiderate efforts of a few irresponsible men ...
Philistines equally deficient in aesthetic sense and religious instinct'. A deputation
to the city council bearing a petition with 734 signatures followed – and the
proposal was dropped.[40] The location of the pig market was considered again in
1912 and in 1934, but proposals to move the market to the Newmarket area in
the Liberties, which previously had held a pig market, were unsuccessful.[41]

Following the ending of the sales of store cattle at Smithfield in 1883, there
were limited sales of store cattle in a special section of the cattle market for the
next decade or so. However, in November 1895, Ganlys decided to put their
existing private occasional store cattle auctions on a regular footing, stating 'we
have decided to hold a series of sales of store cattle ... [starting] ... on 28
November 1895 in our paddocks, 63 Prussia Street'. The trade blossomed. By
1898, store cattle auctions were also being held by Gavin Low, a Scotsman who

40 *Mins*, 7 April 1884; *Mins*, 5 May 1884; *Mins*, 16 July 1894; *Rep 205 of 1897*; Rep 122 of
1898; Mins, 23 October 1865; *Rep 33 of 1899*; *FJ*, 13 March 1899; *FJ*, 11 April 1999; *Mins*,
15 April 1891; *Mins*, 2 October 1899.   **41** *FJ*, 6 February 1912; *FJ*, 7 May 1912; *FJ*, 4 June
1912; *Rep 77 of 1912*; *Mins*, 5 February 1912; *Mins*, 6 May 1912; *Mins*, 3 June 1912; *Mins*, 9
April 1934.

had built up a business in Dublin, at 50 Prussia Street, and by a third firm, R. and J. Wilkinson of 40/41 Prussia Street. The result was almost weekly sales, which were attended by feeders from all over Ireland and graziers from 'the home counties and across channel'. In one week alone, although late in the season, Wilkinson had sold 400, and Ganly 500 animals.[42]

The city council, concerned with the growth of this toll-free and unregulated competition, made provision in the Dublin Corporation (Markets) Act 1899, for the banning of sales outside the cattle market. However, the act provided that, until an auction ring had been provided within the cattle market and at least ten years had elapsed, the existing store cattle sales on the premises of Ganly, Gavin Low, Wilkinson and Charles Keogh (a smaller auctioneer) could continue.[43]

The milch cow market was moved with the stores from Smithfield to the cattle market in 1883, and remained there. In 1911, a proposal emerged to move the milch cow market to the paddock beside the church. Once again the 'Vigilance Committee' of Aughrim Street parish, led by Canon Burke, successfully objected. In 1930, part of the paddock was sold to the parish for a presbytery.[44]

In October 1888, the Royal Commission on Market Rights and Tolls heard that the Dublin Cattle Market provided accommodation for 4,800 cattle and 14,000 sheep. The maximum numbers sold in a single week were 4,500 and 11,000 respectively. There were a couple of large sales in each year. There was plenty of room, except in the pig section, with much room for expansion. Pens were allocated both to salesmasters and to producers who wished to sell directly. Only 2,000 casual sales, directly from producer to consumer, were recorded in five years. Suggested reasons for the small number of direct sales were the security of payment by means of a salesmaster's cheque, and the avoidance of direct haggling with dealers. Perhaps the established links between salesmasters and their regular customers was also a factor. During the period 1883–7, 538,171 fat cattle, 41,291 stores (Smithfield had been closed), 1,335,360 sheep, 24,956 calves and 175,539 pigs had been exposed for sale.[45] Pigs were sold at a different hour on market day; dairy cattle on a different day. The design of the market was considered satisfactory. The capital cost to date was £36,829: despite the limitation on tolls, income just about covered expenses and interest.[46]

---

42 *FJ*, 2 May 1866; *FG*, 1 November 1884; *FG*, 8 August 1885; *FG*, 2 November 1895; *FG*, 5 March 1898; *FG*, 12 March 1898; various weekly market reports in *FG*.   **43** *FJ*, 8 November 1898; 62/63 Vict, (1899), Cap. 236.   **44** *Royal comm. market rights, mins, 1890–91*, p. 40 et seq.; *Rep 172 of 1911; Mins*, 6 November 1911; *Mins*, 13 November 1911; *FJ*, 7 November 1911; *Mins*, 5 February 1912; *Mins*, 8 December 1930.   **45** The official returns were of animals exposed for sale rather than numbers sold. However the Royal Commission on market rights and tolls heard in November 1888 that salesmasters made their own returns based on sales, and that they could save money, though lose pen allocation, by understating their numbers. The system of salesmasters making their own returns was again in operation in the 1960s. All statistics must be viewed in this light.   **46** *Royal comm. market rights, mins*, 1890–91, p. 40 et seq.

Figure 3 Cattle stalls.

Animals were handed over to the salesmasters who sold 'to best advantage', charging commission, deducting tolls and 'gifts' and guaranteeing the sale price to the buyers. They sold to local butchers and to exporters who transported their purchases to Liverpool, Manchester, Wakefield, London and other private markets for resale. Selling was 'by eye' or 'by hand' rather than by weight, even though there had been a weigh scales in the market since January 1888. Reasons given for not using this new machine included loss of time, the charge for weighing, and a general prejudice against change.[47]

Ten years later, in 1898, the Royal Commission on Inland Transport of Cattle was concentrating on cruelty to animals during transport. Evidence was given of cattle being walked to Dublin from as far away as Edenderry. There were two complaints about cruelty by drovers in the market. Controlling the cattle drovers had been a matter of continuing contention in managing the market. The first bylaws in 1864 provided for licensing of drovers and for the wearing of drovers' badges. Proposed new bylaws in 1891 were to incorporate eighteen new rules for drovers in lieu of one existing general rule, but they were never implemented. The drovers had 'raised a society against it', had held a protest meeting, and had refused to co-operate.[48]

47 Ibid.   **48** NAI, CSORP 17849/1864; *Departmental committee appointed by the Board of*

A delegate at a conference of cattle traders in 1911 described the supply of animals to the Dublin dairy trade, saying that five-year-old cows purchased in the Dublin Cattle Market in March and April each year were put out on grass in the suburbs for the summer months, and were taken into sheds around October, before being resold as beef during the following March or April. Milch cows were never sold in November or December. City cowkeepers fed about 3,000 cows at any one time.[49]

'THE BIGGEST AND BEST IN EUROPE'[50]

In 1917, the *Journal of the Department of Agriculture and Technical Instruction* published a comprehensive report on the Dublin Cattle Market. It was handling nearly 200,000 cattle and over 300,000 sheep every year and had recently recorded its highest ever weekly totals of cattle at 6,728 and of sheep at 10,940. Sales were still made 'on the head basis', though the weight was often known. Business was transacted from 5 a.m. until 10 a.m. Disease and sanitary controls were in place.[51]

Most stock came by rail, though local animals were walked in. The peak trading period was from August to November, when grass-fed cattle exchanged hands. The slackest period was the early summer. Largest sheep sales were in the summer time. Cattle came mainly from Meath, Dublin, Kildare, Westmeath and Offaly in that order, although some animals came from as far away as Tipperary and North Cork. Sheep came, in order of numbers, from Meath, Dublin, Westmeath, Offaly and Kildare, while Wicklow provided a small year-round supply to home victuallers.[52]

Fat-stock buyers included Irish shippers, English and Scottish buyers, and local contractors and victuallers. Birkenhead was the main English destination. Local exporters bought sheep to order, while agents of victualling firms throughout England took up most of the supplies offered. Dublin was Ireland's main export centre, and six steam-ship companies operated some thirty-six regular weekly sailings to British ports – to Liverpool, Holyhead, Glasgow, Manchester, Heysham, and Silloth. Dublin victuallers took about 10 per cent of available supplies for city consumption. The milch cow situation remained as described in 1911. Pigs came to the market from Dublin and from parts of Wicklow and Kildare. Fat pigs were typically purchased by Dublin-based and sometimes Limerick-based curers, or by exporters. Store pigs and bonhams were bought by pig keepers, farmers and farm labourers for fattening and resale.[53]

Agriculture, to inquire into and report on the inland transit of cattle, minutes of evidence, H.C. 1898 [C8929], xxxiv, various pages; *Mins*, 15 April 1891; *FJ*, 16 April 1891. **49** *Rep 227 of 1911.* **50** Michael Dillon in *IT*, 20 July 1972. **51** *Journal of the Department of Agriculture and Technical Instruction for Ireland*, xvii (October 1916-July 1917), pp. 57–63. **52** Ibid. **53** Ibid.

Store cattle, as we have seen, were sold outside the market, mainly during spring and autumn. They came from rearers and graziers as well as from provincial buyers. Scottish and English buyers were the typical purchasers as well as farmers and graziers from Dublin, Meath and Kildare.[54]

If one examines the first fifty years of the market's operation, some long term trends emerge from the considerable yearly and seasonal fluctuations in the market's business. Fat cattle exposed for sale gradually increased from around 100,000 to 200,000 per year. Sheep, more consistently, averaged 300,000 to 350,000 on a rising trend. Some limited correlation can be noticed between these trends and the statistics of national exports of fat cattle. There is less correlation with regard to sheep, reflecting the greater role of foreign buyers of cattle than of sheep in the market.[55]

The niche markets had their own patterns. Pigs had been sold in the market since 1883. Their numbers ranged between 35,000 and 60,000 per annum. After the move from Smithfield in 1883, store cattle statistics also appeared. They reached 10,000 head in 1884, but were no longer recorded by the early 1900s. Dairy cattle figures reached 10,000 to 12,000 per annum in the early 1900s, before dropping to a plateau of around 8,000 during the 1914/18 war. Calf numbers fluctuated generally between 3,000 and 5,000 animals per year and represented only a marginal market. Small numbers of goats were sold, the last being in 1934. A small number of horses were traded in the early days as well as a few hundred carts and vehicles per year.[56]

The various statistics reflect the national crisis of the foot-and-mouth outbreak in 1883 and a slump in 1913. The two main markets, fat cattle and sheep, continued their upward trend until they peaked in 1923. In that year, 739,915 animals were exposed for sale in the Dublin Cattle Market. Fat cattle marginally exceeded their 1923 figure just once – many years later – in 1957. The booming sales provoked a proposal in 1915 to move the entire cattle market to the 'sloblands' at Fairview or to the North Wall. This proposal proved abortive.[57]

The success of the Dublin Cattle Market reflected the favourable economic environment of the time. The modern, extensive, sanitary and well-managed facility had only limited competition from the small-scale, diffused and chaotic cattle fairs. Its strategic position close to the traditional areas for finishing animals and at the hub of Ireland's main railway systems gave it an added competitive advantage. Moreover, as a convenient gateway to industrial northern England, with a concentrated population and growing demand for meat, it attracted a host of visiting purchasers to join local victuallers.

The expanding market attracted ancillary business into the area. In particular, the catering trade, hotels, public houses, shops and boarding houses benefited. When Hanlon's, the major public house, opened in 1894, there were already eleven public houses in the area. Banks established local branches. However, the

54 Ibid.   **55** *Accounts*, various; John O'Donovan, *The economic history of livestock in Ireland*, (Cork, 1940), pp. 214 *et. seq.*   **56** *Accounts*, various.   **57** Ibid.; *Mins*, 15 February 1915.

market's export orientation, together with the limited use of the abattoir, restricted the emergence of local 'spin-off' industries such as hide, skin and bone products. Moreover, business and employment opportunities were dissipated beyond the immediate locality into neighbouring districts. Despite the market's one-day-a-week operation, it nevertheless represented a source of income for local men, such as drovers, seeking casual work. But in the context of a city of 157,000 population, only 104 drovers and 197 dealers in cattle, sheep and pigs were recorded for the entire city in the 1911 census. The long term absence of local community support for the market, reflected its limited economic impact.[58]

Many older Dubliners' sole memory of the cattle market is the driving of cattle along the North Circular Road. As early as 1870, there were complaints of 'great inconvenience and danger' arising from the practice. In 1895 and again in 1902, the city council considered the regulation of cattle traffic. The police responded that they could not send a policeman to accompany every drove of cattle. James Joyce and other writers described the driving of cattle from the market to the North Wall, emphasising the danger to passers-by, the cruelty to the animals, the difficulties for drovers meeting oncoming trams or the mixing up of cattle and sheep. This traffic problem ended in the early 1960s, with the introduction of restrictions on the walking of cattle under bovine T.B. controls.[59]

The Dublin Cattle Market was closed for five months during an epidemic of foot-and-mouth disease between February and July 1941, and even after resumption of trading, the market was severely regulated. Animals sold had to be slaughtered immediately or otherwise exported directly for slaughter. Butchers could not attend the market, but had to purchase through an Emergency Purchasing Committee. Disinfection was rigidly enforced. On reopening, the market day was changed from Thursday to Wednesday.[60]

In 1941, steps were initiated to site both the municipal abattoir and the cattle market at East Wall. The corporation's town planning consultants advocated an alternative site at Blackhorse Avenue, which was in turn opposed by the Gardaí on grounds of traffic generation and congestion. The Dublin Cattle Salesmasters' Association opposed any relocation. The city council held a conference of all interested parties in November 1943. After this conference, a site to the north of the East Wall Road and Tolka Quay was recommended for acquisition.[61]

58 Kevin C. Kearns, *Stoneybatter* (Dublin, 1989), pp. 36 & 180; James Joyce, *Ulysses* (New York, 1934 edition) pp. 35, 633, 162, etc.; *Mins*, 3 September 1894; Kenneth Milne, *A history of the Royal Bank of Ireland* (Dublin, 1964), p. 55; Kevin C. Kearns, *Dublin Pub Life and Lore* (Dublin, 1996), p. 177; *Census of Ireland 1911, area, houses and population etc., province of Leinster, city of Dublin*, pp. 18 & 25 [cd 6049–II], H.C., 1912/13, cxiv; *FJ*, 25 November 1879; *FJ*, 5 June 1883. **59** *Mins*, 2 May 1870; *Mins*, 15 July 1895; *Mins*, 3 March 1902; *FJ*, 3 March 1902; Cyril Pearl, *Dublin in Bloomtime* (London, 1969), p. 51; Kearns, *Stoneybatter*, pp. 135–6; Kearns, *Dublin Street Life*, pp. 177–92. **60** NAI, Dept of Agriculture files L4146–41 and L3655–41; *FG*, 15 February 1941 to 10 January 1942; *Evening Herald*, 11 July 1941. **61** *Rep 40 of 1942; Rep 17 of 1943; Rep 16 of 1945; Rep 15 of 1947.*

The proposal envisaged a cattle market with three covered sales rings, a large abattoir, a covered lairage or holding area for 6,000 cattle to replace the existing lairages around Prussia Street, together with rail sidings and loading banks. However, in March 1950, when the project was well advanced, the City Manager advised that the estimated cost had increased from £2,000,000 to an unaffordable £5,500,000. The proposal was then abandoned.[62]

During the 1950s, business in the market was again increasing. From the previous peak in 1923, the number of animals exposed had been dropping throughout the late 1920s and 1930s, reaching its nadir in 1941/2, the year of the foot-and-mouth disease. The post-war rising trend in business reached its peak at 684,158 animals in 1957, after which the final decline set in.[63]

The two main markets, fat cattle and sheep, generally followed similar trends in the period from 1923 to 1960. The cattle figures dropped more suddenly in the early 1930s, due to the imposition of U.K. restrictions on imports of Irish cattle during the 'Economic War'. The sheep figures dropped more slowly. The longer-term trend for fat cattle recovered immediately after the war, aided by increased exports, while sheep began a recovery after 1948. Fat cattle numbers peaked in 1957 at 249,776 per annum; sheep numbers peaked in 1960 at 425,097.[64]

With regard to the smaller markets, pig statistics fluctuated considerably, although their final decline did not commence until 1963; dairy cattle sales had started their long-term decline after the war, and had died out by 1964; calf sales, although fluctuating wildly from year to year, remained viable until 1961 when numbers rapidly declined.[65]

Changes in bovine tuberculosis controls in 1958 and during the following years, caused a major disruption of trade in the market around 1960. Special Tuesday sales of 'once-tested' cattle, that is cattle for whom the disease-free attestation process was incomplete, and fully attested cattle were organised for a period. As attestation progressed, the number of non-attested cattle in the main market progressively decreased. In 1962, sales of attested animals were introduced on every second Wednesday, and by 1963 all sales in the Dublin Cattle Market were of attested cattle.[66]

It will be recalled that sales outside the market were restricted in 1899 to store cattle sales in four designated company premises. By 1958, the store cattle auctions were of considerable size and growing. Three of the four companies were still trading, Ganlys, Gavin Lows, and Craigies (selling from Wilkinsons' former lairage). They sold over 220,000 cattle in 1963. However, by 1971, only Ganlys were still trading seriously.[67]

---

62 *Rep 25 of 1950; Mins*, 3 October 1949; *Mins*, 1 May 1950.   **63** *Accounts*, various.
64 Ibid.; Dept of Agriculture, *Report of the Store Cattle Study group* (A 62) (Dublin, 1969), pp. 24–7.   **65** *Accounts*, various.   **66** Law Department, Dublin Corporation, file of papers related to case taken by L. F. Kelly and others against Dublin Corporation, 1972/3, document no. 74 (hereafter LA).   **67** LA, 70, 236, 206.

DECLINE AND DEMISE

On 3 October 1963, the Dublin Cattle Salesmasters' Association called on the corporation to provide auction sales for fat cattle within the Dublin Cattle Market. The corporation knew, however, that because of a clause in the Dublin Corporation (Markets) Act of 1899, this move would legally trigger the closure of the private auction sales – an outcome which neither they nor most of the salesmasters wanted. The auction firms reacted strongly, claiming that 25–30 per cent of all store cattle exports to Britain passed through their sales rings, and that they were providing considerable local employment as well as essential outlets for thousands of farmers. They had invested heavily in their premises, and had created a strong cross-channel customer base from 'new business', rather than from the traditional market.[68]

Meanwhile, on 15 January 1964, the salesmasters had warned the corporation of the critical threat from auction marts, and had formally proposed the establishment of a company to operate three covered auction rings in the market. The corporation saw legal problems in a private company running the public market. In June 1964, the council's finance committee noted that sales in the market were declining even as the sales (of stores) in the outside lairages increased. Indeed more cattle were now being sold in adjoining premises than within the market. After many meetings with interested parties and government departments, and after considerable lobbying, a proposal emerged among councillors for auction rings in the market to be co-operatively managed by the salesmasters, but incorporating protection for the private auctions. In September 1964, the finance committee recommended the construction of two auction rings. This proposal involved the compulsory incorporation of a half acre of Ganlys' yard.[69]

By now the Salesmasters' Association and the auctioneering firms were at loggerheads over the continuation of private auction sales. The auctioneers made the point that if they were to relocate outside the city their regular customers would follow. Nearing the date of a final decision by the city council, lobbying by the opposing parties intensified, while additional interests joined in. The Marine Port and General Workers' Union was concerned about the future of Ganlys' staff; the National Farmers' Association urged avoidance of 'sudden interference with the delicate mechanism of the export trade'; the national executive of the Irish Livestock Trade supported the new auction marts; the Pedigree Cattle Breeders' Association wished to see the role of the auctioneers maintained as specialists in pedigree livestock; the Dublin Chamber of Commerce supported the four auctioneers; the Dublin Master Victuallers' Association feared that increased costs of the new auction rings would impact on meat prices.[70]

The city council deferred a decision, but sent a deputation to the Minister for Local Government. The deputation acknowledged that the market in its present form was dying, but stated that 'there was a consensus of disagreement'

68 LA, 236.   **69** LA, 236.   **70** LA, 83, 236.

Figure 4 Cattle being driven from the market.

among the councillors over what to do. The Minister surprised the councillors
by questioning why the corporation was in the cattle-selling business at all.
Councillor Robert Briscoe responded immediately that the corporation would
indeed consider giving up their responsibilities for the market. A new agenda
had been created.[71]

In February 1966, the city council considered alternative suggestions that
either the corporation should transfer the market to a new statutory marketing
board, or that the Minister should sanction increased tolls to finance the new
auction rings in conjunction with the closure of the outside sales. They sought
legal advice which identified certain difficulties, and on 3 October 1966, they
further deferred their own decision pending a Ministerial decision to allow an
increase in market tolls.[72]

The question of tolls was always contentious. After ten years without an
increase, the city council had fixed new rates in January 1966, but these were
subject to Ministerial sanction. They had also called on the Minister to subsidize
the losses on the market. The Minister eventually approved the increases in

71 LA, 236; *Mins*, 12 October 1965.   **72** *Rep 32 of 1966*; *Rep 132 of 1966*.

November 1967 despite intensive lobbying against them, but in doing so he called for a full review of the organization and control of the markets.[73]

The corporation's response was that, as the market adequately fulfilled the victualling needs of the city, no further capital expenditure on auction rings could be justified. It was later held by the corporation that the salesmasters themselves had balked at the financial implications and had acquiesced in the suspension of the proposals.[74]

The writing was on the wall. Up to 1962, there had typically been a small, annual surplus on the cattle market, while occasional annual shortfalls were limited to around £1,000. In 1963, however, a deficit of £2,836 appeared, increasing to £11,000 in 1967, to £22,000 in 1970, and peaking at £39,000 in 1972. These increased losses occurred despite a policy of retrenchment initiated in 1963, which resulted in shorter opening hours, closing of weigh scales and staff reductions. Later, pens were reallocated and reduced in number as portions of the market area were progressively abandoned.[75]

Ganlys and Craigies jointly launched a new sales mart at Ashbourne in April 1970, with modern customer facilities. Rumours spread of the impending closure of the cattle market. In June 1970, the corporation confirmed this possibility, noting that the average throughput had dropped from 4107 cattle per week in 1960 to 796 in 1969, and was still declining. The deficit was increasing yearly and an increase in tolls of the size required to recover costs would drive away the remaining business. The closure would have little effect on the economy of the city except to save money, the *lacuna* in service could easily be met by other marts, and there would be little loss of employment.[76]

Heated recriminations took place during the winter of 1970/71 between corporation officials and the salesmasters. By this time, the city council had been removed from office for reasons unconnected with the cattle market. The officials were now actively planning closure while the salesmasters were actively resisting. However, the number of active salesmasters had dropped from forty-eight to twenty-eight in the previous seven years. By now it was not only the market that was being hit; even the outside auction sales were disappearing, with Ganlys the only firm still active.[77]

Ganlys were approached by the corporation to secure their premises as an alternative weekly sales venue if the cattle market itself was closed. Ganlys did not object, but were not prepared to take the initiative themselves. Finally, in July 1971, the corporation announced a closure to take effect on 1 October 1971.[78]

The cattle salesmasters sought an injunction to stop the closure, arguing that the corporation were obliged by law to maintain the service. An interlocutory injunction was secured to keep the market open until the hearing of the case. The salesmasters lost their action in the High Court in July 1972, and their

73 LA, 68, 148, 152, 161, 170, 172.   **74** LA, 179, 186.   **75** LA, 84, 187, *Accounts*, various. **76** *Irish Farmers' Journal*, 4 April 1970; *Evening Press*, 15 June 1970.   **77** LA, 188, 191, 203, 204, 205, 206.   **78** LA, 209, 210, 211.

appeal to the Supreme Court on 10 May 1973. The courts held that the corporation had the power but not the duty to operate the markets. The market never opened again: the last sales, totalling 325 animals, had been held on Wednesday, 9 May 1973. The salesmasters rented lairages from Ganlys and Gavin Lows in an attempt to continue trading, but this effort soon petered out.[79]

Why did the market have to close? The corporation blamed the inexorable rise of the cattle marts, particularly those at Blessington, Maynooth and latterly at Ashbourne. Although the first co-operative cattle mart in the country had commenced operations as late as 1956, there were already twenty-one co-operative marts, and fifty-one private marts in operation in 1960, claiming a combined turnover of £35m. By 1970, 116 co-operative and sixty-one private marts had a combined turnover of £160m. As had been foreseen by various commentators as early as 1959, there was an over-provision of marketing facilities. The reasons for the decline of the Dublin Cattle Market were, however, considerably more complicated, with a number of interacting factors. It is true that the marts were the major immediate cause. Modern sales facilities, often owned by the farmers themselves, were now competing with Dublin. They were more convenient to the farm, eliminated the discomfort and disadvantages previously encountered when selling at fairs, and provided opportunities for social contact. Similarly, the buyers now had a choice of organised sales venues, where they could purchase their needs directly from the producers. An additional factor appeared to be the inner-city location of the market. Already Ganly-Craigies had fled the urban centre for Ashbourne.[80]

But there were other causes. In the export trade, the granting of subsidies to nearly-finished stores in the U.K. had reduced the overseas demand for fat cattle, which was the main business of the Dublin Cattle Market. Indeed, between 1960 and 1970, stores and dead meat exports expanded, while fat cattle exports virtually disappeared. There was also a drastic decline in sheep exports. The rise of the meat factories also had a considerable effect. Roscrea meat factory had been opened in 1935 'to use up all the old and uneconomic cows in the country', but in the last years of the market, much larger companies such as International Meat Products and Dublin Meat Packers had been established to process cattle and sheep respectively. While factories still purchased some 50 per cent of the cattle sold in the Dublin market in its final years, they were increasingly tending to purchase elsewhere.[81]

The introduction and modification of the TB-testing programme disrupted the Dublin Cattle Market from 1958 to 1964, and broke the long-established

79 *IT*, 30 September 1971; *IT,* 14 July 1972; *IT*, 11 May 1973; *IT*, 17 May 1973; N. Lloyd-Blood (ed.), *Irish Law Reports, 1974* (Dublin, 1974). **80** Lloyd-Blood, *Law Reports 1974*, p. 35; LA 206, 207; Patrick Bolger, *The Irish Co-operative Movement* (Dublin, 1977), p. 323; Joseph G. Knapp for Department of Agriculture, *An appraisal of Agricultural Co-operation in Ireland* (Dublin, 1964), p. 43; V. Vial, E. Potts and M. O'Sullivan, *Irish Agriculture: a decade of development* (Dublin, 1973), pp. 31–3. **81** Ibid.; *FG*, 17 August 1935.

habits of its regular participants at the very time that the cattle marts were expanding to provide an alternative. The Dublin Cattle Market, because of the wide area from which it drew its suppliers, was particularly vulnerable to disruption as the scheme, which required segregation of attested and non-attested cattle, progressed geographically from region to region. Changes in the organization of the local meat trade also had adverse effects. The new supermarkets were buying from wholesale butchers, while local butchers, instead of purchasing their own needs in the market, were also switching to the wholesalers who could supply them with the particular cuts which their customers favoured. These wholesalers accounted for 85 per cent of the home market by the time the Dublin Cattle Market closed, and much of their meat was purchased from the expanding meat processors. The municipal abattoir's loss of its licence to slaughter for export to the continent in 1966 was a further, though minor, factor.[82]

The specialized markets were also losing out. The Dublin dairymen, who had dealt in the milch cow market, were losing their suburban fields to urban development, while the large milk plants, which were gradually taking over, were purchasing their milk from suppliers throughout a very wide area. A high proportion of pigs had been supplied to the market by city pig-rearers who were latterly being squeezed out both by environmental pressures, and by a switch in demand away from their fat pigs towards leaner country-bred animals.[83]

Could the corporation have saved the situation by acting more decisively? There were many factors impeding effective action. These included an outdated and inflexible legal framework which restricted its scope for action, the dissipation of the corporation's concentration over a huge range of interests – from abattoirs to zebra crossings – and the organisational structure of the city council, composed of forty-five individuals, virtually all non-specialists in the issues of the cattle trade, each of them with his or her own agenda, and each of them subject to pressures from a wide range of opposing vested interests. To have successfully adapted to the rapid re-organization of cattle marketing in the sixties would appear to have been organizationally impossible.

Michael Dillon was by far the best known agricultural correspondent in Ireland during the decline of the Dublin Cattle Market. His radio reports on the Dublin prices, were listened to all over the country. He recalled that 'we used to boast about Dublin as being the biggest and best [cattle market] in Europe' but concluded that the market had become such a travesty of its former self that it should finally close. It was indeed a sad end to a hugely important venture.[84]

It has been stated that the closure was not only an economic disaster, but also an immense psychological blow to the Stoneybatter area, due to local identification between the market and 'cowtown'. The importance of the economic impact of the closure on the general area must, however, be queried in the

---

82 'Bovine TB Eradication Scheme 1954–1963' in *Journal of Department of Agriculture*, lxi, (n.d. – circa 1965), pp. 210–20; *Mins*, 14 February 1966; LA 208, persons mentioned in note 87 below.   **83** LA 208; persons mentioned in note 87 below.   **84** *IT*, 20 July 1972.

Figure 5 Cattle being driven to the docks.

absence of local representations to keep the market open. Indeed, there was no local pressure to secure alternative wealth-generating activity in the area, but considerable local support for changing the zoning of the cattle market site from 'general business' to 'residential', so that the Drumalee housing estate could be built there. The slow death of the market over many years, and its essentially one-day-a-week contribution to the local economy no doubt lessened its economic impact locally. Drumalee estate physically replaced the remains of the Dublin Cattle Market and Aughrim Street sports hall was built on the paddock.[85]

The closure of the cattle market had a fatal knock-on effect on the municipal abattoir. Already obsolescent and deemed unsuitable for export killings, the advent of meat processing and wholesaling had eroded its business with local butchers. It closed its doors in 1976.[86]

---

85 Kearns, *Stoneybatter*, p. 42; *Mins*, 5 November, 1975 and various dates in 1975.   86 *Rep 61 of 1976*; *Mins*, 1 March, 1976.

PERSONAL RECOLLECTIONS[87]

It is still possible to piece together from the recollections of participants in the Dublin Cattle Market, a vignette of a typical market day during its closing years. Walking in of animals was dying out and road transport was replacing rail. Cattle being walked in might be in the charge of a drover riding a bicycle and accompanied by a dog, starting from Naas, Oldtown or Navan on the day before the market, and might be allowed to graze at the roadside along the way. There were drinking troughs for watering cattle in Aughrim Street, in Manor Street and in the market itself. The drovers, all city men, numbered perhaps a hundred. They worked in all weathers. They could control and tie by the neck a 13-hundredweight-bullock which had never been tied up before. Cattle arriving by rail during the summer might be left at an overnight 'park', possibly in Cabra or Finglas, before being walked in to Prussia Street at 1 a.m. or 2 a.m. In winter they might be lodged in a lairage overnight. Some drovers were in regular employment but most were casuals. One drover was allowed to drive five cattle; two together could handle twenty beasts. In its final years, farmers tended to send their cattle to market rather than attend personally.

There were different sections in the market. The fat cattle which were sold to butchers were mainly heifers, while factories or English buyers preferred bullocks. Store cattle were not traded. Sheep came by rail or arrived by tractor and trailer. Fat sheep were sold mainly to local victuallers but also to provincial butchers. Some breeding ewes were sold seasonally. The milch cow market was supplied by dealers, not farmers. Cows were bought by Dublin dairymen, who would resell them a year later as poor quality fat cattle. These were purchased by factories. The pig market was supplied by local back-lane producers. The heavier animals were bought by factories, the smaller animals by pork butchers. There was a small veal market in the sheep area. Calves were fed on milk and bought mainly by Jewish butchers, and by large hotels. Slaughtering to provide kosher meat took place in the municipal abattoir.

Selling started at 5 a.m. and the largest firms might have up to six salesmen on a cattle stand, or eight on a sheep stand. A 'salesmaster' could be a large firm or an individual. Many salesmasters were also farmers or dealers buying to resell on their own stands. The supplier would leave his cattle with the salesmaster and later be told how much they fetched. A large buyer would be welcomed to a stand as he approached, but as soon as he moved on, custom required that he could not be followed to press a sale. During a sale, a visit might be paid to Conroy's (The City Arms), or to Hanlon's, but in practice there was little time for socializing. The salesmen got to know an enormous number of people even

---

87 The information from which this section was compiled was supplied mainly by Tom Robinson, Theo. Robinson, Tim Gallagher, Larry Lenehan and Christy Geoghegan, together with some recollections of other persons. The responsibility for collating the material is my own.

though many buyers or sellers never attended in person. Long-term business relationships were built up. Sales were paid for by weight. One could buy a 'pen' of ten cattle or a group of two or three. Selling continued until about 10 a.m. or even later, but many buyers, particularly butchers, wanted to get away very early. Prices on the Dublin market tended to set the baseline for prices around the country.

As at fairs, there were 'blockers' who sought to engage in a purchase negotiation until their principals came along to complete the sale. After a sale, the purchaser would make his own distinct scissors cut, to record the purchase. Cattle were seldom lost. Jobbers who bought to resell at the market were regarded as 'the lowest form of life'. The market was 'slow, noisy, dirty and costly'.

English buyers would arrive the evening before the market via the mailboat and lodge overnight in the City Arms Hotel or in local bed and breakfast accommodation. Alternatively, they might come in on a 'dawn flight', assemble their lots of 300 or 400 cattle, go off for breakfast, settle their account, hand over their purchases to a shipping agent and fly out again. Payment was typically by cheque, and credit might be given to regular customers. Breakfast was an important facility. Conroy's and the Parkside hotel, Corcoran's and the Golden Spaniel Restaurant in Prussia Street, as well as many public houses, served large breakfasts such as steak and eggs. The Methodist Church ran a tea room in the market to combat the attractions of the pubs.

Unsold animals could be sent to a park or grazing area for a week before being re-offered for sale, or could be returned to the supplier. Animals for export would be walked directly to the docks until the introduction of Bovine T.B. regulations forbade the practice.

CONCLUSION

The saying 'you must adapt to survive', like all catch-phrases, oversimplifies the situation in real life. The complexities of economic change, involving a multitude of factors, events and agents interacting with each other, create ever-changing situations, which may alternately draw the participants into the centre of activity or alternatively side-line them. To manage this process successfully, those involved must be aware of the changing – often imperceptibly changing – situation, and be willing and able to adapt to the extent required. In the case of the Dublin Cattle Market we see two occasions when the concurrence of factors had reached the stage that the corporation as operator of the Dublin market had to adapt radically to a new milieu, or let it fade into oblivion. In the 1860s, developments in the agricultural, economic, social, political and technological fields conspired to make substantial changes in the marketing of cattle logically inevitable. The long-established Smithfield market which had been developed at a time when its only role was seen as one of ensuring regular supplies of meat to meet the citizens' needs, could not be adapted to meet the new role now determined by external events, of facilitating cattle producers throughout the country to supply meat in the quantities required not only by the growing city of Dublin but in addition by the expanding, newly affluent urban population of Britain. Though for long unwilling to modernize, a time had come when the corporation had to adapt to survive and they did so successfully albeit reluctantly, when faced by another player who was more than willing to supplant them as a marketing agency. We saw how the economic conditions subsequently enabled the Dublin market to expand until it became at one stage, the biggest cattle market in Europe.

A hundred years after its first modernization, a new concurrence of changed circumstances in the same fields overwhelmed the capacity of the corporation to adapt, although it was not unwilling to do so. The growth of cattle marts represented much more effective competition than had been hitherto experienced from the dozens of traditional fairs, as buyers and sellers alike now had a greater choice of options; improvements in travel and transport also facilitated the growth of competition; the fall off in exports of fat cattle to Britain; the centralizing of butchering in meat factories; and the increased scale of retailing of meat products all coincided to have a fatally detrimental effect on sales. The resultant closure of the Dublin Cattle Market, indicates that mere willingness to change, is not in itself sufficient to achieve survival in a competitive world; maintaining the ability to adapt is equally essential.

At The Cross: a shop in rural Ireland, 1880–1911

MIRIAM LAMBE

I

The Stapleton family has been in retail business at The Cross of Pallas for over a hundred years. At the crossroads four minor roads meet; one leads to the town of Borrisoleigh, a mile and a half away, another to the Catholic chapel of ease in Ileigh, while two other roads lead to the village of Upperchurch. Nenagh, the county town, is seventeen miles distant, while Thurles, the largest town in north Tipperary, is seven miles away.

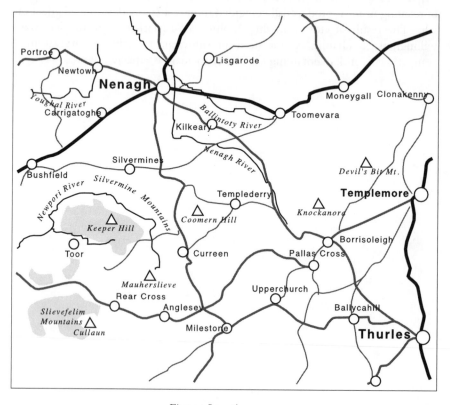

Figure 1 Location map.

Up to the 1980s Stapleton's shop was both a grocery shop and public house, but now it trades only as a pub. The outward appearance is that of one elongated two storey building, but closer inspection shows two buildings; a two storey and a single storey building which was raised to two storeys. There is nothing to indicate which of the two is the original structure; the surviving rate books show no change in valuation. The two buildings were interconnected internally at upstairs and downstairs level. The shop is in what was originally the single storey building, part of the upper floor addition was used as a loft, reached by an outside stone stairway. Outoffices were arranged at right angles to the main building thus forming three sides of a rectangular yard with the fourth side opening directly onto the public road. The original shop was one room with a single counter running along two sides, the bar was at one end of the counter, the grocery at the other. An area of the grocery was partitioned to serve as a snug.

The time frame for this study has been determined by the surviving Stapleton business records and the census returns of 1911, an important source for profiling the business community in the area. The collection of records is very small. There are two books of numbered customer accounts, one book with fifty eight accounts for the year 1881 and the second book with only three accounts for the year 1897. Two day-books span the years 1903 to 1929. The records themselves are fragmentary with many blank pages in the customer accounts' ledgers. The day book for 1918 has only four pages with nothing recorded for September and only one transaction recorded for November.

That any records have survived is fortuitous: changes in ownership of the business, inadequate storage conditions, children looking for scribbling paper, all reduced the chances of survival of the account books. Nevertheless, it is possible by examining these records, together with some public records, to gain an insight into the role of the shop in the economic and social life of rural Ireland at the turn of the nineteenth century.

II

If this study is be more than a simple analysis of the shopping habits of the inhabitants of the neighbourhood of The Cross, it is necessary to put it into the context of the wider retail trade in Ireland during the period 1880 to 1911. A breakdown of the Irish population according to occupational groups shows that, during the years, 1881 to 1901, there was an rise in the number of people engaged in the various branches of the retail trade. This growth was not simply a rise in numbers, but as an occupational group, retailers of various kinds increased as a proportion of the total population, giving credence to the claim that 'Ireland has always suffered from a plague of small shopkeepers'.[1] The following table illustrates this change in the occupational structure of Irish society.

1 Liam Kennedy, 'Retail markets in rural Ireland at the end of the nineteenth century' in *Irish Economic and Social History*, vol. v (1978), pp. 46–63.

Table 1 Occupational classification (excluding Dublin and Belfast) 1881–1901.

Occupation	1881	1891	1901
Publicans	7,012	8,679	8,548
Grocers	11,592	12,970	12,209
General Shopkeepers	24,221	23,277	24,581
No. per 1000 population	9.5	11.16	12.32

Source: Liam Kennedy, 'Traders in the Irish rural economy, 1880–1914'.

Among the reasons given for the large number of retailers in Ireland was the increasing commercialization of the economy in the nineteenth-century. The growth in bank deposits, which rose from £8m in 1850 to £43m in 1900, and the increase in rail traffic, both passenger and freight, are some of the features of the Irish economy in the latter half of the nineteenth century which are cited as evidence of growing commercialization. The proportion of the population living in towns of 1,500 people or more, increased from one sixth in 1845 to one third of the population in 1914 and this was another factor underpinning the commercialization of the economy.[2]

The provincial newspapers reflect this growth in business enterprise. In particular, the advertisements confirm the growing significance of local commercial activity. In 1882, *The Tipperary Leader,* based in Thurles, carried advertisements for a wide range of consumer goods available from traders in towns such as Nenagh, Clonmel, Thurles, Templemore and Dublin.[3]

There were advertisements for side cars from Moylan's of Nenagh and for painting and decorating contractor, Jamieson Stewart of Cashel. Readers were informed that winnowing machines could be hired from Daniel McCormick, Borrisoleigh. Bicycles could be purchased on easy terms from Carson's of 21 Bachelor's Walk, Dublin, who, it was stated, were sole agents for the Coventry Machinists Company. Other goods advertised were monuments and tombs, Peruvian guano (a fertiliser), Danish butter and Cantrell and Cochrane club soda. The network of agents which the newspaper had in Borrisoleigh, Cahir, Capote, Cashel, Carrick-on-Suir, Dublin, Dundrum, Dungarvan, Inch, Clonmel, Limerick Junction and Waterford is also evidence of the linking of local economies with the national economy.

III

From the eighteenth century onwards, various directories were published and from these the outlines of local commercial activity can be sketched.

2 Cormac O Grada, *Ireland: a new economic history, 1780–1939* (Oxford, 1994), pp. 264–70.
3 *Tipperary Leader,* 14 Jan. 1882, 18 Jan. 1882, 3 June 1882, 26 July 1882.

Borrisoleigh was described in one such directory as the centre of an area which was 'good for pasture and tillage'.[4] Three fairs were held annually in the town, on 6 June, 6 August, and the most important fair, a cattle and sheep fair, was held on 27 November. This latter fair was preceded by a pig fair held on the previous day.

Over time, some business names disappeared from the directories but, nevertheless, there was a continuity of families in Borrisoleigh in business, particularly from the last decades of the nineteenth century. Of the businesses listed in 1870, three were still trading in 1915: Chadwick's grocery, Coffey's spirit dealer and Finn's hardware. Between 1883 and 1893 there was a higher survival rate for businesses, with only two of the original thirteen listed in the 1883 directory missing from the 1893 edition. There were six new entries in the 1915 edition: one publican, three general dealers, one grocer and one grocer/spirit dealer. By this time, the Munster and Leinster Bank had opened a branch in Borrisoleigh.

The advertisements in *Bassett's book of Tipperary*, published in 1883, indicate the range of goods and services which an individual business might provide. John Cormack of Borrisoleigh, described as a family grocer, was also a baker, a wine and spirit dealer, a butter merchant, an auctioneer and flour importer. Horse and cattle medicine, oils, colours, paints and stationery could be purchased at Chadwick's, the druggist, which also traded as a family grocer/wine and spirit merchant.

IV

The level of commercial activity in the rural areas is difficult to measure because the directories provide no information on retail establishments in the surrounding countryside. For the early twentieth century, the distribution of shops and pubs in rural areas may be determined from the 1901 and 1911 censuses which have occupational information for each household. Some court records which survived the destruction of the Four Courts in 1922 can be used to map the distribution of public houses in the hinterland of Borrisoleigh. These are the records of the Crown and Peace Office for Tipperary, which include publicans' licence registers dating from 1885 and excise collectors' lists dating from 1886.

When granting licences, account was taken of the number of previously licenced houses in the neighbourhood. The following table shows the distribution of public houses in north Tipperary in 1871, together with the number of pubs per head of population.[5] The towns and villages listed all had populations of over 500 people.

4 George Henry Bassett, *county Tipperary 100 years ago, a guide and directory 1889* (Belfast, 1991), p. 359.   **5** *Return showing the number of houses licensed for the sale of intoxicating liquors in Ireland for the year ending 31 March 1871*, H.C. 1872 (434) xlvii, p. 787.

Table 2 No. of houses licensed for the sale of intoxicating liquors in
north Tipperary in 1871.

Town	No. of Pubs	Population	Ratio
Nenagh	66	5,531	84
Templemore	57	3,443	60
Thurles	58	5,332	92
Borrisoleigh	17	773	45
Borrisokane	15	1,130	75
Cloghjordan	11	668	61
Newport	13	1,013	78
Roscrea	35	3,165	90
Total	272	21,055	77
Rest of county	97	70,902	731

The concentration of public houses varied as has been shown in table number
two, from an average urban ratio of one pub to seventy-seven people to a rural
distribution of one to 731 people. The reason for this is unclear. More than likely
it was a combination of a scarcity of suitable applicants for licences and adequate
premises. Rural pubs were generally located on main roads or at the junctions
of minor roads. Ryan's pub of Ballyboy, Upperchurch, was strategically located
on the Limerick-Thurles road; Ryan's of Latteragh was on the main Thurles-
Nenagh road. There were two pubs at the Milestone in the townland of
Graneria in Upperchurch, an important cross road on the Nenagh-Tipperary
road. Minor cross road locations include Pallas Cross, Killeen Cross on the road
from Templederry to Nenagh, Dolla on the Templederry-Silvermines road and
Foilnamon on the Templederry-Upperchurch road.

At the Petty Sessions held in 1886 in the towns of Borrisoleigh, Thurles and
Nenagh, thirty-four publicans' licences were granted to publicans in the greater
Borrisoleigh area, eleven of which were to publicans in the town. Table 3 shows
that over a twelve-year-period the number of publicans' licences granted in this
area increased by five. Two of these new licences were in the village of
Silvermines, one in nearby Dolla, another was granted to George Wallace in
Templederry and one to Mathew Stapleton of Pallas Cross.[6] In the meantime
some other publicans had ceased to trade. Adam Hodgins of Garryglass was
issued a licence in 1894 but was not listed in 1989. George Powell of
Templederry and Denis Ryan of Upperchurch were both delisted in 1889.

6 NAI, Crown and Peace Office, county Tipperary, Publicans' Licence Register, 1C7/25.

Table 3 Distribution of publicans' licences in Borrisoleigh and surrounding areas.

District	1886	1889	1898
Borrisoleigh	11	11	10
Upperchurch/Drombane	10	10	12
Kilcommon	4	4	4
Silvermines	3	3	6
Templederry	6	6	7
Total	34	34	39

The distribution of shops and pubs during the period 1901–11 can be mapped from the census returns in the Borrisoleigh area. Excluding the town itself, there were fourteen shops and/or public houses in the area. By far the largest concentrations of business were in the villages of Upperchurch and Silvermines, with six businesses in the former and eight in the latter. Shops/pubs in the rural areas were located, as has been previously noted in the case of pubs, at cross roads or on main roads, with the exception of a shop which was beside the chapel of ease in Ileigh, a mile and a half from The Cross of Pallas. All of the new businesses which opened between the census years 1901 and 1911 were to be found in the vicinity of recently established creameries. By 1911 two new shops had opened in Greenane and at Currabaha Cross, near the newly established creameries.[7]

V

Mathew Stapleton was first recorded by the Crown Court as the holder of a publican's licence in 1896. There is no evidence to suggest that prior to this date he was dealing as a spirit grocer. A spirit grocer was restricted in the quantity of alcohol which he could sell for any one order, usually two quarts at a time, for consumption off the premises. A person who sold tea, cocoa-nuts, chocolate or pepper was defined as a grocer. Such a trader could get a spirit licence on payment of an excise fee. The first records of alcohol sales to be found in the Stapleton ledgers date from 1896. The earliest business accounts for 1881 have a couple of references to 'cash lent for drink', but no actual sales of drink.[8]

A certificate of good character, issued by the recorder or magistrate at the quarter sessions, was necessary in order to obtain a publican's licence. A fee, based on the rated valuation of the licensed premises, had to be paid to the excise authority, who then issued the licence. In urban areas, the cost of a publican's licence for a house under £10 valuation was £3 6s.1½d., that of a

7 NAI, Census 1911, county Tipperary, Enumerators' returns DED 125/1, 124/1.
8 Stapleton ledger of account, 1881–96, in the possession of Mathew Stapleton, Pallas Cross, Borrisoleigh, county Tipperary.

spirit grocer cost £9 18s. 5¼d.[9] The authorities would not license a 'poor miserable cabin' and the house had to be properly furnished. The quality of buildings used as pubs varied. Mary Carroll's pub, in the village of Upperchurch, had a slated roof and had a rateable valuation of £3 10s. In nearby Milestone a thatched pub was rated at 10s.[10]

There were four types of publicans' licences; a seven-day licence, a six-day licence, and seven-day and six-day early-closing licences. An early-closing licence meant that the premises opened one hour later and closed one hour earlier than the ordinary licensed premises.[11] The majority of licences were seven day trading licences. Out of 16,654 publicans' licenses in existence in 1877, 13,920 were seven day licences.[12] The licence held by Mathew Stapleton was an ordinary or seven-day licence. The licensing laws were complex, with at least fourteen different types in existence during the period of this study, and a lack of understanding of these laws resulted in many people being summoned for having unlicensed premises. A licence had to be renewed annually on production of two certificates, one signed by six householders in the area and the other by two or more magistrates attesting to the good character of the licensee.

The varied responses to summonses reflect the social and economic differences between publicans. Sometimes solicitors appealed on behalf of their clients who were in breach of the law. Most publicans appealed on their own behalf. One publican in Borrisoleigh, William Small, in a letter to the local excise office, explained his failure to pay the appropriate excise duty, stating 'it is my first time the like to happen and wat [sic] costs is on up to this I will remit to you'. A publican in Friar Street in Thurles, Mary Smyth, accounted for her lapse by saying, 'I am a poor widow and it never will occur during my time again'. A third correspondent stated 'I am after burying a young girl … true [sic] her illness I forgot … the licence lately transferred to me after the death of my mother. I am a poor orphan'. A letter written by an RIC constable based in Kilcommon in 1887 illustrates the different economic circumstances of two rural publicans, both named Ryan. William Ryan at the Cross of Kilcommon, 'near our barracks', had paid the excise duty but did not register. Denis Ryan, Churchquarter, did not pay the ordinary excise duty, 'he being too poor to do so. He sells no drink whatsoever, as if he did I would treat him as an unlicensed person and have him punished by the magistrate'.[13]

9 Elizabeth Malcolm, '*Ireland sober, Ireland free*': *drink and temperance in nineteenth-century Ireland* (Dublin, 1986), p. 209.   10 Tipperary county Libraries, North Tipperary county Council Rate Books, 1889.   11 Malcolm, *Ireland sober*, p. 206.   12 *Report from the select committee on the sale of intoxicating liquors on Sunday (Ireland) Bill together with the proceedings of the committee minutes of evidence and appendix*, H.C. 1877 (198) xvi, I.   13 NAI, Crown and Peace Office, county Tipperary, Publicans' Licences Excise Collectors' Lists, Correspondence etc. 1886–9, 1 C 7/22, 26 Dec. 1887, 18 Dec. 1887, Dec. 1887.

VI

The census returns of 1901 and 1911 are an invaluable source of information on publicans. They not only indicate the size of this occupational group, but the details contained in the enumerators' forms also facilitate sociological profiling of the group. Most of the traders were male and married. Women involved in business were, with a couple of exceptions, widows or shop assistants to their husbands. One woman seemed to have been living apart from her husband as her household consisted of her two children and a female lodger.[14] Two single women were shopkeepers. One lived near the chapel in Ileigh with her son and her own sister, while the other, who was in her forties, lived on her own. Thus, shopkeeping, for at least some women, provided an opportunity of earning a living in a time of restricted opportunities for employment outside the home. The women in the hinterland of Borrisoleigh in 1901 were either farmers' wives, daughters, housekeepers to unmarried brothers or general domestic servants, with the exception of one dressmaker, one national school teacher, one beggar and the female shopkeepers.

There were more openings for men to earn a living outside of farming and farm labouring, in both urban and rural areas. The creameries, in particular, provided new opportunities for males as separators, engine drivers and creamery managers. It is evident from advertisements in the local papers, all seeking male employees, that there were also more opportunities for males in the retail trade in the larger towns … *The Nenagh News* advertised for a 'strong country lad', 'a well educated boy', 'a respectable youth over 18' as an apprentice to the grocery and retail spirit business in a good home where he will be treated as a member of the family and taught his business, … serve two years … a small fine'.[15]

Twenty-seven people described themselves as shopkeepers in the two censuses. Twelve of these were also involved in other activities, the majority in farming, two as creamery managers, two as sub post masters and one as a flour merchant. Very few people described themselves solely as publicans. It was the usual practice for publicans to trade as grocers, to the extent that apprentice barmen were known as 'grocers' assistants'.[16] In an era of restricted employment opportunities, shopkeeping was an attractive option which could be combined with other income-generating activities.

The low cost of entry into retailing, particularly in terms of the capital needed to acquire premises, was another factor which made shopkeeping attractive.[17] Most businesses in Irish towns were family run, and families usually resided above the shop. The majority of businesses in the hinterland of

14 NAI, Census 1901, county Tipperary, Enumerators' returns, DED 122/30. 15 *Nenagh News*, 2 Oct. 1899. 16 In conversation with Mathew Lambe, former manager of the *Big Tree* public house, Dorset Street, Dublin 1, July 1999. 17 Liam Kennedy, 'Traders in the Irish rural economy, 1880–1914' in *Economic History Review*, 2nd series, nos 1–4, p. 204.

Borrisoleigh operated from 'private dwellings' according to the censuses.[18] The investment in goods depended on the amount of stock carried and this could be kept low. Very few of the businesses employed shop assistants or barmaids. Mathew Stapleton was one of the few in the area to employ a shop assistant . Labour requirements were by and large met by the families, wives, daughters or relatives, in one case by a niece and in another by a son-in-law. In one family, the father was a sub post master, his wife a post office assistant, one daughter a merchant, another a shop assistant and a son a rural postman.

VII

The Stapleton accounts provide a good insight into the trading activities of rural publicans/grocers. In the 1880s, for example, the shop carried a wide range of goods. The staple purchases, however, were tea, bread, sugar and tobacco. It was also possible to purchase cart grease, brandy, bread soda, castor oil, eggs, polish, arrowroot, Epsom salt, hair oil, candles, soap, sweets, coffee, pepper, starch, 'blue', laces, caraways, raisins, currants, thread, magenta, blacking, 'perle barley', saltpetre, 'chiplogwood', matches, jam, snuff, washing powder, barley sugar, pipes, striped rock, senna leaves, paraffin oil, mottled soap, note paper, saffron and *The Freeman's Journal*. By 1903 the range of goods on sale had been extended to include pigs' heads, herrings, strainers, boots, cups, feeding bottles, bacon, bowls, knives, mugs, perfume, 'unity malt' and flax seed.[19] Also on sale were school bags, hemp, painting oil, farmers' blue, calico, raspberry wine and chamber pots. By 1914 the branded product had truly arrived at The Cross, when sales of 'Rinso', price one penny, were recorded.

Between the years 1903 and 1910 the sale of meal, flour, bran and 'Pollard' accounted for a substantial proportion of the daily transactions.[20] Pollard was the brand name of an animal feed usually given to pigs, already noted as an important element in the local economy. If sales of animal feed stuffs are excluded from calculations, the value of daily transactions at The Cross was quite low. John Cormack of Drumtarsna called to the shop seven times in June 1881 and ten times in July 1881, yet the amount he spent at any one time never amounted to more than 4s. 2d. The amount outstanding on John Bradshaw's account in April 1881 was £3 12s. 2½d. These transactions were very low compared with the value of sales of flour and animal feeds. In 1903, one hundredweight of pollard cost 8s., flake bran 8s. 9d., ten stone of flour 17s. 6d. However, from 1910 sales of animal feeds no longer featured in the shop's day-books.

The evidence from the day-books suggests that shops in rural areas were the precursors of today's convenience store. The majority of customers came from

---

18 NAI, Census 1901, county Tipperary, Enumerators' returns, DED 101–6, 111, 123–7, Census 1911, DED 102–7, 112, 123–8.   **19** Stapleton day-book 1903, Day-book 1914, in the possession of Mathew Stapleton, Pallas Cross, Borrisoleigh, county Tipperary. **20** Stapleton day-book 1903.

the adjoining townlands. While allowing for the fact that the day-books only recorded credit transactions, the volume of business on a daily basis was small, suggesting that people went to the local shop mainly for such staples as tea, sugar and tobacco and for emergency supplies. Some customers did their Christmas shopping at The Cross and usually they bought currants, raisins, caraway seeds and rice, some minerals, perhaps some coffee and 'a bottle of special'. Rice pudding was at that time the Christmas treat. A bereavement might necessitate a visit to the shop to buy supplies for the wake, such as '5 gals of malt @ £4.10s, 4 bottles of best port wine, 1oz of snuff, bread, 6 lb candles, 2 lb tobacco, 2 st sugar, 3 lbs of tea, 6 doz pipes, 3 lbs of biscuits, 1 pt malt, 3 gals malt and 1 doz porter'.[21] These items were purchased by Pat Hayes of Gurtahoola in January 1900.

Changes in consumer behaviour can be detected in the business records. The earlier ledgers show that the usual quantity of tea bought was two ounces but by 1903 this had risen to a half pound or more, and the order for sugar had increased from a pound to a half stone or more. The sale of alcohol, as a proportion of transactions recorded in the records, also increased quite considerably. There are several possible reasons for these changes. An increase in the consumption of tea, sugar and alcohol could be attributable to rising incomes. There may also be a connection between the opening of the creamery in nearby Pallas in 1899 and an increase in the sale of alcohol. Indeed, it was argued by those opposed to the establishment of creameries that farmers might patronise the local public house on their route home.[22] There may also be an association between the development of the co-operative creamery movement in the district and the decline in the sale of Pollard, with farmers now purchasing animal feed from co-operatives. However, without further information, no definite conclusions can be drawn from the evidence presented in the day-books.

VIII

Mathew Stapleton was involved in the butter trade as a butter factor and it is clear from his records that the development and expansion of the activities of creamery co-operatives brought an end to this commercial activity. Prior to the development of creameries, most butter was farm produced. Cream was left to separate naturally and was churned into butter and packed as it became available into firkins. A firkin held about 70 lbs of butter. The butter was sold directly from the farm or at butter markets to dealers who acted as agents for merchants who graded and packed the butter for the export market. The merchant weighed and tasted the butter. The firkin was stripped and drained at the merchant's stores and then branded and finally sold on to the export merchant.[23]

21 Stapleton day-book 1900. **22** William Hayes, *Drombane Co-operative Agricultural and Dairy Society Ltd. Drombane Turraheen Pallas 1897–1997, celebrating a century of success* (Drombane, 1997), p. 5. **23** William Jenkins, *Tipp Co-op: Origin and development of*

The development of the centrifugal separator in Germany and Denmark made butter-making more efficient and produced a better, more uniform product.[24] As a result, Irish butter faced strong competition from Danish butter in the English market. The Irish Agricultural Organisation Society was established in 1894 to promote the development of co-operative creameries modelled on the Danish system. The agricultural co-operative movement came under intense pressure from many quarters and in particular from traders, who saw their butter buying and the sale of their goods threatened. There was also opposition from Cork butter merchants, 'some of whom did a good bit of gombeening'.[25] The art of butter-making, it was said, would be lost if the co-operative creameries established a foothold.

The first dairy co-operative was started in Ireland in 1889[26] in Drumcollogher, county Limerick. In the Borrisoleigh area, Drombane creamery was established in 1897 and Pallas creamery, an auxiliary of Drombane, opened for business in September 1899. There was a creamery in existence in Rathcardan, the townland adjacent to The Cross of Pallas, but nothing is known of its activities.[27] The new creamery at Pallas, 'between the road and the river', was less than half a mile from the shop at The Cross. By 1901, there were several other creameries in the neighbourhood, in Currabaha, in Greenane, in Killeen and, by 1911, there were new creameries at Knockmaroe, Foilnamon and Fantane. Some occupations, those of creamery manager, butter-maker and butter-separator, appear for the first time in the census returns.[28]

There had been a weekly butter market in Borrisoleigh, but by 1880 this had fallen into abeyance, due partly it was said, to the absence of a rail link. Several attempts were made to establish such a link, which it was felt would lead to the re-establishment of the weekly butter market.

> It is 30 years since this [butter market] flourished and attempts at revival have only helped to corroborate the opinion that buyers will not undertake tedious journeys by car when there are so many market towns with railway facilities. It is different with the fairs, and they continue to retain public favour.[29]

In these circumstances a local trader like Mathew Stapleton, in his capacity as a butter-factor, would have played an important role in the local economy and the extent of this very local trade can be partially reconstructed from the records of Stapleton's shop. He was the link between the butter-maker and the butter

Tipperary Co-operative Creamery Ltd, (Dublin, 1999), p. 7.   **24** William Jenkins, 'Restructuring of Irish dairy co-operatives since 1950: an example from county Tipperary' in *Irish Geography*, vol. 29, no. 1 (1996), p. 38.   **25** R.A. Anderson, With *Horace Plunkett in Ireland* (London, 1935), p. 20.   **26** Hayes, *Drombane*, p. 5.   **27** Bassett, *county Tipperary*, p. 359.   **28** NAI, Census 1911, DED 102–7, 112, 123–8.   **29** Bassett, *county Tipperary*, p. 359.

market in Cork. In October 1897 he supplied Cronin and Nolan of Devonshire Street in Cork with 407 pounds of butter valued at £13 19s. 9d. Cronin and Nolan also had offices in Manchester. The following July he supplied Charles M'Cartie, also of Cork, with 575 pounds of butter, valued at £16 1s. 10d. The largest quantity of butter bought from local farmers was 1,144 lbs, roughly sixteen firkins of butter, which was worth £38 3s., and this was bought in May 1897. The amount of butter made by individuals varied considerably. For example, on 18 October 1897, Mrs Delaney of Cronavone was paid for five pounds of butter, William Stapleton for six and Mrs Richard Bourke for thirty-five.[30]

Because the butter accounts are fragmentary, it is not possible to state with any degree of accuracy the number of farmers who regularly supplied butter to Mathew Stapleton. Butter-making was highly seasonal. Farmers accumulated stocks of butter during the summer months which they sold off during the winter.[31] The number of suppliers varied from fourteen in October 1894 to forty-five in April 1897, the higher figure being partly accounted for by the time of year, as milk was more plentiful in spring following calving. Many of these suppliers of butter, named in the 'account of fresh butter', were women. Thirteen people supplied Mathew Stapleton with butter on 7 December 1894, ten of these were women.[32] Butter-making was considered women's work. Women milked the cows, made butter for home consumption with any surplus being sold at the butter market or shop. The money was then used to pay off shop debts.[33]

The people who supplied butter to the shop at The Cross came from a wider catchment area than the regular customers. Several were from the neighbouring parishes of Upperchurch and Templederry as the map overleaf illustrates. Perhaps a more complete set of customers' accounts might reveal a different picture, but most of the butter makers do not feature in the surviving customer account book. It is difficult to determine the impact of the establishment of co-operative creameries and the mechanisation of butter-making on Mathew Stapleton as the value of his butter trade is unknown. While farmers received a higher price for their milk from the creameries and creamery butter fetched a higher price in the shops, milking was now redefined as men's work. At this stage one can only speculate as to whether the increase in farm incomes compensated the shopkeeper for the loss of the butter-makers' trade.[34]

IX

There were several reports published in the late nineteenth century and early twentieth century which were quite critical of rural shopkeepers.[35] Shopkeepers were described as a 'parasitical class swollen to an extent which renders it

30 Stapleton ledger of account, 1881. **31** Jenkins, *Tipp-Co-op*, p. 13. **32** Stapleton ledger of account, 1881–96. **33** Jenkins, p. 29. **34** Hayes, *Drombane*, p. 5. **35** *Report from the select committee on money lending*, H.C. 1898 [260], x, pp. 227–47.

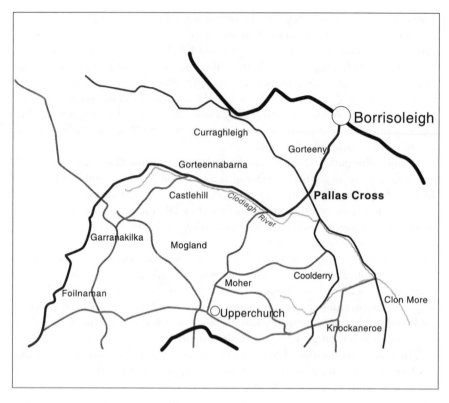

Figure 2 Map of Mathew Stapleton's butter catchment area.

impossible for them to make a living except by extorting prices'.[36] They were accused of charging high prices for goods bought on credit. An example given of this dual price structure was of meal being charged at 12*s.* cash per bag while the credit price was 13*s.* 6*d.*[37] Profits were said to be exorbitant, the mark up on tea for example was claimed to be 100 per cent. Butter and eggs were often exchanged for goods instead of cash, usually for tea, sugar and tobacco. It would seem that the practice at The Cross was to pay cash for butter. Interest charged on retail credit transactions were said to be excessive. Recent research, however, suggests that a difference of 10–15 per cent between the cash price and the

36 Anderson, *With Horace Plunkett in Ireland*, p. 101.   **37** O Grada, *Ireland*, p. 269.

credit price was the norm, which it is contended was modest.[38] As the source of much of the unfavourable comments on shopkeepers in Ireland were the reports of the Congested Districts Board and comments of supporters of the co-operative movement, it would be unsound to use these as evidence of sharp practices throughout the country.

The extant Stapleton ledgers record only credit transactions, so it is not possible to calculate the difference between credit and cash prices. With goods such as tea and sugar which were sold loose, there was a slight difference in prices charged for a pound and a quarter or half-pound. However, without information on wholesale prices, one cannot draw any significant conclusions as to whether Stapleton's mark up was excessive. It can safely be said that there was a remarkable similarity between prices in rural and urban areas, based on a comparison of prices at Stapleton's and Murray's shop in Dunshaughlin, county Meath, as Table 4 illustrates.[39] Again, ten years later, there were few differences between prices at Stapleton's and those charged in Maher's of Thurles.[40] Some of the variation in price may in fact reflect differences in quality. Prices in the three shops were remarkably stable during in this ten-year period

Table 4 Comparison of prices between Murray's, Dunshaughlin, county Meath, 1902 and Stapleton's, Pallas Cross, county Tipperary, 1903.

Item	Murray's	Stapleton's
Tea (lb)	2s. 4d.	2s. 6d.
Sugar (lb)	2d.	2d.
Butter (lb)	1s. 2d.	1s. 8d.
Flour (st)	1s. 9d.	13s. 6d. (half sack)
Raisins (lb)	6d.	4½d.
Candles (lb)	5d.	6d.
Oil (gal)	10d.	10d.
Tobacco (2 oz)	6d.	6d.
Blacking	1d.	2d.
Soap (lb)	3d.	3d.
Porter (gal)	1s. 4d.	10d.
Whiskey	7d.	8d.
Flour	1s. 4d.	14s. (half sack)
Pollard	11d.	10½d.
Bran (st)	1s. 0d.	1s. 0d.

38 Kennedy, 'Retail markets', pp. 50–1. **39** Information supplied by Jim Gilligan, Ratoath, county Meath. **40** Michael Callanan's pass book, account with James Maher, The Square, Thurles, county Tipperary, 25 Nov. 1912, Dec. 1916, in the possession of Ms Phina Callanan, Ardbawn, Thurles, county Tipperary.

Table 5 Comparison of prices between James Maher, Thurles, 1913 and
Stapleton's, Pallas Cross, 1912.

Item	James Maher	Stapleton's
Tea (½ lb)	1s. 4d.	1s. 4d.
Sugar (st)	2s. 4d.	3s. 6d.
Stout (doz)	2s. 0d.	2s. 0d.
Stout (bottle)	2s. 0d.	2d.
Candles (lb)	2d.	2d.
Whiskey	5s. 6d. (qt malt)	3s. 0d. (pt)
Blue	1d.	1d.
Tobacco	7d.	7d.
Porter (gal)	1s. 4d.	1s. 8d.
Lemonade	2d.	2d.

X

The relationship between the shopkeeper and customer was a complex one
because in addition to supplying goods on credit, the shop was also a small-scale
quasi bank. This aspect of the relationship was particularly important in a farming
economy. The seasonal nature of farming and the uncertainty of agricultural
incomes meant that farmers experienced cash flow difficulties, hence the importance of credit purchases and short term loans. Commercial banks at the time were
reluctant to advance loans to small farmers and labourers, partly because of the
difficulties associated with bad debts and the small sums of money involved.
Banks invariably demanded security for even the smallest of loans. Mathew
Stapleton at The Cross was no different from his contemporaries in loaning
money to his customers and from his business records it can be seen that some
of these loans were extremely modest. The sums varied from 2d., 3½d., 1s. 3d.,
to a £1 and occasionally the reasons for these loans were noted. Money was lent
to pay the county cess (a local tax), £4 to pay a 'bill in the bank', and in 1903,
2s. to pay Fr Hackett.[41]

This economic relationship between the shopkeeper and rural dweller was said,
by contemporary observers, to be biased in favour of the trader.[42] Customer
indebtedness and the availability of credit facilities could be used to tie a customer
to a particular shop, thus restricting choice. It was said that shopkeepers encouraged
indebtedness to keep customers. It was asserted that credit dealings encouraged
certain abuses such as the sale of poor quality or adulterated products. With high
levels of illiteracy and innumeracy in the country, there were also opportunities for
the unscrupulous trader to cheat such disadvantaged customers.

41 Stapleton day-book, 3 June 1903.   **42** Kennedy, 'Rural markets' pp. 48–53.

From the shopkeeper's perspective, the risk of bad debts was exacerbated by the difficulties in foreclosing on such debts in a small community. Most of the accounts rolled over from year to year. While the majority of the balances on customers' accounts were quite small, payments were irregular, as a customer's pass book with James Maher, family grocer, The Square, Thurles, indicates. This customer, Michael Callanan, lived in the townland of Ardbawn, a mile outside Thurles. During the period January 1913 to September 1914, only one payment was made, £3 on a balance of £25 3s. 11½d.[43] Three cash payments amounting to £28 6s. 2d. were made, on 5 January 1915 and two separate payments on 2 March 1915, leaving £5 14s.10½d.unpaid until August. In comparison the picture that emerges from the Stapleton accounts is one of a higher level of indebtedness to the shopkeeper. In September 1909, John Heffernan paid £1 off the balance of his pass book which was £10 1s. 5d.[44] In 1923, Mrs Willie Hayes, Junior, of Clonmore, paid £10 on account, while in February of the same year another customer's outstanding balance was £23 10s. An additional risk which the shopkeeper took was to sell alcohol on credit, as Mathew Stapleton did, as debts incurred through the purchase of alcohol on credit could not be proceeded with through the courts. Mutual trust was essential to good relations between shopkeeper and customer.

XI

A critical role has been attributed to shopkeepers and publicans in social and political matters in late nineteenth century Ireland, particularly with regard to the Land League.[45] This dominant role was attributed to the social origins of shopkeepers which were, it was argued, to be found among the farming community. These kinship connections, whether through birth or marriage, were further cemented by the fact that shopkeepers were themselves often farmers.[46] Some of the evidence cited to support the claim for the pivotal role played by shopkeepers in political affairs comes from an analysis of occupations of people arrested under the Protection of Person and Property Act, 1881. The commercial and industrial sectors were over represented among those arrested, with innkeepers and publicans primarily responsible for this skewed picture. This group, which represented only 0.4 per cent of the labour force, accounted for 8.1 per cent of arrests under the aforementioned act. The fact that their premises could be used for illegal meetings and posting of placards might account for this imbalance in the number of arrests from this class.

43 Michael Callanan's pass book, 25 Nov. 1912, Dec. 1916. **44** Stapleton day-book, 1909. **45** Samuel Clarke, 'The social composition of the Land League' in *Irish Historical Studies*, vol. xvii, no. 68 (1971) pp. 447–69. **46** Samuel Clarke, *The social origins of the Irish land war* (Princeton, N.J. 1979), p. 268.

The shopkeeper was well placed to emerge as a local leader. Premises were often well located, as has been shown to be the case in the hinterland of Borrisoleigh and as the following passage illustrates

> The junction of these roads are known as 'Crosses' by various names, Ballyroan, Summerhill, Currabaha, neighbours meet on Sunday afternoon and play pitch and toss, skittles and marbles ... buyers come and buy rabbits every ... evening at the cross roads.[47]

Shopkeepers were largely literate and numerate. In the census returns examined in the course of this research, only one shopkeeper described himself as illiterate. As a group, they had more opportunities for social contact, not only with customers but with agents and sales representatives. Mathew Stapleton, as has previously been noted, had business dealings with Cork butter merchants. These contacts, combined with the physical location of the shops within the community, made them transmitters and receivers of information, news and gossip. These advantages, together with the significance of their economic role and strong kinship ties in the community enabled shopkeepers to enjoy an important social and political role, and to wield power and patronage at a local level.

This perception of shopkeepers as very active in nationalist politics and agrarian issues has been based on research which has relied heavily on evidence from the west of Ireland.[48] An in-depth study of Thomastown, county Kilkenny, produced results which run counter to some of these common generalisations.[49] The shopkeepers in the Thomastown area appeared to exercise very little political influence or leadership. They were not, for example, over-represented on the Board of Guardians which was the most important public forum for expressing political and social opinion. They played only a minor part in famine relief. A study of local government covering the period 1872 to 1886 describes the participation by shopkeepers in public affairs as minimal.[50] A study of the first local elections in north Tipperary, to select members of the newly formed county councils would seem to support this view. These elections were contested primarily by farmers. In only four districts did shopkeepers present themselves as candidates.[51] None of these aspiring local politicians came from any of the townlands surveyed in this study and the anecdotal evidence is that in latter years there was only one publican/farmer active in local politics in the hinterland of Borrisoleigh.[52]

---

47 UCD, Department of Folklore, Primary schools' collection, microfilm P. 155. **48** W.L. Feingold, Transformation of local government in Ireland 1872–1886, revolt of the peasantry (Boston, 1984). **49** Marilyn Silverman and P.H. Gulliver (eds), *Approaching the past, historical anthropology through Irish case studies* (New York, 1992) pp. 190–3. **50** Feingold, *Transformation of local government in Ireland*, pp. 196–8. **51** Donal Murphy, *Blazing tar barrels and standing orders: North Tipperary's first county and district councils 1899–1902* (Nenagh, 1999), pp. 196–204. **52** Personal conversation with Norah Lambe, formerly of Cronavone, Borrisoleigh, county Tipperary, August 1999.

There is a strong case for caution in generalising about people categorised as traders or shopkeepers in Ireland at the turn of the nineteenth century. Comparing experiences it would seem that the role played by shopkeepers in economic and political life was different in the west of Ireland from that in the more prosperous areas of the country. The picture that emerges from this micro-study of rural shopkeepers is not as sharp as one would like due to the absence of critical evidence which made it impossible to measure in any quantitative sense the extent of farmer or labourer indebtedness, of profit margins and interest charged on loans by shopkeepers. It is hoped that the value of this study lies in its focus on the shop as a hub in neighbourhood communities and its examination of commercial developments and specialisations on the small rural shopkeeper.

Murray's of Dunshaughlin, 1896–1910

JIM GILLIGAN*

I

For a century Murray's general store was a Dunshaughlin landmark. Situated at the northern end of the village, it opened for business in May 1896 and remained in the Murray family until sold in 1998. Peadar Murray, who was a publican, draper, cycle salesman, hardware merchant, Gaelic League activist, writer and noted photographer presided over its fortunes until the 1940s. His wife, Margaret, who was prominent in local politics, continued to run the business until the 1960s, when their son, Brendan, took over. When Murray first opened his doors to the public Dunshaughlin consisted of a single long street with little or no development off it. Situated approximately half way between the city of Dublin and the market town of Navan, it was overshadowed by its much larger neighbours and never developed as a business or commercial centre until late in the twentieth century.

Griffith's *Valuation* of 1851 lists three public houses, a grocery and a post office in Dunshaughlin.[1] Trade in the village seems, in general, to have been poor. The Valuation Office house books for Dunshaughlin contain a number of remarks suggestive of this. Bridget Begg's public house benefited from a good passing trade 'because night and day cars stop here … it is the best situation in town.' At Patrick Markey's, on the other hand, 'not much business is carried on'.[2] An account of the area dating from 1845 describes Dunshaughlin as 'so greatly decayed as to become a mere village'.[3] One is also struck by the lack of advertisements in the local press from the business people of Dunshaughlin. The local fairs seem to have been poorly supported. Graziers such as Edward Delany, whose main business was fattening store cattle for the Dublin and English markets, travelled west to buy their cattle in places like Ballinasloe, Strokestown and Moate.[4] A report of a 1907 fair in Dunshaughlin noted that buyers were

* I would like to record my thanks to Brendan Murray for his assistance in researching this study and for access to various documents in his possession relating to his father's business.
1 *General valuation of rateable property in Ireland, Union of Dunshaughlin, valuation of the several tenements,* (Dublin, 1854), p. 47–8.   2 NAI, Valuation Office House Books, county Meath, Barony of Ratoath, Dunshaughlin Town, OL 54212.   3 *The parliamentary gazeteer of Ireland, 1844–5* (2 vols, Dublin, 1845), ii, p. 164.   4 Jim Gilligan, *Graziers and grasslands, portrait of a rural Meath community, 1854–1914* (Dublin, 1998), p. 29.

scarce and 'the supply of stock was very limited.' Yet this represented a marked increase on the previous year.[5]

Dunshaughlin's location and its small and declining population were the main reasons for its failure to develop as a commercial centre. Population in the town had declined from the pre-Famine figure of 524 to a low of 291 in 1891. There was a slight increase to 315 in 1901 but ten years later numbers dropped to 265, the lowest recorded.[6] The 315 inhabitants in 1901 comprised seventy-five households. It was from this small base that Murray drew most of his immediate custom.

Table 1 Population of Dunshaughlin Town, 1841–1911.

1841	1851	1861	1871	1881	1891	1901	1911
524	422	403	362	354	291	315	265

The rural hinterland presented an equally discouraging picture for the local shopkeeper. Population decline was rapid and continuous here also after the Famine, caused mainly by the trend towards grassland farming and away from tillage. Dunshaughlin was at the centre of the richest grazing lands in Ireland, and out of the 130 Poor Law Unions in the country the Dunshaughlin Union consistently had the highest proportion of its area under grass.[7] As a result, the labouring population declined in the post Famine years. A noted local political activist, Bernard Carolan, described Dunshaughlin's hinterland as 'reverting to a howling wilderness' due to the large grazing farms which required little or no farm labour.[8]

By 1901, 270 households amounting to 1,255 people lived in the Catholic parish which had supported 2,447 in 1851 and 3,221 in 1841.[9] Many of the households in the western part of the parish would have found it inconvenient to shop in Dunshaughlin but, on the other hand, Murray's shop attracted some custom from the neighbouring parishes of Dunsany and Ratoath. Nevertheless, it is unlikely that the total number of households who were potential customers ever exceeded 400. Many of the households were poor, and about half lived in third- or fourth- class housing, according to the 1901 Census. Many sons were employed as farm servants or labourers and daughters as domestic servants or housekeepers and would have had little or no disposable income.[10] There is no doubt that many in the area lived close to poverty. In February 1905, ninety-two 'tramps' visited Dunshaughlin Workhouse in one week and as many as 100 arrived in one week in April. Though the Poor Law Union covered a much wider area than Dunshaughlin many probably came from the immediate locality.[11]

5 *Drogheda Independent*, 20 April 1907.   **6** Gilligan, *Graziers and grasslands*, p. 14.   **7** Ibid., p. 20.   **8** *Drogheda Independent*, 20 April 1907.   **9** Gilligan, *Graziers and grasslands*, p. 14. **10** Calculations based on NAI, Census of Ireland 1901, Enumerators' forms, Meath, DED 10, Culmullen 1–13 and 27, DED 14, Killeen 1–11 and DED 19, Dunshaughlin 1–21c. **11** *Drogheda Independent*, 11 February and 1 April 1905.

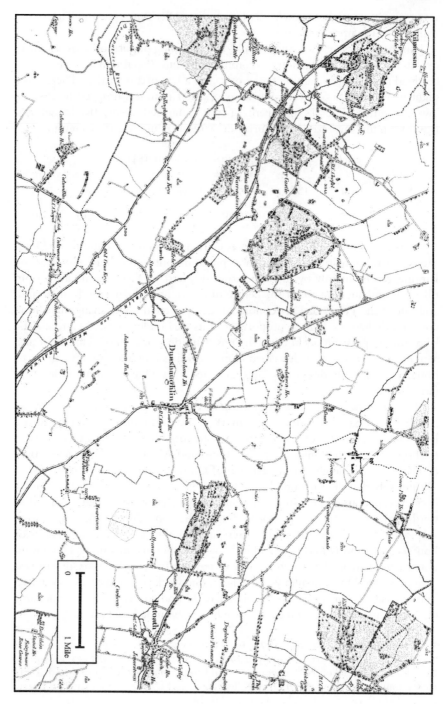

Figure 1 Dunshaughlin, county Meath and locality.

There was only a small commercial element in the village when Peter Murray commenced business. By the 1890s, trade directories of Dunshaughlin listed up to six publicans: Brien's, Murphy's, Foley's, Blake's, Kelly's and Swan's, the last three of which doubled as grocers. The village also had a hotel, two bakers, a tailor and a bootmaker.[12] By 1901, there were still six public houses. Kelly's and Swan's had become Daly's and Murray's respectively. The only grocery shop recorded in the 1901 census was Murray's, but some of the pubs probably still doubled as small grocery shops, a common practice at the time. In addition, it is known that Bernard Carolan had a shop, though his house is recorded as a private dwelling in the census. Laurence Canning described himself as a master-baker and three others living on the same premises were also bakers.[13] It is known that Canning supplied the local workhouse but it is not clear what other outlets he had for his bread. Murray bought bread from suppliers in Kilcock, Trim and Dublin but there is no reference in his accounts to payments to Canning. Within the parish the other public houses were the Spencer Arms beside Drumree railway station, about one and a half miles from Dunshaughlin, Jane Cluskey's in Warrenstown, Caffrey's in Batterstown and Patrick Kevlin's at the Hatchet, at the western end of the parish. The nearest village of equivalent size, Ratoath, also had few businesses.[14] It appears that many of the farmers in the Dunsany area, a few miles to the north of Dunshaughlin, frequented the Dunsany Co-operative Stores, which had a turnover of £10,901 in 1893.[15]

This was the context in which Murray commenced trade as a general merchant. In the grocery and drapery business he had little opposition, but there was a fairly large concentration of public houses in the vicinity. However, the population was low and continuing to decline. Most were dependent on farming for an income and there was only a small well-off element of large farmers and gentry to support a business such as Murray's. Such people however had a ready access to Dublin via the railway from Drumree or Batterstown stations and many had their own horse-drawn transport.

II

The Murrays were natives of Garristown, county Dublin and Peter's parents ran a public house there.[16] He spent over half a century in Dunshaughlin and became almost synonymous with it. Yet, when he died in 1949 he was buried in the family grave in his native Garristown. His reasons for moving to Dunshaughlin are not known but since he was no stranger to the shop business, it is likely he availed of the first opportunity which arose to start business on his own.

12 *Royal national directory of Ireland* (London, 1894), p. 89.　**13** NAI, Census 1901, Enumerators' forms, Meath DED 19, Dunshaughlin.　**14** *Royal national directory*, pp. 193–4.
15 David Lynch, John Donohoe, Michael Smith, *Dunsany 1894–1994* (Navan, 1994), p. 149.
16 Brendan Murray, Dunshaughlin, in conversation with the author, 8 Jan. 2000.

Figure 2 Peter Murray. © B. Murray.

The premises where Murray began trading was not always a business premises. Griffith's *Valuation* indicates that in the middle of the nineteenth century the house was the residence of the local Church of Ireland clergyman, who leased it from Willoughby Bond. Bond also had an interest in a number of properties in the town as well as over 250 acres in Mooretown, three miles from the town. By the 1890s, Bond's interest in the property had passed to Peter Moran of Blackwater House, Ratoath, who leased the property to Sylvester Lamb initially, and from 1884 to William Swan of Skryne.[17] Both used the premises as a public house. The premises were transferred to James Swan on 1 November 1895 on the death of William Swan and to Murray on 1 May 1896, at Trim Quarter Sessions.[18]

James Swan had paid Moran £100 in February 1896 to have his father's lease assigned to him and also agreed an annual rental of £14 for a lease of 60 years.[19] However, a month later, Swan sublet the premises to Murray but no details of the rental are available. Moran was not entirely happy with this arrangement and put pressure on Murray to surrender and renew the lease. In July 1900, Murray's

17 VO, Revised valuation books, county Meath, Town of Dunshaughlin, Dunshaughlin ED. **18** NAI, Publicans' Licence Applications (Court Book), county Meath, 1891–1909, IC 2781, pp. 46, 49 and handwritten note in Account of Spirits Book, in possession of Brendan Murray, Dunshaughlin. **19** RD, 1896/12/193.

diary records that he 'was over this morning with my landlord, he was very hard ... [I] could get a new lease on condition that I gave him £100 and £18 per year rent.'[20] The following month he recorded that he 'rode to town, signed surrender of old lease and signed new one.'[21] The new lease was for sixty years at an annual rental of £18 but the lease does not specify if the £100 Moran demanded was paid.[22] Later that month Moran 'wiped out half a year's rent'.[23] Murray could now continue business with the premises secured for his lifetime. Such an annual rental appears to have been the norm in the area. Daly's public house next door to Murray's was held on a rent of £14 while Alicia Caul's public house in Ratoath was held on a lease of £16, which a sale prospectus described as a 'very moderate yearly rent'.[24]

A selection of records survives from Murray's early years in business. Although they are extensive, they vary in their usefulness to the historian. From the opening of business in 1896 to mid-1899, Murray kept an account of cash received and paid out.[25] Receipts are simply recorded as cash received and are not itemised, whereas expenses are more detailed, with the amounts and the payee listed. This book enables one to estimate Murray's income and expenditure in his first three years of business. A large ledger outlining the accounts of individual customers from August 1900 to August 1902 has survived, showing purchases and payments towards the account. This book gives details of those who had an account with Murray but gives no information on cash customers.[26] However, a day book which covers the period July 1902 to June 1903, thus overlapping partly with the ledger, gives details of cash and credit customers and itemises individual purchases.[27]

In addition, there are a number of diaries, some only partly filled and often containing little more than comments on the weather or scribbled financial calculations. However, a number of them contain interesting remarks on the business and local events and the 1906 volume gives a daily account of sales, comprising cash, credit and payments on account.[28] There are also a number of quotations from various companies for the period 1910–1913. There is also a small file of Cycle Agreement Forms which give details of bicycles bought on the 'Easi Pay Mathod', a type of hire purchase. The cycle file dates from 1910 to 1915.[29]

20 Murray's Diary, 31 July 1900. All diaries are in the possession of Brendan Murray, Dunshaughlin. **21** Ibid., 17 August 1900. **22** RD, 1900/60/253, 1900/60/254 and 1900/66/15. **23** Murray's Diary, 27 August 1900. **24** RD, 1879/73/19 and *Drogheda Independent*, 27 February 1909. **25** Cash Book, 1896–99, in possession of Brendan Murray, Dunshaughlin. **26** Customers' Ledger, 1900–2, in possession of Brendan Murray, Dunshaughlin. **27** Day Book, 1902–3, in possession of Brendan Murray, Dunshaughlin. **28** Murray's Diary, 1906. **29** Quotations, 1910–13 and Cycle Agreement Forms, 1910–15, in possession of Brendan Murray, Dunshaughlin.

Figure 3 Earliest known photo of Murray's shop, early 1900s.
© B. Murray.

III

An analysis of Murray's sales' ledger for the years 1901–02 yielded a list of 348 customers who held an account in the shop. It was possible to identify with reasonable certainty where 278 of those resided. Almost a quarter of the total came from the immediate vicinity of the village or adjoining townlands. Most of those were in the village itself, all within half a mile of the shop. Comparing Murray's list of customers with the 1901 census, it appears that 61.3 per cent of households in the village held an account in Murray's.[30] This is a very large portion of the households, particularly when one considers that Murray was a relative newcomer to the village.

   Another 15 per cent of the customers, fifty-three persons, resided within two miles of the shop. Fourteen of those came from the poorest and most densely populated townland, Red Bog. Ten out of the twelve households in Red Bog held an account in Murray's and the vast majority of those were small tenants or labourers. Approximately a quarter of the shop's clients lived within a two to

30 Calculation based on NAI, Census 1901, Enumerators' forms, Meath, DED 19, Dunshaughlin.

four mile radius of the shop, the vast majority of them in the Culmullen end of the parish, with a sizeable proportion from Dunsany-Killeen, just outside the parish to the north. This left 15 per cent of the shop's named customers who lived over four miles away but the vast majority of those were not far beyond the four mile radius.

Murray stocked a wide range of foodstuffs, drinks both alcoholic and non-alcoholic, drapery and hardware. Food available ranged from basic items such as tea, sugar, butter, loaves of bread, eggs and salt to more luxurious items such as sweet-cakes, biscuits, cakes and pots of jam. It appears that many people made their own bread because flour, sold by the stone, and bread soda were popular items. Tea was expensive, ranging in price from 2*s*. to 2*s*. 4*d*. per pound, while butter was also costly at 1*s*. 2*d*. per pound. Sugar and eggs, on the other hand, were relatively cheap. A pound of sugar cost a mere 2*d*. while a dozen eggs could be had for a shilling.

Meat was sold on the premises but it seems to have been limited to bacon and ham, a pound of which cost seven to nine pence. A tin of salmon could be had for the same price. A wide selection of drinks was available: stout, malt and porter are recorded but there is no mention of beer or lager. Murray stocked whiskey and brandy, sherry, wine, port and even champagne, as well as lemonade and lemon soda. Many customers bought stout by the bottle at a cost of 1*s*. 10*d*. per dozen.

Murray didn't confine his business to food and drink. He also carried a wide selection of clothing and footwear. The records show that boots, stockings, shirts, jackets, gloves, shawls, pinafores, corsets, handkerchiefs and belts were on sale. He also catered for the local seamstresses and tailors, selling material such as wool, muslin and calico. Buttons could be had at one penny per dozen, while lace collars and feathers were also in stock.

By 1912, the shop also sold farm implements, ranging from the simple spade, shovel and rake to more advanced machinery like mowers, reapers and wheel rakes, and also stocked cement, timber and glass. From at least 1909, Murray stocked a range of bicycles which could be bought on the hire purchase system, and to accommodate the slowly growing motor car population he also sold petroleum.

The range and variety of merchandise on offer indicates that Murray had links with numerous suppliers, mainly based in Dublin but including others from much further afield. Surviving letters, with price lists in some cases, indicate that Murray did business with a range of well-known Dublin companies such as Guinness, Arnotts, Jameson, Clerys, Easons and Bolands. He also traded with Winstanley, the boot and leather manufacturers, Williams and Woods, makers of confectionery and preserves, Henshaws, providers of iron goods, Gilbeys, wine and spirit merchants and clothing manufacturers Crowe Wilson and Thomas Guiney. He also ventured further afield to the Dyeing and Woollen Factory in Cork, Boyle Co-Operative in county Roscommon, and the Selskar Iron Works in Wexford. With the increasing popularity of the bicycle, Murray had links with

British firms such as Kynoch's Cycles in Birmingham, who were 'pleased to note that the machines we have sent you are to your satisfaction'. Other overseas suppliers were Humber in Coventry, the Dunlop Rubber Company in Birmingham and Michelin in London.[31]

IV

Murray's clientele ranged over the whole social spectrum of the area. The well-to-do large farmers; the small professional element in the village such as the R.I.C. constables, the schoolmaster and the clergy; tradesmen such as carpenters and tailors; and agricultural labourers, herds, grooms and servants all frequented the premises. Rich and poor depended on the shop and it was probably one of the few places where the different classes met. Such meetings were a rarity in an area which the *Drogheda Independent* described as a 'part of the country where the classes wholly ignore the masses.'[32]

There were some significant differences between the various social groups in the goods they bought and the ways they paid. Edward Delany of Woodtown and Edward Kelly of Creakenstown were both large farmers, whose income came in the main from fattening cattle on their farms for the Dublin and English markets. They owned or leased over 200 acres of land each and were regular customers of Murray's.[33] Delany bought bacon at least once a fortnight and also purchased malt, port and, in the week leading up to Christmas, champagne. He also took home biscuits, cakes, pickles and Bovril.[34] Kelly also bought some foodstuffs such as cakes, lemonade and sugar but seems to have concentrated his purchases on animal feed like bran, pollard and yellow meal, and farmyard hardware like brushes, nails, staples and forks. Both men had accounts which they settled from time to time, often running up substantial bills before payment. By September 1900, Kelly's outstanding bill amounted to £6 19s. 5d. and when the bill was furnished it was promptly paid in full by cheque. By February 1901, Kelly owed £8 14s. 3d., which he again promptly settled, this time in cash. In the fifteen months from June 1900 he spent £27 8s. 2d. in Murray's.[35]

The Thunders of Lagore, who farmed over 200 acres, also accumulated large bills. By August 1900, £11 10s. which was owed was part paid by a cheque for £7 16s. A further cheque for £5 2s. 11d. was paid in October. The Thunders' account also consisted of much hardware and some drink.[36] It is possible that many of the better-off farmers also did some of their shopping in Dublin. Delany was a regular visitor to other towns to buy cattle and the fact that Kelly had a cheque book suggests an account in Dublin, Navan or Trim. The first reference to a bank in Dunshaughlin is in 1905 when the Ulster Bank in Trim

31 Quotations, 1910–11.   **32** *Drogheda Independent*, 14 July 1906.   **33** Gilligan, *Graziers and grasslands*, pp. 34, 37.   **34** Customers' Ledger, p. 61.   **35** Ibid., pp. 117, 271, 430. **36** Ibid., p. 153.

opened a branch office on fair days and on the second and last Tuesdays of each month. However, according to the clerk of the Union, there was very little business done.[37] There was a regular train service to Dublin from Drumree which Peter Murray often used and it is likely that others availed of it also to visit Dublin.

The accounts of Mrs Daly, a substantial farmer from Clonross, suggest however that some of the larger farmers did most of their shopping locally. Mrs Daly was widowed and the household also consisted of three sons, a daughter and two step-sisters. The step-sisters, both in their thirties, each listed their occupation as 'Lady' in the 1901 census. A male servant was also part of the household.[38] It is likely that, as a widow, Mrs Daly had less opportunity to travel to Dublin and consequently seems to have done most of her shopping in Murray's. In October 1901, she shopped there on twelve occasions and by November owed £17 17s. 2d., of which she paid £11 19s. 5d. Mrs Daly purchased a great variety of goods, all of which indicate a high standard of living and a varied diet in the household. Purchases ranged from basics such as tea, butter, sugar and loaves to more luxurious items like bacon, jam, cocoa, lemonade and even sweets, cigarettes, a siphon of soda and different varieties of biscuit.[39]

People of this social status, the medium to large farmers, tended to run up substantial bills but to settle promptly when furnished with an account. They often paid in full, or reduced the amount outstanding substantially, and paid in cash or occasionally by cheque. Although they did buy some foodstuffs locally, such people may well have bought food and other items elsewhere also, probably in Dublin, as there was no other important shopping centre nearby.

The agricultural labourer, herd, groom and others dependent on the local agricultural economy tended to concentrate their purchases on basic items of food but also spent substantial portions of their limited income on drink. James Lynch, an unmarried fifty-four year old agricultural labourer from Red Bog, was a regular customer. In September 1900, he called about once every three days and owed £1 7s. 7d. by the end of the month. He paid off 15s. of this on 26 September and another 14s. 6d in mid-November. In early and late February 1901, he paid 11s. 8d and 6s. respectively. He made two further payments in March of 5s. and 10s.[40] Customers such as Lynch rarely cleared their accounts completely. They tended to pay more often than the large farmer but in much smaller amounts which rarely covered even half the amount outstanding. For example, by January 1901, Lynch still owed £1 6s. 2d. and by March his outstanding bill in was £1 14s. 3d., despite the payments noted above. Lynch's purchases are described in the accounts as 'goods', so it is difficult to analyse them fully, but butter, some bacon in December, tobacco and regular amounts of stout or drink are recorded.

37 *Drogheda Independent*, 4 February 1905 and 1 February 1905. **38** NAI, Census 1901, Enumerators' forms, Meath, DED 19, Clonross. **39** Customers' Ledger, pp. 613, 680. **40** Ibid., pp. 175, 333.

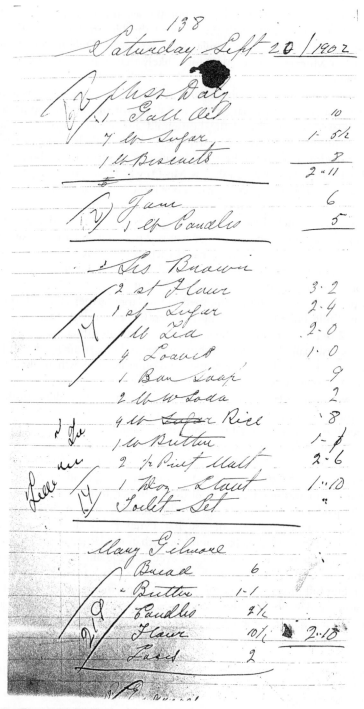

Figure 4 Murray's Day Book, 1902, showing customers' purchases.

Michael Bracken, a seventy-seven year old widower who lived in Red Bog with his unmarried daughter, was another small-scale customer. In August 1900, he owed £2 12s. 5d. and a year later he still owed £2 8s. 8d. Bracken paid off small amounts regularly and also traded eggs and butter in an effort to lessen his bills. His cash payments varied from a few shillings to a pound or more and he also got credit of 4s. and 1s. 3d. for butter and 1s. 6d. and 2s. 2d. for eggs.[41] A few other customers also availed of this method of reducing bills, such as Thomas Cassidy who was paid 2s. for three dozen eggs. Murray, in turn, sold the eggs to other customers, in this case turning a profit of 50 per cent by selling them for 1s. per dozen.[42] It is also very likely that he sold the home-made butter in the shop as well as commercially produced butter like that from Boyle Co-Operative. Cassidy, who was a married agricultural labourer, bought butter, tea, sugar and bacon three times in December and regular amounts of drink and stout. An itemized bill from August 1902 records him spending 1s. 2d. on tea, 8d. on sugar, 6d. on tobacco, 3d. on a loaf, 6d. on butter and 8d. on porter.[43] This appears to be a typical bill for him and others of a similar social standing.

The main problem faced by Murray was that customers rarely cleared their accounts and large amounts were outstanding at all times. A few further examples will illustrate the point. Mr. Browne from Dunsany owed £7 3s. 2d. in August 1900 and by September it had risen to £9 7s. 8d. A payment of £4 reduced his debt but by late October the bill had risen to £12 9s. 1d., which he then cleared in cash. By January 1901, the amount had climbed once again to £11 15s.[44] Mrs Barry, described as a bottlewoman, had a bill for £1 14s. 8d. in August 1900; a year later practically the same amount was outstanding despite cash payments during the intervening year of £1 18s. 7d.[45] Robert Cowley, a carpenter from Cooksland, owed £4 6s. in August 1900 and by the end of September the outstanding balance was £6 9s. 1d. The balance was later reduced by £3 19s. 6d., which was allowed for work Cowley did for Murray.[46] Many other customers behaved in a similar fashion, thus creating a huge cash flow problem for Murray who had to meet his suppliers' bills on a monthly basis or risk going out of business.

V

When he commenced business in May 1896, Murray calculated that his stock, including £40 worth of cash in hand, amounted to over £300. However, his liabilities were greater. Excluding £265 of his own money which he had invested in the business, he owed over £200 to various suppliers and a loan of £240 to Andrew J. Keogh, a Dublin auctioneer.

41 Ibid., pp. 12, 501.   **42** Ibid., p. 884.   **43** Day Book, p. 37.   **44** Customers' Ledger, pp. 10, 272.   **45** Ibid., p. 24.   **46** Ibid., pp. 30, 238.

The shop opened for business on 29 May 1896 and an examination of the cash book reveals that he took in a total of £8 14s. while spending a further £55 18s. 8d. to the end of the month. (See Appendix 1 for monthly details). From June to the end of the year monthly receipts averaged £200, with December the best month at £244 12s. 7d. The turnover for the year was £1,455 9s. 3d. and, with payments of £1,354 16s., Murray was left with a surplus of about £100 for the year, representing about 7 per cent of turnover. Business in 1897 continued in a similar vein, the average monthly taking was up to £321, with December again by far the highest month at £459 8s. 4d. Expenses also rose to over £3,500 leaving a surplus of just over £200, a return of over 5 per cent on the turnover.

However, the profitability did not continue in 1898. Receipts continued to increase, up by 15 per cent on the previous year, but payments to suppliers and other outgoings leaped by 25 per cent, leaving Murray with a yearly loss of £158 in that year.[47] It is not clear why there was such a turnaround. The increase in receipts may have been due to increased demand, with extra customers frequenting the shop as it established itself firmly in the village. The extra custom would have caused Murray to increase his wholesale purchases and, accordingly, his expenditure but this would not explain the lower increase in income compared to expenditure. It seems likely that increasing numbers of customers were availing of credit and not paying immediately for their purchases. This would explain the failure of income to keep pace with expenditure. Indeed, in many cases the amount outstanding increased rather than decreased over time. Murray, as a newcomer to the area, may also have been prepared to offer credit more easily than other shopkeepers in order to attract trade, although there is no direct evidence for this. Refusal to extend credit could have resulted in the loss of customers and even in the refusal to settle bills already due.

The ledger, which commences in August 1900, provides substantial evidence for the view that increasing credit was the cause of the shop's lack of profit. An analysis of the first 100 accounts yielded a sum due of over £250, an average of £2 10s. per account.[48] Applying a similar average to all 348 accounts would indicate that almost £900 was outstanding. Obviously, if it had been possible to collect even a part of this money, Murray's situation would have been greatly improved. Even a quarter of this figure would have been equivalent to the shop's profit in its best year and would have turned around a bad one like 1898.

Purchasing goods on credit was a feature of shopkeeping at this time. Farmers in particular required credit as they didn't have a regular income. They needed to purchase seeds and food for animals in order to generate an income. Credit was not readily available from banks, which were very reluctant to lend to the small farmer. Most small towns didn't even have a bank and in those which did the bank opened for only a few days per month. In 1913, it was estimated that only 62 per cent of Irish bank offices were open on a full-time basis. As noted

47 All calculations based on Cash Book, 1896–9.   48 Customers' Ledger.

previously, Dunshaughlin had an Ulster Bank sub-office as did the neighbouring towns of Ratoath, Summerhill and Kilcock. The Belfast Banking Company had a sub-office in Skryne while the Provincial Bank and the Hibernian Bank had sub-offices in Duleek and Slane respectively.[49] In some areas local credit societies offered loans to farmers. An Agricultural Credit Society based in Ballivor in county Meath loaned a maximum of £10 to farmers with rateable valuations averaging £7 10s. and also arranged loans for labourers in cottages with an acre of land.[50] There is no evidence for the existence of any credit society in Dunshaughlin and accordingly, for many people, the shopkeeper was the only source of credit, whether in goods or in cash. Murray's accounts indicate that cash loans were rarely given.

Many contemporary observers believed that shopkeepers were too willing to extend credit to ensure customers continued to frequent their shop. It was also claimed that shopkeepers charged more for goods bought on credit than for cash. A report on agricultural credit published in 1914 stated however, that there was little difference between the price for the cash customer and one who availed of credit. The report also found some evidence of high levels of indebtedness to shopkeepers but believed those levels were declining.[51] Thomas McArdle, a member of the Agricultural Credit Society in Dromiskin, county Louth, told the committee that shopkeepers 'prefer to deal on credit than on cash. They want to keep these people on their books for as long as they can, to get a better profit' but that in 'a decent house if a customer pays in a few months he will get as good terms as if he paid cash down'.[52] Murray's accounts conform to this pattern and show no evidence of extra charges for credit. Goods bought on credit were added to the customer's account at the same price as if paid for in cash and when the bill was paid, in part or in full, there appears to have been no interest added. Effectively, the shopkeeper was extending short-term credit to customers without the benefit of any security or interest.

The report condemned transactions involving the use of eggs or butter to pay bills as it claimed that this practice gave the shopkeeper the opportunity to make excessive profits.[53] A number of Murray's customers used eggs and butter to reduce their bills. This was akin to a barter system where the eggs were effectively traded for items available in the shop. Murray seems to have allowed 8d. for a dozen eggs, which he sold on for 1s., thus giving him a profit of 50 per cent. Even allowing for occasional breakages and unsold eggs this was a substantial profit. It is not possible to calculate profits for butter as the amounts taken in were never specified. However, while the shopkeeper might make some profit on eggs and

49 *Report of the departmental committee on agricultural credit in Ireland* [Cd 7375], H.C. 1914, xiii, pp. 18, 386. Hereafter referred to as Murnaghan Committee. **50** *Report of the departmental committee on agricultural credit in Ireland: Evidence, appendices and index* [Cd 7376], H.C. 1914, xiii, p. 443. Hereafter referred to as Murnaghan Committee, Evidence. **51** Murnaghan Committee, pp. 71–2. **52** Murnaghan Committee, *Evidence*, p. 433. **53** Murnaghan Committee, pp. 75–6.

butter, such trade represented only a small part of the shop's turnover. The chief stumbling block to regular profit continued to be the amount outstanding in unpaid or partially paid accounts. This created a huge cash flow problem for the shopkeeper who had to meet his suppliers' bills on a monthly basis or risk a court appearance and possibly go out of business.

Murray's 1901 diary reflects this problem. A good day was one when bills were settled, rather than one when large amounts of goods were sold. He noted that 15 May and 14 August were 'a good day' and 'a great day' respectively, 'owing to the Union payment'. He described 31 October as 'a great day's business as Mrs Farnan paid £10'. He declared 27 May 'a good day's business owing to the following having paid accounts, Thomas Delany £7 8s., Mrs Murphy £3 10s., Swan £17, Thomson 5s. 8d'.[54] A day in late March of 1902 was 'a fairly good day chiefly owing to Mrs Edward Kelly and Edward Delany paying accounts'.[55]

The 1901 diary has a number of gloomy references to the lack of business. On 28 May 1901, he remarked that there is 'a bad business doing except that a few cheques were paid' and 'business lately has been very bad'. In mid-January he referred to there being scarcely any business, and another day was 'a wretched day's business' while Saturday 23 February was 'the worst Saturday this long time'. Early March was no better: 'scarcely anyone in, only received a few pounds'. Later that month there was 'a fair day's business … Jem Cahill bought [the] makings of a suit same as my own'.[56] Business continued to fluctuate in 1902. Trade was 'only middling' on a normally busy Saturday 'except that Mrs Rourke was in with cheque [for] £4 5s.' and Mark Cullen paid 'a good lot'. However, in June he recorded 'the best day's business this long time'.[57]

Local events such as a sports' day, funerals or holidays could make the difference between a good and a bad day. For example, 16 August 1901 represented 'a pretty fair day's business owing to prizes having been bought for the sports'. Murray was joint Honorary Secretary of the annual sports. Tom Teeling's funeral took place on 17 April and there were 'a lot of Dunsany people in afterwards,' while 24 June represented 'a great day's business owing to [the] holiday tomorrow.'[58]

Looking at a month at random it is possible to get an idea of how busy the shop was from day to day. During August 1902, Saturday was always the busiest day of the week with 29, 27, 52 and 57 customers on the four Saturdays respectively. Mondays were quiet with 16, 16 and 4 visitors on the first three Mondays. The two Fridays listed were also quiet with 15 and 18 customers respectively. The daily takings ranged from £2 to £4 with Saturday naturally representing the greatest sales at £11 5s. 7d., £6 5s. 1d., £10 17s. 6d. and £9 2s. 3d. respectively. However, while sales for August 1 to 23 amounted to £78 11s. 6d., the amount his customers actually paid was about half that, at £39 19s. 10d.[59]

Matters hadn't improved by 1906. Murray's detailed accounts for that year reveal that in any given month cash paid on account rarely matched credit sales.

54 Murray's Diary, 1901.   **55** Ibid., 1902.   **56** Ibid., 1901.   **57** Ibid., 1902.   **58** Ibid., 1901.   **59** Calculations based on Day Book, August 1902.

(See Appendix 2) For the year as a whole, £513 3s. 6d. was cleared off customers' accounts but twice that amount, £1,145 15s. 2d., was sold on credit. Thus the amount of money due but not paid remained a problem. Worse still, it seems the overall amount of cash received during the year was £2,426, a sum which was less than the 1897-98 figures, and over the whole year Murray recorded a profit of only £46 3s. 2d.[60]

The overall picture one gains from the accounts is that, after a promising start, Murray struggled to make ends meet from the beginning of the century as money outstanding mounted. Evidence in the Registry of Deeds tends to substantiate this view. The initial borrowing of £240 from Andrew J. Keogh was repaid in 1900 but later that year Murray again mortgaged the property and promised to pay Edward Egan, a Dublin merchant, £375 1s. 8d. by April 1901.[61] It appears he may also have had difficulty paying Crowe Wilson, as his diary notes 'Crowe's man down when I came home ... he wants me out Monday week, fairly firm.'[62] In 1903, Murray assigned his house, premises and tenements to Crowe Wilson for the remainder of the lease and in 1905 did the same to another supplier, Cockle and Ashley.[63]

VI

Accounts do not exist for the years immediately after 1907, but Murray continued in business and indeed expanded his range of services. Towards the end of the decade he diversified into the sale of bicycles, an area of great potential at the time. In the 1880s and 1890s, the cycling boom was at its peak and it was 'a craze for young sports' minded men of an athletic bent, as well as being a leisurely pursuit for the more adventurous element of the middle class, both male and female.'[64] Murray was an enthusiastic cyclist himself and set up a cycling club known as The Buffalo Bills. Along with a number of companions, he cycled the length and breadth of Meath and, in June 1902, even cycled to Cork to view the Cork Exhibition.[65] He rode to his native Garristown and to business in Dublin frequently.

In is not clear when Murray began to deal in bicycles but from 1909 onwards the cycle element of his business increased in importance. By then there were a substantial number of cycle agents within a twenty-five mile radius of Dunshaughlin and in 1909 *The Drogheda Independent* was carrying numerous advertisements each week from such outlets. Each supplier attempted to outdo his competitor with claims of superior offers. O Grady claimed to sell 'the bicycle that made Enfield famous' while Deacons of Maynooth cautioned that

60 Calculations based on Murray's Diary, 1906.   61 RD, 1900/55/80 and 1900/66/15.
62 Murray's Diary, 6 March 1902.   63 RD, 1903/60/87 and 1905/4/59.   64 Bob Montgomery, *An Irish roadside camera, Ireland's earliest motorists and their automobiles: the pioneering years, 1896–1906* (Dublin, 1997), p. 23.   65 Murray's Diary, 1902.   66 *Drogheda*

a ṁuinntir na miḋe agus Finegall !

bioḋ sé i niúl dóiḃ.

gur gaeḋilgeoir mise,

agus go mbíonn,

rotair ḋeasa gaeḋealaca,

an **Pierce** agus **Lucania**

ḋá nḋíol agam.

Aoine gur mian leis ceann aca ḋ'faġáil, 'sé
an ruḋ gur fearr ḋó a ḋéanaṁ, ná—litir ḋo
cur ag triall orm sa—i ngaeḋilge nó i mbéarla
—agus ní beiḋ an locht im leit muna mbeiḋ
margaḋ eaḋrainn.

peaḋar S. O Muireaḋaiġ

ḋomnac seacnaill.

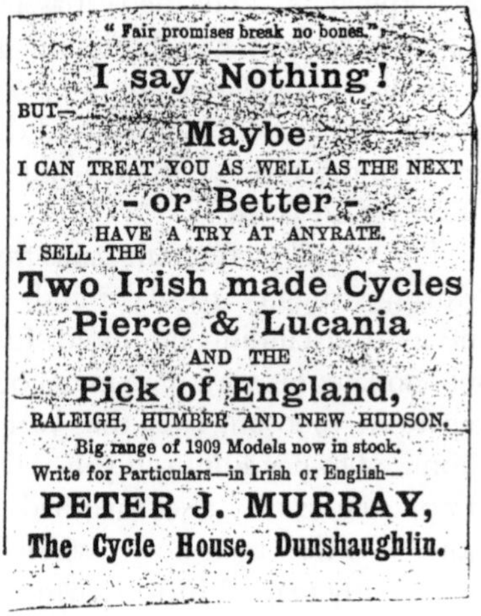

" Fair promises break no bones."

I say Nothing !

BUT—

Maybe

I CAN TREAT YOU AS WELL AS THE NEXT

-or Better-

HAVE A TRY AT ANYRATE.

I SELL THE

Two Irish made Cycles

Pierce & Lucania

AND THE

Pick of England,

RALEIGH, HUMBER AND NEW HUDSON.

Big range of 1909 Models now in stock.

Write for Particulars—in Irish or English—

PETER J. MURRAY,

The Cycle House, Dunshaughlin.

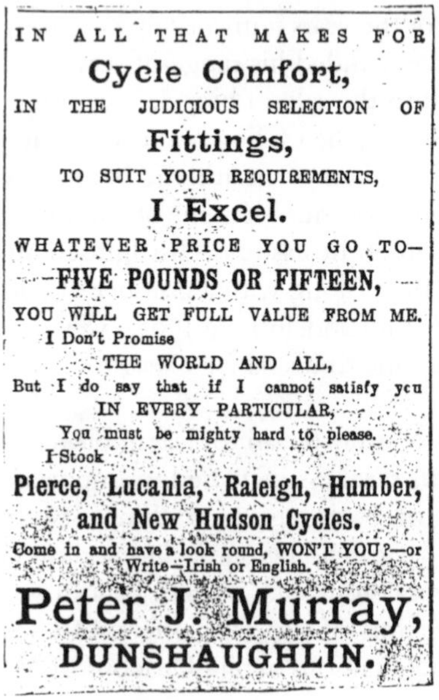

IN ALL THAT MAKES FOR

Cycle Comfort,

IN THE JUDICIOUS SELECTION OF

Fittings,

TO SUIT YOUR REQUIREMENTS,

I Excel.

WHATEVER PRICE YOU GO TO—

FIVE POUNDS OR FIFTEEN,

YOU WILL GET FULL VALUE FROM ME.

I Don't Promise

THE WORLD AND ALL,

But I do say that if I cannot satisfy you

IN EVERY PARTICULAR,

You must be mighty hard to please.

I Stock

Pierce, Lucania, Raleigh, Humber,

and New Hudson Cycles.

Come in and have a look round, WON'T YOU?—or
Write—Irish or English.

Peter J. Murray,

DUNSHAUGHLIN.

Figure 5 Advertisements for Murray's bicycles, *Drogheda Independent*, 1909.

'unscrupulous people claimed they [Deacons] couldn't equal others'.[66] Most advertised that old bicycles were taken as part payment, carriage would be paid to the nearest railway station and the majority, including Murray, offered a system of payment by instalment known as 'Easy Pay' or 'Gradual Payment' as an alternative to paying cash.

The spate of advertising seems to have goaded Murray into joining the fray. Beginning on 27 February 1909, he began an advertising campaign which consisted of a small classified and a larger display advertisement in *The Drogheda Independent*, often appearing on the front page.[67] His display advertisement was more moderate in tone than many of his competitors, stating that 'Maybe I can treat you as well as the next – or Better – Have a Try at any Rate'. The classified small advertisement gave Murray an opportunity to put in verse the virtues of his bicycles, a typical example being:

'WHISPER AND I SHALL HEAR
You call for a one or three Speed Gear
But whether you dwell afar or near
Be SURE to send your ORDER here'.[68]

The verse changed each week to refer to topical or seasonal events and was usually one of many small advertisements inserted by local cycle dealers. Murray by now was giving his address as The Cycle House, Dunshaughlin, suggesting that cycle sales were becoming a central part of the business. He also inserted advertisements completely in Irish addressed to the people of Meath and Fingal, advertising only his Irish made machines, Pierce and Lucania.[69] Advertisements, or indeed articles in Irish, were a rarity in the newspaper at this time and reflected Murray's prominence in the Gaelic League movement. In addition to Murray's personal advertising, companies such as Humber and Lucania inserted their own large display advertisements with line drawings which listed their Meath and Louth agents, including Murray.[70]

All of this suggests that by the end of the decade Murray was more interested in promoting his cycle business than his other interests. The cycle business had a number of attractions. Demand for bicycles seems to have been high and he could attract custom from a wider area than his grocery and pub clientele. The instalment system ensured a regular monthly income and was probably a surer source of ready cash than the grocery business. Eighty-four gradual payment forms survive and they enable one to reconstruct a picture of the business at the time.[71]

The majority of these forms are undated but most refer to 1911 and 1912. Just over a quarter of the buyers were women and the occupations of purchasers,

Independent, 16 January 1909 and 20 February 1909.　**67** *Drogheda Independent*, 27 February 1909 and following weeks.　**68** *Drogheda Independent*, 6 March 1909. **69** *Drogheda Independent*, 17 April 1909.　**70** *Drogheda Independent*, 3 April 1909. **71** Cycle Agreement Forms, 1910–5, in possession of Brendan Murray, Dunshaughlin.

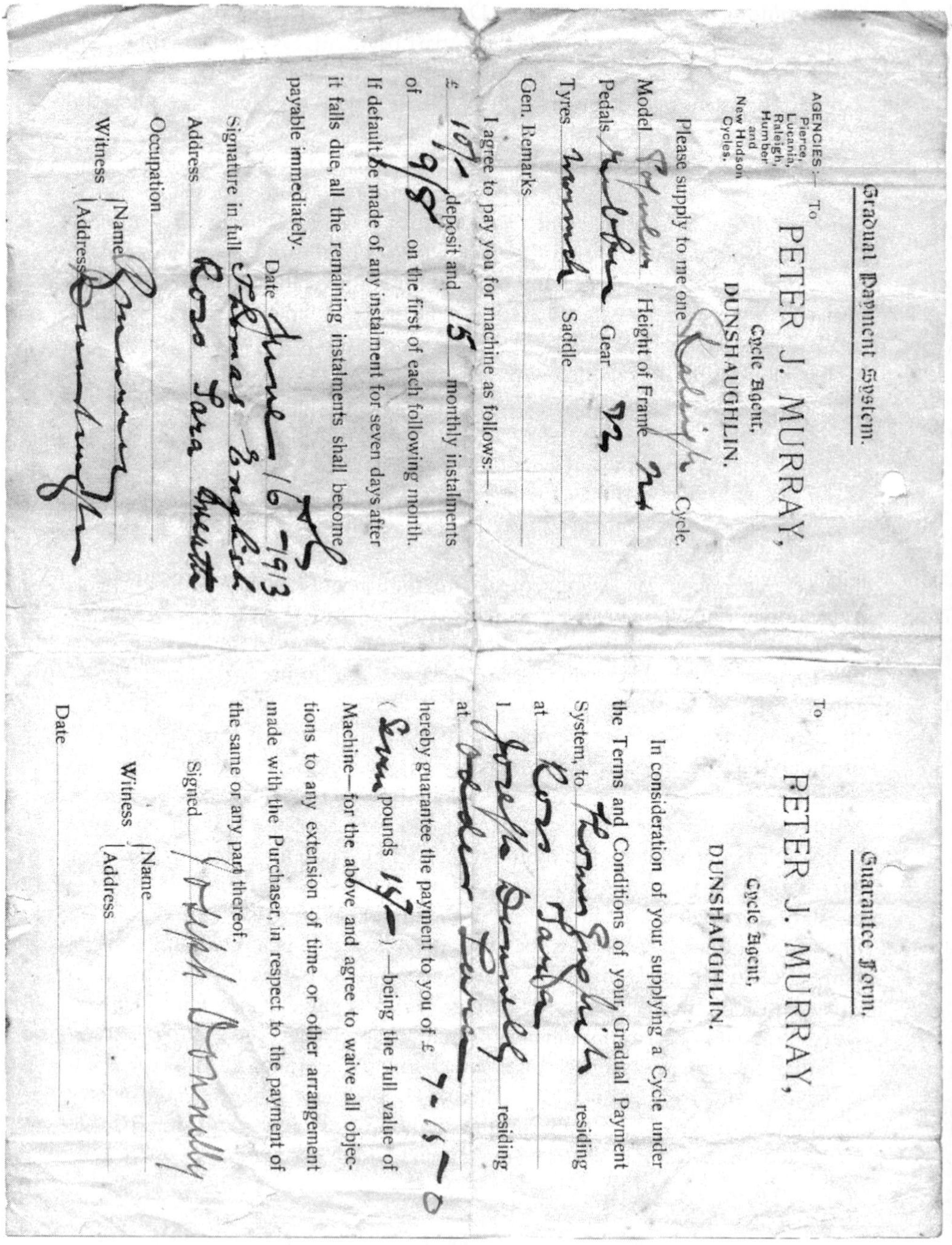

Gradual Payment System.

AGENCIES:— Pierce, Lucania, Raleigh, Humber and New Hudson Cycles.

To PETER J. MURRAY,
Cycle Agent,
DUNSHAUGHLIN.

Please supply to me one Raleigh Cycle.
Model ______ Height of Frame ______
Pedals ______ Gear ______
Tyres ______ Saddle ______
Gen. Remarks ______

I agree to pay you for machine as follows:—
£ 10/- deposit and 15 monthly instalments of 9/8 on the first of each following month.
If default be made of any instalment for seven days after it falls due, all the remaining instalments shall become payable immediately.

Date June 16 1913
Signature in full Thomas English
Address ______
Occupation ______
Witness {Name ______ Address ______

Guarantee Form.

To PETER J. MURRAY,
Cycle Agent,
DUNSHAUGHLIN.

In consideration of your supplying a Cycle under the Terms and Conditions of your Gradual Payment System, to Thomas English residing at ______ I ______ residing at ______ hereby guarantee the payment to you of £ 7-15-0 (______ pounds ______)—being the full value of Machine—for the above and agree to waive all objections to any extension of time or other arrangement made with the Purchaser, in respect to the payment of the same or any part thereof.

Signed ______
Witness {Name ______ Address ______
Date ______

Figure 6 Cycle Agreement Form, 1913.

where given, varied greatly. In the main, they were from the lowly paid working class such as domestic servants, labourers and grooms but they also included a publican, tailor and even an R.I.C. Inspector. The majority paid a small deposit of £1 or £2, amounting to 15 to 20 per cent of the total, and the remainder in twelve monthly instalments ranging from 8s. to 15s. Occasionally, payments were spread out over eighteen months or were made quarterly.

In no instance was the credit price more than the quoted retail price but it is likely that there were discounts for the cash customer. Certainly there were reductions for prompt payment under the 'Gradual Payment' scheme which varied from a discount of 5s. if paid off in eighteen months to 10s. if cleared over twelve months. From Murray's documents it is not possible to calculate profits made on the sale of bicycles as they do not list wholesale prices. However, cycle parts such as tyres and rims allowed profit margins from 30 to 60 per cent. Even allowing for the highest discount noted of 17s. on an £8 7s. bicycle, Murray was probably making from £1 to £2 on each machine sold. Considering the large amount of advertising he engaged in and the variety of merchandise on offer, it is likely that cycle sales became a central part of his business and may have compensated for the large sums of money outstanding in the grocery trade.

The advertising columns of *The Drogheda Independent* indicate that Murray had competition in Enfield, Maynooth, Drogheda, Kells, Navan and Trim. Dublin firms took advertising space also. His neighbour and friend, Bernard Carolan, was also a competitor, while another colleague, Mickey Fitzimons, sold cycles in Dunsany but appears not to have advertised. Despite the competition, demand for Murray's cycles came from a wide radius. The majority of customers were from Dunshaughlin and neighbouring parishes such as Dunsany, Skryne and Ratoath but he also attracted custom from Curraha and Ashbourne, both near his native Garristown, Duleek, and as far north as Drumconrath and Nobber. He also attracted custom from outside Meath with purchasers coming from Kilcock in Kildare and Mulhuddart in Dublin.

VII

There is some evidence that shopkeepers and publicans were active in the political arena in late nineteenth century Ireland. Samuel Clark, writing of the Land War, maintained that

> in the post-famine period their importance was enhanced still further and they came to rival landowners and clergymen as wielders of local power and patronage. They often enjoyed a social relationship with rural people that was comparable even to that of the parish priest.[72]

72 Samuel Clark, *Social origins of the Irish land war* (Princeton, 1979), p. 128.

This degree of political involvement was not found in P.H. Gulliver's survey of Thomastown in county Kilkenny nor does this study of Dunshaughlin support Clark's views.[73] Of course, Murray was a newcomer to the area and as such didn't have kinship links or lengthy involvement in the community, both of which were important factors noted by Clark. Indeed, when Murray married in 1911 his wife was not a local but a native of Milltown in Dublin. None of the other local publicans was politically involved either. However, Bernard Carolan, who sold bicycles, was active in a variety of nationalist organisations. He acted as secretary for a number of bodies, including the local G.A.A. club, the South Meath branch of the United Ireland League and the short-lived Back to the Land movement in the town, but he never stood for election to public office.[74]

Murray's involvement was in nationalist cultural movements, particularly the Gaelic League and the G.A.A. The first Meath branch of the League was set up in Dunshaughlin in 1900 with Peter Murray as its prime mover.[75] He had taken private lessons in Irish in Dublin and persuaded the then President of Maynooth College, Dr O' Hickey, to speak at a branch meeting in Dunshaughlin.[76] He was also instrumental in organising an annual *aeríocht* or open-air *feis* for the town. The 1902 event was attended by Patrick Pearse, while Murray was also a close friend of the Gaelic revivalist Sean T. O'Kelly, later to be Ireland's second President.[77]

The Gaelic League branch was very successful and involved a large cross section of locals, including shopkeepers, some farmers, the local curate and schoolmaster and even a member of the R.I.C. In the 1911 census Murray completed his details in Irish and it has already been noted that he placed Irish language advertisements for his business in *The Drogheda Independent*.[78] Murray was also actively involved in setting up the first hurling club in Dunshaughlin, which was named *Na Fir le Céile* or The United Men.[79] He was also secretary of the annual sports, which were organised by men who were nationalist in outlook. Though Murray was never directly involved in politics, his wife, originally Margaret Hackett, became a member of the Dunshaughlin Rural District Council in the 1920s and was later a member of Meath County Council.[80]

VIII

In many ways, Murray was typical of the shopkeeper of his day. His shop carried a huge range of goods and there was little or no specialization. He was a grocer

73 P.H. Gulliver, 'Shopkeepers and farmers in south Kilkenny, 1840–1981' in Marilyn Silverman and P.H. Gulliver (eds), *Approaching the Past* (New York, 1992), pp. 176–204. **74** See for example *Drogheda Independent*, 17 March 1906 and 26 October 1907. **75** *Drogheda Independent*, 17 November 1900. **76** *Drogheda Independent*, 19 October 1901. **77** *Drogheda Independent*, 20 September 1902. **78** NAI, Census 1911, Enumerators' forms, Meath, DED 19, Dunshaughlin. **79** *Drogheda Independent*, 27 September 1902. **80** *Meath Chronicle*, 5 June 1920 and Denis Boyle, *A History of Meath County Council, 1899–1999* (Navan, 1999), pp. 206–7.

Figure 7 Murray's shop front, 1934. © B. Murray.

and a publican as well as a draper and a vendor of farm supplies. He followed the then widespread custom of extending credit to all his customers and, while this may have enabled him to retain custom, it also meant that large sums of money were always outstanding. Rich and poor availed of this facility and it appears to have been a huge burden on the business. Given the ubiquity of shop credit in Ireland at the time, Murray probably had no alternative but to accommodate his customers in this way.

Murray, however, was in many ways an innovator and risk-taker, open to outside influences and ideas. He came to Dunshaughlin as a complete outsider and, as far as can be ascertained, had no prior kinship links with the area. He seems to have changed the focus of his business in the first decade of the twentieth century, when he diversified into bicycle sales to the extent that he called his shop The Cycle House. He advertized regularly, even using Irish language advertisements to attract business from the supporters of the Gaelic revival. He also made use of the deferred payment system to boost sales. His innovative style was evident in other areas also. He was central to the setting up of the Gaelic League in Dunshaughlin and was successful in attracting a varied membership into the branch. He must have been among the first in the area to own a camera and he developed his own photographs, taking a great interest in the most up to date development techniques.

Despite the many difficulties his business survived. Photographs of the changing shop front over the first half of the twentieth century suggest substantial investment in and development of the business despite the difficulties of making a regular profit. Developments in the period after 1910 are beyond the scope of this essay but the problems identified here appear to have continued to bedevil the business as the Economic War of the 1930s caused Murray to be declared a bankrupt for a time. However, the business recovered and remained in the Murray family for over a century, until it was sold in 1998, one hundred and two years after Peter Murray had first opened to the public.[81]

APPENDIX I

MURRAY'S RECEIPTS AND EXPENDITURE, 1896–98

1896	Recd.	Paid	Balance
End April	8.70	3.32	5.38
May	8.70	32.61	−23.91
June	158.86	126.24	32.62
July	222.40	165.87	56.53
August	200.79	194.82	5.97
September	218.78	209.89	8.89
October	205.15	256.98	−51.83
November	196.45	154.30	42.15
December	244.63	210.76	33.87
1896 Total	£1,464.46	£1,354.79	£109.67
1897			
January	256.55	237.58	18.97
February	267.05	255.06	11.99
March	278.90	258.99	19.91
April	341.29	339.33	1.96
May	282.56	259.16	23.40
June	258.92	259.30	−0.38
July	337.59	335.01	2.58
August	387.54	375.58	11.96
September	283.76	282.13	1.63
October	339.46	285.00	54.46
November	364.39	370.20	−5.81
December	459.42	396.18	63.24
1897 Total	£3,857.43	£3,653.52	£203.91

⟶

81 The building was renovated after the sale and still functions as a public house now known as Catty Ned's. The present proprietor is Mr Peter Duffy.

1898	Recd.	Paid	Balance
January	347.58	379.08	−31.50
February	293.10	284.50	8.60
March	306.52	317.52	−11.00
April	415.05	387.79	27.26
May	357.72	413.56	−55.84
June	260.18	210.02	50.16
July	423.98	397.55	26.43
August	351.35	409.65	−58.30
September	423.50	518.15	−94.65
October	419.48	535.63	−116.15
November	388.54	263.45	125.09
December	449.78	478.09	−28.31
1898 Total	£4,436.78	£4,594.99	£−158.21

APPENDIX 2

MURRAY'S ACCOUNTS, 1906

	Cash on A/c	Cash Sales	Credit Sales	Total Cash	Paid Out	Balance
January	62.57	90.45	40.59	153.01	152.16	0.85
February	44.79	123.40	72.64	168.20	168.51	−0.31
March	64.53	109.37	83.33	173.60	179.61	−6.01
April	68.68	112.38	95.08	181.07	182.60	−1.53
May	79.89	105.78	98.86	185.69	194.88	−9.19
June	81.37	123.21	125.46	225.36	184.88	40.48
July	83.62	121.77	106.07	205.39	212.46	−7.07
August	86.71	153.51	121.16	240.16	234.04	6.12
September	83.44	116.36	97.22	199.79	202.58	−2.79
October	121.29	159.80	114.48	280.92	211.16	69.76
November	76.99	126.54	97.33	203.52	208.50	−4.98
December	61.13	149.96	93.52	209.94	249.13	−39.19
Total	£915.01	£1492.53	£1145.74	£2426.65	£2380.51	£46.14

Index